Contents

BERTOLT BRECHT

The Good Person of Szechwan

Der Gute Mensch von Sezuan

translated by
TONY KUSHNER

Introduction and notes by
CHARLOTTE RYLAND

General Editor: TOM KUHN

METHUEN DRAMA

Methuen Drama Parallel Texts

10 9 8 7 6 5 4 3 2 1

First published in Great Britain by Methuen Drama
Methuen Drama
A & C Black Publishers Limited
36 Soho Square
London W1D 3QY
www.methuendrama.com

This translation first published in Great Britain in 2010 by Methuen Drama.
Original work entitled *Der Gute Mensch von Sezuan*, published by Suhrkamp
Verlag Frankfurt am Main 1955.

ISBN 978 1 408 11150 5

Available in the USA from Bloomsbury Academic & Professional,
175 Fifth Avenue/3rd Floor, New York, NY 10010.
www.BloomsburyAcademicUSA.com

A CIP catalogue record for this book is available from the British Library

Typeset by Mark Heslington Limited, Scarborough, North Yorkshire
Printed and bound in Great Britain by CPI Cox and Wyman, Reading,
Berkshire

Introduction

Bertolt Brecht's *The Good Person of Szechwan* is in many ways one of the most obviously 'Brechtian' of his plays. The use of masks, the split character and the dramatic irony that ensues, the 'alienated' setting in a stylised China, the asides to the audience and the final call-to-arms of the Epilogue – all of these features, and more, contribute to a play that is as 'epic' as they come. Kushner's version effectively reproduces these elements; and where there are inevitable losses, there are also significant gains. In the Prologue, for example, Wang describes the figures that he sees passing as he tries to identify the Gods. He rules out one on the basis that he has ink on his fingers and so must be a factory clerk, to which Kushner adds: 'A cement factory – he's grey' (5). Thus the translator adds to the visual quality of this opening scene – a figure covered in cement dust – as well as bringing out two elements central to Brecht's theory: the domination of the individual's identity by his work; and the epic technique of describing the on-stage action, such that the audience feel that they are being *shown* a situation rather than experiencing a slice of real life. The play's dramatic irony is also brought to the fore at various points by Kushner, such as with Mrs Shin's interjection in Scene Six. 'You can say that again,' she crows, when Sun calls the fact that Shen Te and Shui Ta can never be in the same room 'a mystery' (157).

Mrs Shin's knowing aside here not only enriches the play's theoretical basis, but also renders the scene more dynamic and textured in terms of its dramatic tension. Throughout, Kushner makes more such subtle changes that enhance the action and – above all – its comic potential. With an eye to staging, he occasionally restructures the dialogue to render particular lines more poignant or marked in some way. For example, Shui Ta's plaintive speech in Scene Five is restructured by Kushner so that the question-answer, 'Why are vultures circling in the sky over there? Because they know: A woman's meeting with her lover', can be followed immediately by Shu Fu's entrance. This more immediate juxtaposition of Shui Ta's sinister words with the arrival of Shu Fu make the latter's involvement with Shen Te all the more ominous.

Comedy and word play

It is the comic potential of Brecht's play that Kushner has the most fun with. As agonising as Brecht's play can be, in its portrayal of a situation that seems – at least until the Epilogue – to be hopeless, it is also a very playful text, and one of Kushner's greatest achievements in this particular version is his reproduction of its light moments and comic touches. Brecht's dumb Policeman becomes yet more laughable in his inability even to articulate a simple logical argument: 'First, …' he reasons, then 'Two, …' and finally 'And C and last, …' (71). Such a change to the original (which simply reads 'Firstly … Secondly … Thirdly') perfectly retains the tone of the German and yet increases its comedy. Similarly, the early episode in which Wang tries desperately to keep the Gods away from Shen Te's house, so that they do not see her 'customer' arriving, is extended by Kushner, taking full advantage of the comedic value of that situation, as well as of the dramatic irony that it affords (17).

As well as such additions to the text, there are also moments of equivalence, when Kushner replaces one of Brecht's humorous moments with one of his own making. Take, for example, Mrs Shin's snide comment about the unlikely possibility that Shen Te will do some trade in her tobacco shop: 'Hopefully you'll actually get some customers, too?' (30). Kushner changes this into a pun on a previous mention of 'pointers', which then become, in her mocking tone, pointers 'to the poorhouse' (31). Here, as repeatedly throughout the text, Kushner takes the existing tone and amplifies it, making the most of its comic potential.

Much comedy in both the German and English versions comes from puns and wordplay, which Kushner equally exploits. When Shu Fu assures the audience that his relationship with Shen Te will be no more than an 'exchange of ideas', Kushner's version is laden with innuendo, with the promise that 'the only intercourse will be intellectual' (137). Later, Kushner makes Sun more of a figure of fun through his play on the word 'degree': 'I've got education, not a lot but a degree. Of education, I have a degree of education, I don't have a degree' (205).

Kushner's wordplay serves not only to produce comic effects, but also adds to the texture of the piece, introducing echoes of other lexical fields that enhance its allusiveness. He tends to use, for example, idiomatic phrases drawn from the financial and legal fields, when the topic is something that is – on the surface –

neither financial nor legal. So the fact that, according to Sun, Shen
Te hasn't 'held out anything' is 'to her credit' (119), while later
The First God states that they are all 'banking on' Shen Te (169).
He is referring here to the importance of Shen Te for the Gods'
task of finding 'enough' good people, but the irony of his use of
the financial terminology will not be lost on an audience sensitised
to the negative correlation between economic matters and the
possibility of being 'good'. These additions by Kushner remind the
audience that the economic and the legal are never far away, their
subtle allusiveness increasing the dramatic irony that defines
Brecht's play.

Register

It is the register of Brecht's play that perhaps presents the most
difficulties for the translator. Brecht's language here is
meticulously crafted to reflect his setting, a China where courtesy
and respect – or, at least, the appearance of these graces – are
paramount; where much of the real substance of dialogues
consequently remains below the surface; and where – in Brecht's
Szechwan – the Gods are mere bureaucrats, intent more on ticking
boxes and getting a decent night's sleep than on anything more
'divine'. Linguistic registers between different languages are never
exactly equivalent, circumscribed as they are by cultural norms,
and the rendering of German politeness in English is a case in
point: English is always already far more polite than German ever
can be. Consequently, the overly polite formulae that Brecht uses,
which sound odd in German, cannot be translated into English to
produce the same effect. Similarly, the Gods' bureaucratic
language lends itself more to a Germanic tongue, with its plethora
of technical terms that immediately impart a certain dry and
mechanical tone.

   Kushner does largely succeed in bringing these elaborate
politenesses into the English, such as in the beautifully phrased
words from the acquisitive Husband: 'Such ungenerous thoughts
would perish on our Shen Te's lips' (55). The layers of
dissimulation and deception are palpable in this phrase dripping
with flattery, which at first sounds so complimentary but can
quickly be stripped back to reveal a grasping, proprietorial mode
that fears only losing control over 'our Shen Te'. Similarly, Shu Fu's
sinister desire to help Shen Te is expressed in the most saccharine
of tones: 'Permit me a divergent opinion: the flow of her goodness

should burst the floodgates. It's the young lady's nature to do good' (131). Kushner successfully negotiates Brecht's melding of the overly polite and the drily bureaucratic here, reflecting the apparent impossibility of removing business interests from personal relations, in his juxtaposition of the perfunctory 'Etcetera' with the pompous: 'Mr Shui Ta, might I hope that Miss Shen Te would grant audience to these ideas?' (131).

Nevertheless, it is the light-hearted, mocking tone and the caustic, cutting remarks that Kushner responds to most readily, and indeed there is a tendency for his version to accentuate these tones. So Mrs Shin threatens Shen Te not with leaving her children on his doorstep, but with leaving her children's *corpses* there, 'child-killer!' (29). And Kushner's Sun seems to lose his temper with Shen Te much more quickly than Brecht's, spitting: 'Any other talents? Besides lying?' instead of the original snide 'You're not really much fun right now' (83).

One of the small yet significant ways in which Brecht's language conveys a world where more is going on underneath the surface than above is in the linguistic repetitions, which can take on different meanings in different contexts and so reveal – to the audience – the latent hypocrisy. Sun is the prime proponent of these repetitions in his dealings with Shen Te. Twice he uses the same phrase behind her back and then to her face, managing to make what is originally a slur sound like an affectionate compliment. The terms are 'armes Tier' ('poor animal') and 'dickköpfig' ('fat-headed'); and while Kushner's translations ('poor mutt', 'poor chicken' and 'fat head', 'ox') reflect to a degree the change in Sun's tone, they lose the repetition that lays bare Sun's two-facedness so effectively in the original.

Updating the original

The German-Chinese setting of the original play is shifted westwards to a degree by Kushner, with some linguistic allusions that locate the characters in an American setting. For example, The Policeman threatens Wang with the 'hoosegow', an American slang term for jailhouse used largely in Westerns, as a translation for a German colloquial term, 'das Kittchen' (in British English, 'clink') (135). Similarly, Szechwan's 'Yellow Street' is paired with 'Easy Street' in Kushner's version, rendering the location not German-Chinese but firmly American-Chinese (173). A final nudge westwards and towards the present appears in the Epilogue, with

the reminder that the actors' livelihood depends on the audience's approval:

> But since our jobs depend on you,
> (Not to mention a corporate grant or two)

This knowing nod to the contemporary – and particularly American – reliance on corporate sponsorship and philanthropic support for the survival of the theatre updates Brecht's play and further intensifies his portrayal of the inextricable intertwining of business and art.

This updating of the Epilogue is a final example of the delicate weave of Kushner's text, maintaining the tone and poise of Brecht's original while bringing it towards his own diction, time and place. The result is a vibrant text: at times hilarious, at others desperate, but always convincing.

The Good Person of Szechwan

Der Gute Mensch von Sezuan

Translated by Tony Kushner

Personen

Die drei Götter
Shen Te
Shui Ta
Yang Sun, *ein stellungsloser Flieger*
Frau Yang, *seine Mutter*
Wang, *ein Wasserverkäufer*
Der Barbier Shu Fu
Die Hausbesitzerin Mi Tzü
Die Witwe Shin
Die achtköpfige Familie
Der Schreiner Lin To
Der Teppichhändler und seine Frau
Der Polizist
Der Bonze
Der Arbeitslose
Der Kellner
Die Passanten des Vorspiels

**Schauplatz: Die Hauptstadt von Sezuan, welche halb
europäisiert ist**

Characters

Wang the Waterseller
The First God
The Second God
The Third God
Man
Shen Te/Shui Ta
Mrs Shin
The Wife
The Nephew
The Husband
The Unemployed Man, *then* The Foreman
The Little Man, *then* The Carpenter, *then* The Former
  Carpenter
The Landlady
The Limping Man, *then* The Brother
The Grandfather
The Niece, *then* The Young Prostitute
The Sister-in-Law
The Policeman
The Boy
The Old Woman
Sun
The Old Prostitute
Shu Fu
The Old Man
Mrs Yang
The Bonze
The Waiter

Vorspiel
Eine Straße in der Hauptstadt
von Sezuan

Es ist Abend. **Wang,** *der Wasserverkäufer, stellt sich dem Publikum vor.*

Wang   Ich bin Wasserverkäufer hier in der Hauptstadt von Sezuan. Mein Geschäft ist mühselig. Wenn es wenig Wasser gibt, muß ich weit danach laufen. Und gibt es viel, bin ich ohne Verdienst. Aber in unserer Provinz herrscht überhaupt große Armut. Es heißt allgemein, daß uns nur noch die Götter helfen können. Zu meiner unaussprechlichen Freude erfahre ich von einem Vieheinkäufer, der viel herumkommt, daß einige der höchsten Götter schon unterwegs sind und auch hier in Sezuan erwartet werden dürfen. Der Himmel soll sehr beunruhigt sein wegen der vielen Klagen, die zu ihm aufsteigen. Seit drei Tagen warte ich hier am Eingang der Stadt, besonders gegen Abend, damit ich sie als erster begrüßen kann. Später hätte ich ja dazu wohl kaum mehr Gelegenheit, sie werden von Hochgestellten umgeben sein und überhaupt stark überlaufen werden. Wenn ich sie nur erkenne! Sie müssen ja nicht zusammen kommen. Vielleicht kommen sie einzeln, damit sie nicht so auffallen. Die dort können es nicht sein, die kommen von der Arbeit. (*Er betrachtet vorübergehende Arbeiter.*) Ihre Schultern sind ganz eingedrückt vom Lastentragen. Der dort ist auch ganz unmöglich ein Gott, er hat Tinte an den Fingern. Das ist höchstens ein Büroangestellter in einer Zementfabrik. Nicht einmal diese Herren dort *zwei Herren gehen vorüber* kommen mir wie Götter vor, sie haben einen brutalen Ausdruck wie Leute, die viel prügeln, und das haben die Götter nicht nötig. Aber dort, diese drei! Mit denen sieht es schon ganz anders aus. Sie sind wohlgenährt, weisen kein Zeichen

Prologue
A Street in the Capital
City of Szechwan

Evening. **Wang** *the waterseller introduces himself to the audience.*

Wang   I am a waterseller here in the capital city of Szechwan. My business wears me out. When it's dry I have to walk miles to fetch water to sell, and when it's wet, I go broke. Great poverty rules this province. So we all say: Only the Gods can help us now. And to my unspeakable joy, I've learned from an itinerant cattle dealer that the Heavens have been shaken by the number of complaints floating up from here, and now several of the highest Gods are headed this way and may be expected soon in Szechwan. I've been waiting at the city gates for three evenings, so that I can be first to welcome them. It'll be my only chance, later they'll be surrounded by the high and mighty, clamouring for their attentions. I must recognise them! They might not come in a group; they could arrive individually so as not to stand out.

He sees workers passing.

Wang   It isn't them, their backs are bowed from carrying loads, they're workers. And that one there isn't a God either, just a factory clerk – ink on his fingers. A cement factory: he's grey.* Not even those two gentlemen there —

Two gentlemen pass.

Wang   They have the brutal faces of men who beat people, and the Gods don't need to do that. But these three! With them it's a whole other thing. They're well-fed, they don't look like they do any work, and their shoes are dusty which means they come from far away. It's them! Command me, Awakened Ones!

irgendeiner Beschäftigung auf und haben Staub auf den
Schuhen, kommen also von weit her. Das sind sie!
Verfügt über mich, Erleuchtete!

Er wirft sich zu Boden.

Der Erste Gott (*erfreut*)   Werden wir hier erwartet?

Wang (*gibt ihnen zu trinken*)   Seit langem. Aber nur ich
wußte, daß ihr kommt.

Der Erste Gott   Da benötigen wir also für heute Nacht
ein Quartier. Weißt du eines?

Wang   Eines? Unzählige! Die Stadt steht zu euren
Diensten, o Erleuchtete! Wo wünscht ihr zu wohnen?

Die Götter sehen einander vielsagend an.

Der Erste Gott   Nimm das nächste Haus, mein Sohn!
Versuch es zunächst mit dem allernächsten!

Wang   Ich habe nur etwas Sorge, daß ich mir die
Feindschaft der Mächtigen zuziehe, wenn ich einen von
ihnen besonders bevorzuge.

Der Erste Gott   Da befehlen wir dir eben: nimm den
nächsten!

Wang   Das ist der Herr Fo dort drüben! Geduldet euch
einen Augenblick!

*Er läuft zu einem Haus und schlägt an die Tür. Sie wird
geöffnet, aber man sieht, er wird abgewiesen. Er kommt zögernd
zurück.*

Wang   Das ist dumm. Der Herr Fo ist gerade nicht zu
Hause und seine Dienerschaft wagt nichts ohne seinen
Befehl zu tun, da er sehr streng ist. Er wird nicht wenig
toben, wenn er erfährt, wen man ihm da abgewiesen hat,
wie?

Die Götter (*lächelnd*)   Sicher.

Wang   Also noch einen Augenblick! Das Haus nebenan
gehört der Witwe Su. Sie wird außer sich sein vor Freude.

Er läuft hin, wird aber anscheinend auch dort abgewiesen.

Wang *throws himself on the ground.*

The First God (*overjoyed*)   You were waiting for us?

Wang (*pouring them drinks of water*)   For a long time. Only I knew you were coming.

The First God   We will need rooms for the night. Do you know where we can find any?

Wang   Any? Many! The city awaits your pleasure, oh Awakened Ones! In which house would you like to stay?

The Gods *exchange meaningful glances.*

The First God   Try the nearest house first, my Son. Begin nearby!

Wang   I'm a little worried that I might arouse the wrath of the powerful if I single out one house for the honour.

The First God   And so we command you: whichever's closest!

Wang   Mr Fo lives here! Patience, please, I'll be back in an eyeblink!

He runs to a house and knocks on the door. The door opens; he is turned away. He returns reluctantly.

Wang   Bum luck. Mr Fo isn't at home at present, and his servants are afraid to act in his absence, he's so strict. He'll be furious when he finds out who they refused to let in, huh?

The Gods (*smiling*)   No doubt.

Wang   Another eyeblink, please! The next house is the Widow Su's. She'll be overcome with joy.

He runs to the next house; knocks; and apparently is turned away.

Wang Ich muß dort drüben nachfragen. Sie sagt, sie hat nur ein kleines Zimmerchen, das nicht instand gesetzt ist. Ich wende mich sofort an Herrn Tscheng.

Der Zweite Gott Aber ein kleines Zimmer genügt uns. Sag, wir kommen.

Wang Auch wenn es nicht aufgeräumt ist? Vielleicht wimmelt es von Spinnen.

Der Zweite Gott Das macht nichts. Wo Spinnen sind, gibt's wenig Fliegen.

Der Dritte Gott (*freundlich zu* **Wang**) Geh zu Herrn Tscheng oder sonstwohin, mein Sohn, ich ekle mich vor Spinnen doch ein wenig.

Wang *klopft wieder wo an und wird eingelassen.*

Stimme Aus Dem Hause Verschone uns mit deinen Göttern! Wir haben andere Sorgen!

Wang (*zurück zu den Göttern*) Herr Tscheng ist außer sich, er hat das ganze Haus voll Verwandtschaft und wagt nicht, euch unter die Augen zu treten, Erleuchtete. Unter uns, ich glaube, es sind böse Menschen darunter, die er euch nicht zeigen will. Er hat zu große Furcht vor eurem Urteil. Das ist es.

Der Dritte Gott Sind wir denn so fürchterlich?

Wang Nur gegen die bösen Menschen, nicht wahr? Man weiß doch, daß die Provinz Kwan seit Jahrzehnten von Überschwemmungen heimgesucht wird.

Der Zweite Gott So? Und warum das?

Wang Nun, weil dort keine Gottesfurcht herrscht.

Der Zweite Gott Unsinn! Weil sie den Staudamm verfallen ließen.

Der Erste Gott Ssst! (*Zu* **Wang**.) Hoffst du noch, mein Sohn?

Wang Wie kannst du so etwas fragen? Ich brauche nur ein Haus weiter zu gehen und kann mir ein Quartier für

Wang   I shall have to make further inquiries. She says she has only a very tiny room, and it's a mess. I'll go ask Mr Tscheng.

The Second God   A small room is enough. Tell the widow we are coming.

Wang   But not a small, messy room, surely? It could be crawling with spiders.

The Second God   That doesn't matter. Where spiders crawl, no flies at all.

The Third God (*pleasantly, to* **Wang**)   Go to Mr Tscheng, my son, go anyplace else, I'm not fond of spiders.

Wang *knocks at another house and is let in.*

Voice Within The House   Take your Gods someplace else! We have enough trouble as it is!

Wang (*back to* **the Gods**)   Mr Tscheng is dreadfully sorry, but he has a house full of relatives and he's too ashamed to show himself to you, Awakened Ones. Just between us, I think some of his guests are bad people and he's afraid of your condemnation.

The Third God   Are we so frightening?

Wang   To bad people you are, right? Everyone knows that the Province of Kwan has had flood after flood for centuries.

The Second God   And why do you suppose that is?

Wang   Because the people there don't fear the Gods.

The Second God   Ridiculous! The people there don't maintain the dam properly.

The First God   Sssssssshhhh!

(*To* **Wang**.) Is there any point in looking further, my son?

Wang   How can you even ask that? In the very next house there'll be a room. They're all licking their chops

euch aussuchen. Alle Finger leckt man sich danach, euch zu bewirten. Unglückliche Zufälle, ihr versteht. Ich laufe!

Er geht zögernd weg und bleibt unschlüssig in der Straße stehen.

Der Zweite Gott   Was habe ich gesagt?

Der Dritte Gott   Es können immer noch Zufälle sein.

Der Zweite Gott   Zufälle in Schun, Zufälle in Kwan und Zufälle in Sezuan! Es gibt keinen Gottesfürchtigen mehr, das ist die nackte Wahrheit, der ihr nicht ins Gesicht schauen wollt. Unsere Mission ist gescheitert, gebt es euch zu!

Der Erste Gott   Wir können immer noch gute Menschen finden, jeden Augenblick. Wir dürfen es uns nicht zu leicht machen.

Der Dritte Gott   In dem Beschluß hieß es: die Welt kann bleiben, wie sie ist, wenn genügend gute Menschen gefunden werden, die ein menschenwürdiges Dasein leben können. Der Wasserverkäufer selber ist ein solcher Mensch, wenn mich nicht alles täuscht.

Er tritt zu **Wang**, *der immer noch unschlüssig dasteht.*

Der Zweite Gott   Es täuscht ihn alles. Als der Wassermensch uns aus seinem Maßbecher zu trinken gab, sah ich was. Dies ist der Becher.

Er zeigt ihn **dem ersten Gott**.

Der Erste Gott   Er hat zwei Böden.

Der Zweite Gott   Ein Betrüger!

Der Erste Gott   Schön, er fällt weg. Aber was ist das schon, wenn *einer* angefault ist! Wir werden schon genug finden, die den Bedingungen genügen. Wir müssen einen finden! Seit zweitausend Jahren geht dieses Geschrei, es gehe nicht weiter mit der Welt, so wie sie ist. Niemand auf ihr könne gut bleiben. Wir müssen jetzt endlich Leute namhaft machen, die in der Lage sind, unsere Gebote zu halten.

Der Dritte Gott (*zu* **Wang**)   Vielleicht ist es zu schwierig, Obdach zu finden?

for the opportunity to shelter you. Unfortunate coincidence, the first two. I'll run!

He walks slowly into the street and stands still, bewildered.

The Second God   I told you so.

The Third God   It could be an unfortunate coincidence.

The Second God   Coincidences in Schun, coincidences in Kwan, coincidences in Szechwan. You don't want to face the Naked Truth: There are no more God-fearing people. Our mission's failed.

The First God   At the very next instant we could find them. It isn't supposed to be easy.

The Third God   As it has been decreed: if a few good people can be found, who live lives worthy of human beings, then the world can stay exactly as it is. The waterseller is such a person, unless I'm mistaken.

The Third God *goes to* **Wang**, *who still stands bewildered in the middle of the street.*

The Second God   He's always mistaken. When we were given water I noticed something about the waterseller's drinking cup.

He shows the cup to **The First God**.

The First God   Two bottoms.

The Second God   A swindler!

The First God   So forget him. What does it matter if one man's rotten? We'll find others who are good. There has to be one, at least! For 2,000 years we hear the cry: The World can't go on as is. No one can stay good here. We must search the people to find those who are able to honour our commandments.

The Third God (*to* **Wang**)   Maybe it'll be too hard, finding us lodging?

Wang   Nicht für euch! Wo denkt ihr hin? Die Schuld,
daß nicht gleich eines da ist, liegt an mir, der schlecht
sucht.

Der Dritte Gott   Das bestimmt nicht.

Er geht zurück.

Wang   Sie merken es schon. (*Er spricht einen Herrn an.*)
Werter Herr, entschuldigen Sie, daß ich Sie anspreche,
aber drei der höchsten Götter, von deren bevorstehender
Ankunft ganz Sezuan schon seit Jahren spricht, sind nun
wirklich eingetroffen und benötigen ein Quartier. Gehen
Sie nicht weiter! Überzeugen Sie sich selber! Ein Blick
genügt! Greifen Sie um Gottes willen zu! Es ist eine
einmalige Gelegenheit! Bitten Sie die Götter zuerst unter
Ihr Dach, bevor sie Ihnen jemand wegschnappt, sie
werden zusagen.

Der Herr *ist weitergegangen.*

Wang (*wendet sich an einen anderen*)   Lieber Herr, Sie
haben gehört, was los ist. Haben Sie vielleicht ein
Quartier? Es müssen keine Palastzimmer sein. Die
Gesinnung ist wichtiger.

Der Herr   Wie soll ich wissen, was deine Götter für
Götter sind? Wer weiß, wen man da unter sein Dach
bekommt.

Er geht in einen Tabakladen. **Wang** *läuft zurück zu den dreien.*

Wang   Ich habe schon einen Herren, der bestimmt
zusagt.

*Er sieht seinen Becher auf dem Boden stehen, sieht verwirrt nach
den Göttern, nimmt ihn an sich und läuft wieder zurück.*

Der Erste Gott   Das klingt nicht ermutigend.

Wang (*als* **Der Mann** *wieder aus dem Laden herauskommt*)
Wie ist es also mit der Unterkunft?

Der Mann   Woher weißt du, daß ich nicht selber im
Gasthof wohne?

Der Erste Gott   Er findet nichts. Dieses Sezuan können
wir auch streichen.

Wang   Hard to house the Gods? Don't think that! It's my fault that you aren't already accommodated. I'm just doing a bad job of looking.

The Third God   That's untrue. (*He rejoins the other* **Gods**.)

Wang   They're catching on.

Wang *speaks to a man passing by.*

Wang   Estimable gentleman, please forgive me for speaking to you, but three of the highest Gods are here, for real, in Szechwan, and they desire lodgings. Don't walk away! Take a look! See for yourself! It's a once-in-a-lifetime opportunity, for Godsake, grab it! Be the first to have Gods in your house, invite them, they'll accept, before somebody else snatches them up.

The man has gone. **Wang** *turns to another gentleman.*

Wang   You, sir, you heard, do you maybe have a room, it doesn't have to be swank, it's the thought that counts.

The Man   How can I tell what kind of Gods you have there? No knowing who I'd be taking under my roof.

He goes into a tobacco store.

Wang *goes to* **the three Gods**.

Wang   I've found someone, it's practically a sure thing.

He sees his cup lying on the ground, picks it up, looks uncertainly at **the Gods***, and runs back to the street.*

The First God   It doesn't sound promising.

The man comes out of the tobacco shop.

Wang (*to* **The Man**)   How about that room?

The Man   How do you know I'm not looking for a room myself?

The First God   He's coming up with nothing. Cross off Szechwan too.

Wang Es sind drei der Hauptgötter! Wirklich! Ihre
Standbilder in den Tempeln sind sehr gut getroffen.
Wenn Sie schnell hingehen und sie einladen, werden sie
vielleicht zusagen.

Der Mann (*lacht*) Das müssen schöne Gauner sein, die
du da wo unterbringen willst. (*Ab.*)

Wang (*schimpft ihm nach*) Du schieläugiger Schieber!
Hast du keine Gottesfurcht? Ihr werdet in siedendem
Pech braten für eure Gleichgültigkeit! Die Götter
scheißen auf euch! Aber ihr werdet es noch bereuen! Bis
ins vierte Glied werdet ihr daran abzuzahlen haben! Ihr
habt ganz Sezuan mit Schmach bedeckt! (*Pause.*) Jetzt
bleibt nur noch die Prostituierte Shen Te, die kann nicht
nein sagen.

Er ruft 'Shen Te'. *Oben im Fenster schaut* **Shen Te** *heraus.*

Wang Sie sind da, ich kann kein Obdach für sie finden.
Kannst du sie nicht aufnehmen für eine Nacht?

Shen Te Ich glaube nicht, Wang. Ich erwarte einen
Freier. Aber wie kann denn das sein, daß du für sie kein
Obdach findest?!

Wang Das kann ich jetzt nicht sagen. Ganz Sezuan ist
ein einziger Dreckhaufen.

Shen Te Ich müßte, wenn er kommt, mich versteckt
halten. Dann ginge er vielleicht wieder weg. Er will mich
noch ausführen.

Wang Können wir nicht inzwischen schon hinauf?

Shen Te Aber ihr dürft nicht laut reden. Kann man mit
ihnen offen sprechen?

Wang Nein! Sie dürfen von deinem Gewerbe nichts
erfahren! Wir warten lieber unten. Aber du gehst nicht
weg mit ihm?

Shen Te Es geht mir nicht gut, und wenn ich bis
morgen früh meine Miete nicht zusammen habe, werde
ich hinausgeworfen.

Wang   Three big important Gods! I swear! They look just like their statues in the Temple. Quick, invite them, they may very well accept.

The Man (*laughs*)   Con artists you're trying to pass off as holy houseguests. (*He exits.*)

Wang   Tightassed skinflint! Don't you fear Heaven? Your heart will roast on a spit in Hell! All the Gods will crap on your head! You'll be sorry, your descendants will be sorry, unto the fourth generation you'll be sorry! You have bedecked all Szechwan with shame.

Pause.

There's still Shen Te, the prostitute, who never says no.

He calls 'Shen Te' at a window in which a red light burns. **Shen Te** *looks out.*

Wang   They're here and I can't find a room for them anywhere. Can you take them for the night?

Shen Te   Sorry, no, Wang, a customer is coming over momentarily. Surely you can find them a room?

Wang   Szechwan's one big shithole.

Shen Te   When the customer comes I'll go away with him.* Do you want to ask them inside?

Wang   No! The Awakened Ones mustn't know how you make your living. We'll wait across the street. Hide when your customer comes. Don't leave with him.

Shen Te   I'm having a hard time, if I don't scrape the rent together I'll be evicted.

Wang   In solch einem Augenblick darf man nicht rechnen.

Shen Te   Ich weiß nicht, der Magen knurrt leider auch, wenn der Kaiser Geburtstag hat. Aber gut, ich will sie aufnehmen.

Man sieht sie das Licht löschen.

Der Erste Gott   Ich glaube, es ist aussichtslos.

Sie treten zu Wang.

Wang (*erschrickt, als er sie hinter sich stehen sieht*)   Das Quartier ist beschafft. (*Er trocknet sich den Schweiß ab.*)

Die Götter   Ja? Dann wollen wir hingehen.

Wang   Es hat nicht solche Eile. Laßt euch ruhig Zeit. Das Zimmer wird noch in Ordnung gebracht.

Der Dritte Gott   So wollen wir uns hierhersetzen und warten.

Wang   Aber es ist viel zuviel Verkehr hier, fürchte ich. Vielleicht gehen wir dort hinüber.

Der Zweite Gott   Wir sehen uns gern Menschen an. Gerade dazu sind wir hier.

Wang   Nur: es zieht.

Der Dritte Gott   Ist es dir hier angenehm?

Sie setzen sich auf eine Haustreppe. **Wang** *setzt sich etwas abseits auf den Boden.*

Wang (*mit einem Anlauf*)   Ihr wohnt bei einem alleinstehenden Mädchen. Sie ist der beste Mensch von Sezuan.

Der Dritte Gott   Das ist schön.

Wang (*zum Publikum*)   Als ich vorhin den Becher aufhob, sahen sie mich so eigentümlich an. Sollten sie etwas gemerkt haben? Ich wage ihnen nicht mehr in die Augen zu blicken.

Der Dritte Gott   Du bist sehr erschöpft.

Wang   This is no time to think about money.

Shen Te   I don't know, the stomach grumbles even on the Emperor's Birthday. But good, I'll take them in.

The red light goes out.

The First God   I think all is lost.

The Gods *go to* **Wang**.

Wang (*surprised when he sees them standing behind him*)   A room's been found. (*He wipes the sweat from his brow.*)

The Third God   Indeed? Then we would like to occupy it.

Wang   It needs tidying first.

The Third God   Then we'll wait. Right here.

Wang   Too bustling, too hectic. Perhaps around the corner?

The Second God   We enjoy watching the traffic. That's why we've come.

Wang   So windy! Brrr!

The Second God   Oh, we're a hardy people.*

Wang   Or perhaps you'd appreciate a nice night-tour of Szechwan? A little constitutional? See the sights?

The Third God   Our feet are sore enough. (*smiling*) If you're trying to get rid of us, just say so.

They sit on a stoop. **Wang** *sits a bit apart, on the ground.*

Wang (*nervously*)   You're staying with a single girl. She's the best person in Szechwan.

The Third God   That's nice.

Wang (*to the audience*)   When I picked up my cup they stared at me. Do they know? I'm not going to look them in the eyes anymore.

The Third God   You're exhausted.

Wang   Ein wenig. Vom Laufen.

Der Erste Gott   Haben es die Leute hier sehr schwer?

Wang   Die guten schon.

Der Erste Gott (*ernst*)   Du auch?

Wang   Ich weiß, was ihr meint. Ich bin nicht gut. Aber ich habe es auch nicht leicht.

Inzwischen ist ein Herr vor dem Haus Shen Tes erschienen und hat mehrmals gepfiffen. Wang ist jedesmal zusammengezuckt.

Der Dritte Gott (*leise zu* **Wang**)   Ich glaube, jetzt ist er weggegangen.

Wang (*verwirrt*)   Jawohl.

Er steht auf und läuft auf den Platz, sein Traggerät zurücklassend. Aber es hat sich bereits folgendes ereignet: Der wartende Mann ist weggegangen und **Shen Te**, *aus der Tür tretend und leise 'Wang' rufend, ist,* **Wang** *suchend, die Straße hinuntergegangen. Als nun* **Wang** *leise 'Shen Te' ruft, bekommt er keine Antwort.*

Wang   Sie hat mich im Stich gelassen. Sie ist weggegangen, um ihre Miete zusammenzubekommen, und ich habe kein Quartier für die Erleuchteten. Sie sind müde und warten. Ich kann ihnen nicht noch einmal kommen mit: Es ist nichts! Mein eigener Unterschlupf, ein Kanalrohr, kommt nicht in Frage. Auch würden die Götter bestimmt nicht bei einem Menschen wohnen wollen, dessen betrügerische Geschäfte sie durchschaut haben. Ich gehe nicht zurück, um nichts in der Welt. Aber mein Traggerät liegt dort. Was machen? Ich wage nicht, es zu holen. Ich will weggehen von der Hauptstadt und mich irgendwo verbergen vor ihren Augen, da es mir nicht gelungen ist, für sie etwas zu tun, die ich verehre.

Er stürzt fort.

Kaum ist er fort, kommt **Shen Te** *zurück, sucht auf der anderen Seite und sieht die Götter.*

Shen Te   Seid ihr die Erleuchteten? Mein Name ist Shen Te. Ich würde mich freuen, wenn ihr mit meiner Kammer vorliebnehmen wolltet.

Wang   A bit run down.

The First God   Is it hard for people here?

Wang   It's hard for good people.

The First God (*seriously*)   Including you?

Wang   I take your meaning. I'm not good. But it's hard for me too.

During this a man has appeared before **Shen Te***'s house and is whistling for her.* **Wang** *winces with every whistle. He screws his eyes tight shut. He hunches over, hiding himself.*

The customer gives up.

Shen Te *comes out of the house after the customer has gone. She looks for* **Wang***, and, not seeing him, goes off to find him, softly calling 'Wang'.*

The First God (*softly, to* **Wang**)   Wang . . .

Wang   Yep.

The Third God (*also softly, to* **Wang**)   I believe the client has gone now.*

Wang, *rattled, opens his eyes, then looks up, then runs to* **Shen Te***'s house, leaving his equipment behind. He quietly calls 'Shen Te' at the darkened window. There's no answer.*

Wang   She's left me holding the bag. She's run off, chasing after her rent, and I have no room to offer the Awakened Ones. They're tired, they're waiting, I can't go back to them empty-handed, I can't invite them to stay with me, I live in a sewer-pipe, that's out of the question. And anyway the Gods would refuse to stay with me, they know I'm a swindler. I'm not going back to them, no way in the world. But I've left my gear with them. What'll I do? I'll leave the capital, hide myself from their sight, for I have failed to serve the ones I worship.

No sooner has **Wang** *rushed off when* **Shen Te** *returns. She looks across the street and sees* **the Gods***.*

Shen Te   Are you the Awakened Ones? My name is Shen Te. It would make me very happy to welcome you to my small room.

Der Dritte Gott   Aber wo ist denn der Wasserverkäufer
hin?

Shen Te   Ich muß ihn verfehlt haben.

Der Erste Gott   Er muß gemeint haben, du kämst nicht,
und da hat er sich nicht mehr zu uns getraut.

Der Dritte Gott (*nimmt das Traggerät auf*)   Wir wollen es
bei dir einstellen. Er braucht es.

Sie gehen, von Shen Te geführt, ins Haus.

*Es wird dunkel und wieder hell. In der Morgendämmerung
treten die Götter wieder aus der Tür, geführt von* **Shen Te***, die
ihnen mit einer Lampe leuchtet. Sie verabschieden sich.*

Der Erste Gott   Liebe Shen Te, wir danken dir für deine
Gastlichkeit. Wir werden nicht vergessen, daß du es warst,
die uns aufgenommen hat. Und gib dem Wasserverkäufer
sein Gerät zurück und sage ihm, daß wir auch ihm
danken, weil er uns einen guten Menschen gezeigt hat.

Shen Te   Ich bin nicht gut. Ich muß euch ein
Geständnis machen: Als Wang mich für euch um Obdach
anging, schwankte ich.

Der Erste Gott   Schwanken macht nichts, wenn man nur
siegt. Wisse, daß du uns mehr gabst als ein Nachtquartier.
Vielen, darunter sogar einigen von uns Göttern, sind
Zweifel aufgestiegen, ob es überhaupt noch gute
Menschen gibt. Hauptsächlich um dies festzustellen,
haben wir unsere Reise angetreten. Freudig setzen wir sie
jetzt fort, da wir einen schon gefunden haben. Auf
Wiedersehen!

Shen Te   Halt, Erleuchtete, ich bin gar nicht sicher, daß
ich gut bin. Ich möchte es wohl sein, nur, wie soll ich
meine Miete bezahlen? So will ich es euch denn gestehen:
ich verkaufe mich, um leben zu können, aber selbst
damit kann ich mich nicht durchbringen, da es so viele
gibt, die dies tun müssen. Ich bin zu allem bereit, aber
wer ist das nicht? Freilich würde ich glücklich sein, die
Gebote halten zu können der Kindesliebe und der
Wahrhaftigkeit. Nicht begehren meines Nächsten Haus,

The Third God But what's become of the waterseller?

Shen Te He must be looking for me.

The First God He must have thought you'd rescinded your offer, and he was afraid to tell us.

The Third God (*picking up* **Wang**'s *gear*) We'll leave this with you. He'll need it.

Shen Te *leads them into the house.*

It gets dark and then light again. At dawn, **the three Gods** *come out of the door again, led by* **Shen Te**, *who lights the way with a lamp. They take their leave.*

The First God Dear Shen Te, we thank you for your hospitality. We will not forget that it was you who gave us shelter. And give the waterseller his gear back, and say to him that we thank him as well, for he has showed us a good person.

Shen Te I'm not good. I must tell you something: when Wang approached me desiring shelter for you, I was reluctant.

The First God Reluctance doesn't matter if you triumph over it. Understand that you have given us more than a room for a night. Many, even among the Gods, have doubted whether any good people could be found anywhere. To ascertain if this was indeed the case, we undertook this journey. Happily now we'll continue on our way, knowing that we've already found one. Farewell!

Shen Te Stop, Awakened Ones, I'm not at all sure that I'm good. I'd like to be, but then how would I pay my rent? So I must tell you: I sell myself to make my living, but even doing that I can't manage, because so many are forced to do the same, it drives down the price. I'm willing to do anything, but who isn't? I'd really be happy keeping the commandments, showing a child's love for her parents, telling the truth. Not to covet my neighbour's house would be a joy to me, and to be true to one man

wäre mir eine Freude, und einem Mann anhängen in Treue, wäre mir angenehm. Auch ich möchte aus keinem meinen Nutzen ziehen und den Hilflosen nicht berauben. Aber wie soll ich dies alles? Selbst wenn ich einige Gebote nicht halte, kann ich kaum durchkommen.

Der Erste Gott   Dies alles, Shen Te, sind nichts als die Zweifel eines guten Menschen.

Der Dritte Gott   Leb wohl, Shen Te! Grüße mir auch den Wasserträger recht herzlich. Er war uns ein guter Freund.

Der Zweite Gott   Ich fürchte, es ist ihm schlecht bekommen.

Der Dritte Gott   Laß es dir gut gehn!

Der Erste Gott   Vor allem sei gut, Shen Te! Leb wohl!

Sie wenden sich zum Gehen. Sie winken schon.

Shen Te (*angstvoll*)   Aber ich bin meiner nicht sicher, Erleuchtete. Wie soll ich gut sein, wo alles so teuer ist?

Der Zweite Gott   Da können wir leider nichts tun. In das Wirtschaftliche können wir uns nicht mischen.

Der Dritte Gott   Halt! Wartet einen Augenblick! Wenn sie etwas mehr hätte, könnte sie es vielleicht eher schaffen.

Der Zweite Gott   Wir können ihr nichts geben. Das könnten wir oben nicht verantworten.

Der Erste Gott Warum nicht?

Sie stecken die Köpfe zusammen und diskutieren aufgeregt.

Der Erste Gott (*zu* **Shen Te**, *verlegen*)   Wir hören, du hast deine Miete nicht zusammen. Wir sind keine armen Leute und bezahlen natürlich unser Nachtlager! Hier! (*Er gibt ihr Geld.*) Sprich aber zu niemand darüber, daß wir bezahlten. Es könnte mißdeutet werden.

Der Zweite Gott   Sehr.

would be very nice. I too would prefer not to make a
profit off others, I too would like to not rob the helpless.
But how can I do all this? And if I break only a few
commandments, I can't make ends meet.

The First God   These, Shen Te, these are only the
doubts of a good person.

The Third God   Live well, Shen Te! Give our best to the
waterseller. He proved to be a good friend.

The Second God   I fear we didn't prove to be the same
for him.

The Third God   May things go well for you!

The First God   Above all, be good, Shen Te! Live well!

They turn to leave. They wave.

Shen Te   But I'm so unsure of myself, Awakened Ones.
How will I stay good when everything's so expensive?

The Second God   Unfortunately we cannot address
ourselves to economic matters.

The Third God   Wait! One moment please! If she had a
little more, she might be good more easily.

The Second God   We can't give her anything. We'd
never explain that upstairs.

The First God   Why not?

They put their heads together and talk excitedly.

The First God (*shyly, to* **Shen Te**)   We've heard that you
can't scrape your rent together. We aren't paupers and of
course we pay for having had a good night's sleep! Here!

He gives her money.

But don't tell anyone that we paid. It might be
misunderstood.

The Second God   You can say that again.

Der Dritte Gott   Nein, das ist erlaubt. Wir können ihr ruhig unser Nachtlager bezahlen. In dem Beschluß stand kein Wort dagegen. Also auf Wiedersehen!

Die Götter schnell ab.

The Third God We can't give, but it's perfectly permissible to pay in exchange for a good night's rest. In what's been decreed there's nothing against that. And so again farewell!

The Gods *make a fast exit.*

1
Ein Kleiner Tabakladen

Der Laden ist noch nicht ganz eingerichtet und noch nicht eröffnet.

Shen Te (*zum Publikum*) Drei Tage ist es her, seit die Götter weggezogen sind. Sie sagten, sie wollten mir ihr Nachtlager bezahlen. Und als ich sah, was sie mir gegeben hatten, sah ich, daß es über tausend Silberdollar waren. – Ich habe mir mit dem Geld einen Tabakladen gekauft. Gestern bin ich hier eingezogen, und ich hoffe, jetzt viel Gutes tun zu können. Da ist zum Beispiel die Frau Shin, die frühere Besitzerin des Ladens. Schon gestern kam sie und bat mich um Reis für ihre Kinder. Auch heute sehe ich sie wieder über den Platz kommen mit ihrem Topf.

Herein **Die Shin**. *Die Frauen verbeugen sich voreinander.*

Shen Te Guten Tag, Frau Shin.

Die Shin Guten Tag, Fräulein Shen Te. Wie gefällt es Ihnen in Ihrem neuen Heim?

Shen Te Gut. Wie haben Ihre Kinder die Nacht zugebracht?

Die Shin Ach, in einem fremden Haus, wenn man diese Baracke ein Haus nennen darf. Das Kleinste hustet schon.

Shen Te Das ist schlimm.

Die Shin Sie wissen ja gar nicht, was schlimm ist, Ihnen geht es gut. Aber Sie werden noch allerhand Erfahrungen machen hier in dieser Bude. Dies ist ein Elendsviertel.

Shen Te Mittags kommen doch, wie Sie mir sagten, die Arbeiter aus der Zementfabrik?

Die Shin Aber sonst kauft kein Mensch, nicht einmal die Nachbarschaft.

1
A Little Tobacco Shop

The shop is not fitted out and is not yet opened.

Shen Te (*to the audience*)   Three days have passed since the Gods went away. They said they wanted to pay for a good night's rest. And when I looked at what they'd given me, I saw it was over a thousand silver dollars. With the money I've bought the lease on a tobacco shop. Yesterday I moved in, and I hope I'll be able to do a lot of good here. For instance, there's Mrs Shin, the shop's previous tenant. She was here first thing yesterday asking for rice for her children. And here she is again, crossing the square with her rice-pot.

Mrs Shin *enters. The women bow to each other.*

Shen Te   Good day, Mrs Shin.

Mrs Shin   Good day, Miss Shen Te. Are you happy in your new home?

Shen Te   Very. Did your children sleep well?

Mrs Shin   Oh, well, in a strange house, not that you could call that barracks a house. The littlest has a cough now.

Shen Te   That's terrible.

Mrs Shin   You don't know from terrible, things are going nicely for you. But you'll learn, this shack will teach you about terrible. This whole place, it's a slum.

Shen Te   But at noon the workers from the cement factory come by?

Mrs Shin   Yes, but nobody else buys anything, not the cheap people who live round here.

Shen Te   Davon sagten Sie mir nichts, als Sie mir den Laden verkauften.

Die Shin   Machen Sie mir nur nicht jetzt auch noch Vorwürfe! Zuerst rauben Sie mir und meinen Kindern das Heim und dann heißt es eine Bude und Elendsviertel. Das ist der Gipfel. (*Sie weint.*)

Shen Te (*schnell*)   Ich hole Ihnen gleich den Reis.

Die Shin   Ich wollte Sie auch bitten, mir etwas Geld zu leihen.

Shen Te (*während sie ihr den Reis in den Topf schüttet*)   Das kann ich nicht. Ich habe doch noch nichts verkauft.

Die Shin   Ich brauche es aber. Von was soll ich leben? Sie haben mir alles weggenommen. Jetzt drehen Sie mir die Gurgel zu. Ich werde Ihnen meine Kinder vor die Schwelle setzen, Sie Halsabschneiderin!

Sie reißt ihr den Topf aus den Händen.

Shen Te   Seien Sie nicht so zornig! Sie schütten noch den Reis aus!

Herein ein ältliches Paar und ein schäbig gekleideter Mensch.

Die Frau   Ach, meine liebe Shen Te, wir haben gehört, daß es dir jetzt so gut geht. Du bist ja eine Geschäftsfrau geworden! Denk dir, wir sind eben ohne Bleibe! Unser Tabakladen ist eingegangen. Wir haben uns gefragt, ob wir nicht bei dir für eine Nacht unterkommen können. Du kennst meinen Neffen? Er ist mitgekommen, er trennt sich nie von uns.

Der Neffe (*sich umschauend*)   Hübscher Laden!

Die Shin   Was sind denn das für welche?

Shen Te   Als ich vom Land in die Stadt kam, waren sie meine ersten Wirtsleute. (*Zum Publikum.*) Als mein bißchen Geld ausging, hatten sie mich auf die Straße gesetzt. Sie fürchten vielleicht, daß ich jetzt nein sage. Sie sind arm.
Sie sind ohne Obdach.

Shen Te   You didn't tell me that when you sold me the lease on the shop.

Mrs Shin   Oh now you're complaining too! First you steal my children's home from them and then you call it – what'd you call it? – a shack in a slum. You're too much! (*She cries.*)

Shen Te (*quickly*)   I'll get your rice.

Mrs Shin   I also need to borrow some money.

Shen Te (*as she pours rice into the pot*)   I can't. I haven't sold anything yet.

Mrs Shin   But I need it. What am I going to live on? You've taken everything from me, and now you're strangling me on top of that. I'll leave my kids' tiny corpses on your doorstep, you child-killer!*

Mrs Shin *tears the rice-pot from* **Shen Te**'s *hands.*

Shen Te   Don't get so excited, you're spilling the rice!

The Husband *and* **The Wife** *enter, followed by* **The Nephew**, *dressed shabbily.*

The Wife   Oh, my dear Shen Te, we'd heard it was going good for you. You're a businesswoman now! And imagine! We have no place to live! Our tobacco shop went under. So we asked ourselves, she won't mind putting us up for the night. You know my nephew? He's come along, he can't stand to be apart from us.

The Nephew (*looking around*)   Nice!

Mrs Shin   Who're these characters?

Shen Te   My first landlords, when I came to the city from the country.

(*To the audience.*) When the little money I had was gone they threw me out on the street. Maybe now they're afraid I'll tell them no. They are poor.
They have no shelter.

Sie sind ohne Freunde.
Sie brauchen jemand. Wie könnte man da nein sagen?

(*Freundlich zu den Ankömmlingen.*) Seid willkommen! Ich
will euch gern Obdach geben. Allerdings habe ich nur
ein kleines Kämmerchen hinter dem Laden.

Der Mann   Das genügt uns. Mach dir keine Sorge.
(*Während* **Shen Te** *Tee bringt.*) Wir lassen uns am besten
hier hinten nieder, damit wir dir nicht im Weg sind. Du
hast wohl einen Tabakladen in Erinnerung an dein erstes
Heim gewählt? Wir werden dir einige Winke geben
können. Das ist auch der Grund, warum wir zu dir
kommen.

Die Shin (*höhnisch*)   Hoffentlich kommen auch Kunden?

Die Frau   Das geht wohl auf uns?

Der Mann   Psst! Da ist schon ein Kunde!

Ein **Abgerissener Mann** *tritt ein.*

Der Abgerissene Mann   Entschuldigen Sie. Ich bin
arbeitslos.

Die Shin *lacht.*

Shen Te   Womit kann ich Ihnen dienen?

Der Arbeitslose   Ich höre, Sie eröffnen morgen. Da
dachte ich, beim Auspacken wird manchmal etwas
beschädigt. Haben Sie eine Zigarette übrig?

Die Frau   Das ist stark, Tabak zu betteln! Wenn es noch
Brot wäre!

Der Arbeitslose   Brot ist teuer. Ein paar Züge aus einer
Zigarette, und ich bin ein neuer Mensch. Ich bin so
kaputt.

Shen Te (*gibt ihm Zigaretten*)   Das ist wichtig, ein neuer
Mensch zu sein. Ich will meinen Laden mit Ihnen
eröffnen, Sie werden mir Glück bringen.

Der Arbeitslose *zündet sich schnell eine Zigarette an, inhaliert
und geht hustend ab.*

They have no friend.
They need someone. How could anyone say no?

(*Friendly, to the new arrivals.*) Please come in! I'll be glad
to give you shelter. Even though there's only a tiny little
room behind the shop.

The Husband   Don't worry, we'll manage.

As **Shen Te** *brings tea.*

The Wife   We should just settle in back here, out of your
way while you get to work. You probably decided on a
tobacco shop because it reminded you of our place, your
first home, of which you were so fond. We know
everything there is to know, that's another reason we
came, to give you pointers!

Mrs Shin (*sarcastically*)   Like the way to the poorhouse.*

The Wife   Who invited you?

The Husband   Ssssh! A customer!

A man in rags enters.

The Man in Rags   I beg your pardon. I'm unemployed.

Mrs Shin *laughs.*

Shen Te   What can I do for you?

The Unemployed Man   I heard you were opening
tomorrow. So I thought, when things are being
unpacked, sometimes there are damaged goods. Got any
bent cigarettes you can spare?

The Wife   That's rich, begging for cigarettes! They're
not bread!

The Unemployed Man   Who can afford bread? A few
drags on a cigarette and I'm a whole new person. I'm
totally kaput.

Shen Te (*giving him a cigarette*)   That's important, to be a
whole new person. I'm going to open my shop giving this
to you, you'll bring me luck.

The Unemployed Man *quickly lights up, inhales and goes out
coughing.*

Die Frau   War das richtig, liebe Shen Te?

Die Shin   Wenn Sie den Laden so eröffnen, werden Sie ihn keine drei Tage haben.

Der Mann   Ich wette, er hatte noch Geld in der Tasche.

Shen Te   Er sagte doch, daß er nichts hat.

Der Neffe   Woher wissen Sie, daß er Sie nicht angelogen hat?

Shen Te (*aufgebracht*)   Woher weiß ich, daß er mich angelogen hat!

Die Frau (*kopfschüttelnd*)   Sie kann nicht nein sagen! Du bist zu gut, Shen Te! Wenn du deinen Laden behalten willst, mußt du die eine oder andere Bitte abschlagen können.

Der Mann   Sag doch, er gehört dir nicht. Sag, er gehört einem Verwandten, der von dir genaue Abrechnung verlangt. Kannst du das nicht?

Die Shin   Das könnte man, wenn man sich nicht immer als Wohltäterin aufspielen müßte.

Shen Te (*lacht*)   Schimpft nur!* Ich werde euch gleich das Quartier aufsagen, und den Reis werde ich zurückschütten!

Die Frau (*entsetzt*)   Ist der Reis auch von dir?

Shen Te (*zum Publikum*)
Sie sind schlecht.
Sie sind niemandes Freund.
Sie gönnen keinem einen Topf Reis.
Sie brauchen alles selber.
Wer könnte sie schelten?

Herein ein kleiner Mann.

Die Shin (*sieht ihn und bricht hastig auf*)   Ich sehe morgen wieder her. (*Ab.*)

Der Kleine Mann (*ruft ihr nach*)   Halt, Frau Shin! Sie brauche ich gerade!

The Wife   Was that appropriate, dear Shen Te?

Mrs Shin   If that's how you open your shop you'll be closing it in three days.

The Husband   I bet he could have paid for it.

Shen Te   But he said he couldn't.

The Nephew   How do you know he wasn't lying?

Shen Te (*getting angry*)   How do I know he was?

The Wife (*shaking her head*)   She can't say no! You're too good, Shen Te. If you want to hang on to your shop, you must be able to refuse requests occasionally.

The Husband   Just tell 'em none of this belongs to you. Tell 'em it's all the property of some tight relative, let's say a cousin who keeps close accounts. Try that. Worked for us.*

Mrs Shin   One could try something like that if one weren't playing a saint.

Shen Te (*laughing*)
They are awful.
They are nobody's friend.
They begrudge each other bowls of rice.
They need everything themselves.
Who could scold them?

A little man enters. **Mrs Shin** *sees him and starts to leave, hastily.*

Mrs Shin   See you tomorrow. (*Exits.*)

The Little Man (*calling after her*)   Stop, Mrs Shin! You're who I've come to see!

Die Frau Kommt die regelmäßig? Hat sie denn einen Anspruch an dich?

Shen Te Sie hat keinen Anspruch, aber sie hat Hunger: das ist mehr.

Der Kleine Mann Die weiß, warum sie rennt. Sind Sie die neue Ladeninhaberin? Ach, Sie packen schon die Stellagen voll. Aber die gehören Ihnen nicht, Sie! Außer Sie bezahlen sie! Das Lumpenpack, das hier gesessen ist, hat sie nicht bezahlt. (*Zu den andern*) Ich bin nämlich der Schreiner.

Shen Te Aber ich dachte, das gehört zur Einrichtung, die ich bezahlt habe?

Der Schreiner Betrug! Alles Betrug! Sie stecken natürlich mit dieser Shin unter einer Decke! Ich verlange meine 100 Silberdollar, so wahr ich Lin To heiße.

Shen Te Wie soll ich das bezahlen, ich habe kein Geld mehr!

Der Schreiner Dann lasse ich Sie einsteigern! Sofort! Sie bezahlen sofort, oder ich lasse Sie einsteigern!

Der Mann (*souffliert* **Shen Te**) Vetter!

Shen Te Kann es nicht im nächsten Monat sein?

Der Schreiner (*schreiend*) Nein!

Shen Te Seien Sie nicht hart, Herr Lin To. Ich kann nicht allen Forderungen sofort nachkommen.

(*Zum Publikum*) Ein wenig Nachsicht und die Kräfte verdoppeln sich.
Sieh, der Karrengaul hält vor einem Grasbüschel:
Ein Durch-die-Finger-Sehen und der Gaul zieht besser.
Noch im Juni ein wenig Geduld und der Baum
Beugt sich im August unter den Pfirsichen. Wie
Sollen wir zusammenleben ohne Geduld?
Mit einem kleinen Aufschub
Werden die weitesten Ziele erreicht.

(*Zum* **Schreiner**.) Nur ein Weilchen gedulden Sie sich, Herr Lin To!

The Wife   Is she always around? Does she have some claim on you?

Shen Te   She's hungry.

The Little Man   She better run. You're the new shopkeeper? So you've already started loading up the shelves. But they're not your shelves! Not unless you pay for them! That sack of trash previous to you, she didn't pay for them. (*To the others.*) I'm the carpenter, see.

Shen Te   I thought the fittings came with the shop.

The Little Man, *who is now* **The Carpenter**   Cheaters! Everybody cheats! You and that Shin woman, you're probably in bed together on this! I'm getting my 100 silver dollars or my name's not Lin To!

Shen Te   But I've got no more money!

The Carpenter   Then I'll make you sell off. Now! Pay me my money now or I'll make you auction it all.

The Husband (*a whisper to* **Shen Te**)   Cousin!

Shen Te   How about next month?

The Carpenter (*screaming*)   NO!

Shen Te   Don't be hard-hearted, Mr Lin. I can't satisfy everyone all at once.

(*To the audience.*) A little forbearance and your strength
    returns to you.
Think of the carthorse stopping to graze a tuft of grass:
Turn your head, let her eat, and the horse will pull better
    after.
Show patience in June and the tree
In August sags with the weight of its pears. How
Can we live together without patience?
Only tarry a little,
You'll reach your most remote destination.

(*To* **The Carpenter**.) A little more patience, Mr Lin To!

Der Schreiner Und wer geduldet sich mit mir und mit meiner Familie? (*Er rückt eine Stellage von der Wand, als wolle er sie mitnehmen.*) Sie bezahlen oder ich nehme die Stellagen mit!

Die Frau Meine liebe Shen Te, warum übergibst du nicht deinem Vetter die Angelegenheit? (*Zum* **Schreiner**.) Schreiben Sie Ihre Forderung auf und Fräulein Shen Tes Vetter wird bezahlen.

Der Schreiner Solche Vettern kennt man!

Der Neffe Lach nicht so dumm! Ich kenne ihn persönlich.

Der Mann Ein Mann wie ein Messer.

Der Schreiner Schön, er soll meine Rechnung haben.

Er kippt die Stellage um, setzt sich darauf und schreibt seine Rechnung.

Die Frau Er wird dir das Hemd vom Leibe reißen für seine paar Bretter, wenn ihm nicht Halt geboten wird. Erkenne nie eine Forderung an, berechtigt oder nicht, denn sofort wirst du überrannt mit Forderungen, berechtigt oder nicht. Wirf ein Stück Fleisch in eine Kehrichttonne, und alle Schlachterhunde des Viertels beißen sich in deinem Hof. Wozu gibt's die Gerichte?

Shen Te Er hat gearbeitet und will nicht leer ausgehen. Und er hat seine Familie. Es ist schlimm, daß ich ihn nicht bezahlen kann! Was werden die Götter sagen?

Der Mann Du hast dein Teil getan, als du uns aufnahmst, das ist übergenug.

Herein ein hinkender Mann und eine schwangere Frau.

The Carpenter   And who'll have patience for me and my family?

He rips a rack of shelves from the wall, threatening to take it with him.

Pay me or I'm taking the shelves.

The Wife   My dear Miss Shen Te, you should turn this unpleasantness over to your cousin.

(*To* **The Carpenter**.) Submit your bill and Miss Shen Te's cousin will pay it.

The Carpenter   Oh her cousin, I'll bet.

The Nephew   Don't laugh, dummy. Her cousin's my personal friend.

The Husband   He's sharp as a knife.

The Carpenter   Oh alright, alright. Give him my bill, then.

He puts the shelves on the ground, sits on them and begins to tot up the bill.

The Wife   Without us stopping him he'd've torn the shirt off your back, for that wormy lumber. Accept one bill, correct or incorrect, and you'll be drowning in bills, correct or incorrect. Toss one scrap of gristle in your ashcan and soon every slaughterhouse hound in town'll find your yard, fighting over it. That's what the courts are for.

Shen Te   The courts won't help him get his money back.* He's worked and now he's got nothing to show for it. And he's got a family. It's bad that I can't pay him anything! What will the Gods say?

The Husband   You did your bit when you took us in; that's plenty enough.

A limping man and his pregnant wife enter.

Der Hinkende (*zum Paar*)   Ach, hier seid ihr! Ihr seid ja
saubere Verwandte! Uns einfach an der Straßenecke
stehen zu lassen!

Die Frau (*verlegen zu* **Shen Te**)   Das ist mein Bruder
Wung und die Schwägerin. (*Zu den beiden.*) Schimpft
nicht und setzt euch ruhig in die Ecke, damit ihr Fräulein
Shen Te, unsere alte Freundin, nicht stört. (*Zu* **Shen Te**.)
Ich glaube, wir müssen die beiden aufnehmen, da die
Schwägerin im fünften Monat ist. Oder bist du nicht der
Ansicht?

Shen Te   Seid willkommen!

Die Frau   Bedankt euch. Schalen stehen dort hinten.
(*Zu* **Shen Te**.) Die hätten überhaupt nicht gewußt, wohin.
Gut, daß du den Laden hast!

Shen Te (*lachend zum Publikum, Tee bringend*)   Ja, gut, daß
ich ihn habe!

Herein **Die Hausbesitzerin** *Frau Mi Tzü, ein Formular in der
Hand.*

Die Hausbesitzerin   Fräulein Shen Te, ich bin die
Hausbesitzerin, Frau Mi Tzü. Ich hoffe, wir werden gut
miteinander auskommen. Das ist ein Mietskontrakt.
(*Während* **Shen Te** *den Kontrakt durchliest.*) Ein schöner
Augenblick, die Eröffnung eines kleinen Geschäfts, nicht
wahr, meine Herrschaften? (*Sie schaut sich um.*) Ein paar
Lücken sind ja noch auf den Stellagen, aber es wird
schon gehen. Einige Referenzen werden Sie mir wohl
beibringen können?

Shen Te   Ist das nötig?

Die Hausbesitzerin   Aber ich weiß doch gar nicht, wer
Sie sind.

Der Mann   Vielleicht könnten wir für Fräulein Shen Te
bürgen? Wir kennen sie, seit sie in die Stadt gekommen
ist, und legen jederzeit die Hand für sie ins Feuer.

Die Hausbesitzerin   Und wer sind Sie?

Der Mann   Ich bin der Tabakhändler Ma Fu.

The Limping Man (*to* **The Husband** *and* **The Wife**)   So here you are! Some swell relatives! Leave us stranded on a street corner!

The Wife (*embarrassed, to* **Shen Te**)   This is my brother, Wung, and my sister-in-law.

(*To Wung and his wife.*) Now stop grousing and sit quietly in the corner so you don't bother Shen Te, our old friend.

(*To* **Shen Te**.) She's in her fifth month, we have to take them in, don't you think?

Shen Te   Please, come in.

The Wife   Say thank you. There are bowls in the back. (*To* **Shen Te**.) They just didn't know where else to turn. Good thing you have this shop!

Shen Te (*laughing to the audience, bringing tea*)   Yes. It's good that I have it.

Mrs Mi Tzu, **The Landlady**, *enters with a document in her hand.*

The Landlady   Miss Shen Te, I'm your landlady, Mrs Mi Tzu. I hope we'll get along. This is your lease.

As **Shen Te** *reads through the lease,* **The Landlady** *continues.*

Isn't it grand, opening day of a small business, don't you think, my fine gentlemen? (*She looks around.*) The shelves aren't full yet, but soon they will be. You can provide me with references?

Shen Te   Is that necessary?

The Landlady   I've no idea who you are.

The Husband   Might we vouch for Miss Shen Te? We've known her since she first came to our city, and for her sake we'd eagerly stick our hands in an open fire.

The Landlady   And you are ...?

The Husband   Ma Fu, the tobacconist.

Die Hausbesitzerin Wo ist Ihr Laden?

Der Mann Im Augenblick habe ich keinen Laden.
Sehen Sie, ich habe ihn eben verkauft.

Die Hausbesitzerin So. (*Zu* **Shen Te**.) Und sonst haben
Sie niemand, bei dem ich über Sie Auskünfte einholen
kann?

Die Frau (*souffliert*) Vetter! Vetter!

Die Hausbesitzerin Sie müssen doch jemand haben, der
mir dafür Gewähr bietet, was ich ins Haus bekomme. Das
ist ein respektables Haus, meine Liebe. Ohne das kann
ich mit Ihnen überhaupt keinen Kontrakt abschließen.

Shen Te (*langsam, mit niedergeschlagenen Augen*) Ich habe
einen Vetter.

Die Hausbesitzerin Ach, Sie haben einen Vetter. Am
Platz? Da können wir doch gleich hingehen. Was ist er?

Shen Te Er wohnt nicht hier, sondern in einer anderen
Stadt.

Die Frau Sagtest du nicht in Schung?

Shen Te Herr Shui Ta. In Schung!

Der Mann Aber den kenne ich ja überhaupt! Ein
Großer, Dürrer.

Der Neffe (*zum* **Schreiner**) Sie haben doch auch mit
Fräulein Shen Tes Vetter verhandelt! Über die Stellagen!

Der Schreiner (*mürrisch*) Ich schreibe für ihn gerade
die Rechnung aus. Da ist sie! (*Er übergibt sie.*) Morgen
früh komme ich wieder! (*Ab.*)

Der Neffe (*ruft ihm nach, auf* **Die Hausbesitzerin** *schielend*)
Seien Sie ganz ruhig, der Herr Vetter bezahlt es!

Die Hausbesitzerin (**Shen Te** *scharf musternd*) Nun, es
wird mich auch freuen, ihn kennenzulernen. Guten
Abend, Fräulein. (*Ab.*)

The Landlady   Where is your shop located?

The Husband   At present, located noplace in particular.
You see, I liquidated.

The Landlady   Aha.

(*To* **Shen Te**.) There's no one else who could give me a
reference for you?

The Wife (*whispering*)   Cousin! Cousin!

The Landlady   There must be someone who can tell me
what sort of person I have as a tenant. It's a respectable
property, my dear. Without some assurances I absolutely
cannot let you sign that lease.

Shen Te (*slowly, eyes downcast*)   I have a cousin.

The Landlady   Oh, a cousin. Close at hand? Then we'll
speak to him right away. What's he do?

Shen Te   He's not from around here, he's from
elsewhere.

The Wife   Didn't you tell me he lives in Schun?

Shen Te   Mr ... Shui Ta. In Schun!

The Husband   You don't say! Small world! I know him!
Really great, real honest.

The Nephew (*to* **The Carpenter**)   You! You've done
business with Miss Shen Te's cousin! For the shelves!

The Carpenter (*sullen*)   I'm finishing up his bill right
now. There!

He hands the bill to **Shen Te**.

The Carpenter   I'll be back early tomorrow! (*Exits.*)

The Nephew (*calling after him, glancing at* **The Landlady**)
Don't worry, her cousin pays!

The Landlady (*looking sharply at* **Shen Te**)   Mmmm-
hmm. I'm looking forward to meeting him too. Good
evening, Miss. (*Exits.*)

Die Frau (*nach einer Pause*)   Jetzt kommt alles auf! Du kannst sicher sein, morgen früh weiß die Bescheid über dich.

Die Schwägerin (*leise zum* **Neffen**)   Das wird hier nicht lange dauern!

Herein ein Greis, geführt von einem **Jungen**.

Der Junge (*nach hinten*)   Da sind sie.

Die Frau Guten Tag, Großvater. (*Zu* **Shen Te**.)   Der gute Alte! Er hat sich wohl um uns gesorgt. Und der Junge, ist er nicht groß geworden? Er frißt wie ein Scheunendrescher. Wen habt ihr denn noch alles mit?

Der Mann (*hinausschauend*)   Nur noch die Nichte.

Die Frau (*zu* **Shen Te**)   Eine junge Verwandte vom Land. Hoffentlich sind wir dir nicht zu viele. So viele waren wir noch nicht, als du bei uns wohntest, wie? Ja, wir sind immer mehr geworden. Je schlechter es ging, desto mehr wurden wir. Und je mehr wir wurden, desto schlechter ging es. Aber jetzt riegeln wir hier ab, sonst gibt es keine Ruhe.

Sie sperrt die Türe zu, und alle setzen sich.

Die Frau   Die Hauptsache ist, daß wir dich nicht im Geschäft stören. Denn wovon soll sonst der Schornstein rauchen? Wir haben uns das so gedacht: Am Tag gehen die Jüngeren weg, und nur der Großvater, die Schwägerin und vielleicht ich bleiben. Die anderen sehen höchstens einmal oder zweimal herein untertags, nicht? Zündet die Lampe dort an und macht es euch gemütlich.

Der Neffe (*humoristisch*)   Wenn nur nicht der Vetter heut nacht hereinplatzt, der gestrenge Herr Shui Ta!

Die Schwägerin *lacht.*

Der Bruder (*langt nach einer Zigarette*)   Auf eine wird es wohl nicht ankommen!

Der Mann   Sicher nicht.

The Wife (*after a pause*)   The pigeons are coming home to roost! Tomorrow morning she'll be on to you.

The Sister-in-Law (*softly to* **The Nephew**)   This can't last, we'll have to leave here soon.

An old man enters, led by a boy.

The Boy (*to the old man*)   They're here.

The Wife   Grandfather. (*To* **Shen Te**.) The old darling, he was worried about us. And hasn't the boy gotten big? He eats everything, like an ostrich. Did you bring anyone else with you?

The Husband (*looking outside*)   Just your niece.

The Niece *enters.*

The Wife (*To* **Shen Te**.)   A young country girl, like you. I hope we're not crowding you. We weren't such a big group back when you lived with us, were we? We multiplied. The worse things got, the more that came. And the more that came, the more things got worse. But now we'd better lock that door or there'll never be peace.

She locks the door, and everyone sits.

What really matters is that we let you get on with your business. Otherwise, what'll put fuel in the furnace? This is what we thought: during the day the young people will go out, and only grandfather, my sister-in-law and perhaps I will stay behind. The others will just stick their noses in once, maybe twice a day, right? Light that lamp and make yourselves at home.

The Nephew (*making a joke*)   We better hope her fiscally responsible cousin Mr Whatsisface —

The Husband   Shui Ta!

The Nephew   Better pray he doesn't show up tonight, boot us out.

The Sister-in-Law *laughs.*

The Limping Man, *who is now* **The Brother** (*taking a cigarette*)   No one'll mind if I take just one.

The Husband   Who'd begrudge you?

Alle nehmen sich zu rauchen. **Der Bruder** *reicht den Weinkrug herum.*

Der Neffe   Der Vetter bezahlt es!

Der Grossvater (*ernst zu Shen Te*)   Guten Tag!

Shen Te, *verwirrt durch die späte Begrüßung, verbeugt sich. Sie hat in der einen Hand die Rechnung des* **Schreiners**, *in der andern den Mietskontrakt.*

Die Frau   Könnt Ihr nicht etwas singen, damit die Gastgeberin etwas Unterhaltung hat?

Der Neffe   Der Großvater fängt an!

Sie singen Das Lied vom Rauch.

Der Grossvater
Einstmals, vor das Alter meine Haare bleichte
Hofft mit Klugheit ich mich durchzuschlagen.
Heute weiß ich, keine Klugheit reichte
Je, zu füllen eines armen Mannes Magen.
  Darum sagt ich: laß es!
  Sieh den grauen Rauch
  Der in immer kältre Kälten geht: so
  Gehst du auch.

Der Mann
Sah den Redlichen, den Fleißigen geschunden
So versucht ich's mit dem krummen Pfad
Doch auch der führt unsereinen nur nach unten
Und so weiß ich mir halt fürder keinen Rat.
  Und so sag ich: laß es!
  Sieh den grauen Rauch
  Der in immer kältre Kälten geht: so
  Gehst du auch.

Die Nichte
Die da alt sind, hör ich, haben nichts zu hoffen
Denn nur Zeit schafft's und an Zeit gebricht's.
Doch uns Jungen, hör ich, steht das Tor weit offen
Freilich, hör ich, steht es offen nur ins Nichts.
  Und auch ich sag: laß es!
  Sieh den grauen Rauch
  Der in immer kältre Kälten geht: so
  Gehst du auch.

Everyone takes something to smoke. **The Brother** *passes around a jug of wine.*

The Nephew   Her cousin'll cover it!

The Grandfather (*gravely, to* **Shen Te**)   Good morning!

Shen Te, *bewildered by the late greeting, bows. She has* **The Carpenter**'*s bill in one hand, the lease in the other.*

The Wife   Sing something, let's entertain our hostess.

The Nephew   Grandfather! Sing!

They sing The Song of the Smoke.

The Grandfather
Back before age bleached me white,
I thought that I'd get by on brains:
But nothing comes of being bright;
Smart but poor means hunger pains.
   And so I say: let go!
   Observe the grey smoke rise:
   It flies from cold to colder, that's
   How everybody dies.

The Husband
The faithful servant, good and true,
Gets nowhere, so I turned to crime.
But criminals get nowhere too,
And every road's a waste of time.
   And so I say: let go!
   Observe the grey smoke rise:
   It flies from cold to colder, that's
   How everybody dies.

The Niece
The old should hope for nothing more;
Hope's time, and time runs out, I guess:
The young stand at the open door:
It opens on to Nothingness.
   And so I say: let go!
   Observe the grey smoke rise:
   It flies from cold to colder, that's
   How everybody dies.

Der Neffe   Woher hast du den Wein?

Die Schwägerin   Er hat den Sack mit Tabak versetzt.

Der Mann   Was? Dieser Tabak war das einzige, das uns noch blieb! Nicht einmal für ein Nachtlager haben wir ihn angegriffen! Du Schwein!

Der Bruder   Nennst du mich ein Schwein, weil es meine Frau friert? Und hast selber getrunken. Gib sofort den Krug her!

Sie raufen sich. Die Tabakstellagen stürzen um.

Shen Te (*beschwört sie*)   Oh, schont den Laden, zerstört nicht alles! Er ist ein Geschenk der Götter! Nehmt euch, was da ist, aber zerstört es nicht!

Die Frau (*skeptisch*)   Der Laden ist kleiner, als ich dachte. Wir hätten vielleicht doch nicht der Tante und den andern davon erzählen sollen. Wenn sie auch noch kommen, wird es eng hier.

Die Schwägerin   Die Gastgeberin ist auch schon ein wenig kühler geworden!

Von draußen kommen Stimmen, und es wird an die Tür geklopft.

Rufe   Macht auf! Wir sind es!

Die Frau   Bist du es, Tante? Was machen wir da?

Shen Te   Mein schöner Laden! O Hoffnung! Kaum eröffnet, ist er schon kein Laden mehr!

(*Zum Publikum*) Der Rettung kleiner Nachen
Wird sofort in die Tiefe gezogen:
Zu viele Versinkende
Greifen gierig nach ihm.

Rufe (*von draußen*)   Macht auf!

The Nephew Where did the wine come from?

The Sister-in-Law He pawned the bale of tobacco.

The Husband He did what!? That tobacco was the last thing we owned! We didn't even pawn it to rent a room for the night. Pig!

The Brother My wife was freezing? Who're you calling a pig, pig? You've drunk as much as anyone else. Gimme my jug!

They fight. The racks of tobacco fall down.

Shen Te (*imploring*) Oh please, stop, the shop, you're destroying everything! This is a gift from the Gods! Take what you want, but don't destroy it!

The Wife (*sceptical*) This shop is smaller than I'd been led to believe. Maybe we shouldn't have sent word to Auntie and the others, when they arrive it's going to get uncomfortable.

The Sister-in-Law Already our hostess feels colder towards us.

Voices outside, and knocking at the door.

Voices Open up! It's us!

The Wife Is that you, Auntie? What should we do?

Shen Te My beautiful shop! Oh I had such hopes! Barely opened, and it's not even a shop anymore.

To the audience.

The little life raft
Is instantly pulled under.
Too many drowning people,
Greedy, grab hold.

Voices (*outside*) Open up!

ZWISCHENSPIEL
UNTER EINER BRÜCKE

Am Fluß kauert der Wasserverkäufer.

Wang (*sich umblickend*)   Alles ruhig. Seit vier Tagen
verberge ich mich jetzt schon. Sie können mich nicht
finden, da ich die Augen offenhalte. Ich bin absichtlich
entlang ihrer Wegrichtung geflohen. Am zweiten Tage
haben sie die Brücke passiert, ich hörte ihre Schritte
über mir. Jetzt müssen sie schon weit weg sein, ich bin vor
ihnen sicher.

*Er hat sich zurückgelegt und schläft ein. Musik. Die Böschung
wird durchsichtig, und es erscheinen die Götter.*

Wang (*hebt den Arm vors Gesicht, als sollte er geschlagen
werden*)   Sagt nichts, ich weiß alles! Ich habe niemand
gefunden, der euch aufnehmen will, in keinem Haus!
Jetzt wißt ihr es! Jetzt geht weiter!

Der Erste Gott   Doch, du hast jemand gefunden. Als du
weg warst, kam er. Er nahm uns auf für die Nacht, er
behütete unseren Schlaf, und er leuchtete uns mit einer
Lampe am Morgen, als wir ihn verließen. Du aber hast ihn
uns genannt als einen guten Menschen, und er war gut.

Wang   So war es Shen Te, die euch aufnahm?

Der Dritte Gott   Natürlich.

Wang   Und ich Kleingläubiger bin fortgelaufen! Nur
weil ich dachte: sie kann nicht kommen. Da es ihr
schlecht geht, kann sie nicht kommen.

Die Götter
  O du schwacher!
  Gut gesinnter, aber schwacher Mensch!
  Wo da Not ist, denkt er, gibt es keine Güte!
  Wo Gefahr ist, denkt er, gibt es keine Tapferkeit!
  O Schwäche, die an nichts ein gutes Haar läßt!
  O schnelles Urteil! O leichtfertige Verzweiflung!

Wang   Ich schäme mich sehr, Erleuchtete!

INTERLUDE
UNDER A BRIDGE

Wang *the waterseller squats by the river.*

Wang (*looking around*)   Everything's calm. I've been
hiding for four days. I'm keeping my eyes open, they'll
never find me. I deliberately fled in the direction they
were headed. On the second day I heard their footsteps
as they crossed this bridge. They must be far away by now.

*He lies down and falls asleep. Music. The embankment becomes
transparent and* **the Gods** *appear.*

Wang (*covering his face with his arms, as if expecting blows*)
Don't say it, I know it all already, no one wanted to take
you in, I couldn't find anyone! Now you know too! Go
away!

The First God   No, but you found someone. After you'd
fled, this person arrived, she sheltered us for the night,
watched over us as we slept, lit our path with a lamp at
dawn when we took our leave. You told us this person was
good, and you were right.

Wang   Shen Te?

The Third God   None other.

Wang   And I who have no faith fled away! Because I
believed she couldn't do it. Because she has no money, I
thought she couldn't.

The Gods
    Oh, weak one!
    Well-intended but weak man!
    Where there is Need, he thinks there is no Goodness!
    Where there is danger, he thinks there is no Bravery!
    Oh weakness that doubts the existence of Good!
    Oh Rush-to-Judgement! Oh giddy despair!

Wang   Very ashamed, Awakened Ones!

Der Erste Gott   Und jetzt, Wasserverkäufer, tu uns den
Gefallen und geh schnell zurück nach der Hauptstadt
und sieh nach der guten Shen Te dort, damit du uns von
ihr berichten kannst. Es geht ihr jetzt gut. Sie soll das
Geld zu einem kleinen Laden bekommen haben, so daß
sie dem Zug ihres milden Herzens ganz folgen kann.
Bezeig du Interesse an ihrer Güte, denn keiner kann lang
gut sein, wenn nicht Güte verlangt wird. Wir aber wollen
weiter wandern und suchen und noch andere Menschen
finden, die unserm guten Menschen von Sezuan
gleichen, damit das Gerede aufhört, daß es für die Guten
auf unserer Erde nicht mehr zu leben ist.

Sie verschwinden.

The First God   And now, waterseller, do us the favour of returning quickly to the capital city and look after the good Shen Te there, keep us informed. It is said she's obtained money somehow, she's purchased a small business, so that she'll be able to follow fully the pull of her gentle heart. Solicit her Goodness, for only when Goodness is demanded of one can one remain Good. We for our part will wander hither and yon searching out others like our good person of Szechwan, so that it will no longer be bruited about that the good cannot live on this earth.

They disappear.

2
Der Tabakladen

Überall schlafende Leute. Die Lampe brennt noch. Es klopft.

Die Frau (*erhebt sich schlaftrunken*)   Shen Te! Es klopft!
Wo ist sie denn?

Der Neffe   Sie holt wohl Frühstück. Der Herr Vetter
bezahlt es.

Die Frau *lacht und schlurft zur Tür. Herein ein* **Junger Herr**,
hinter ihm **Der Schreiner**.

Der Junge Herr   Ich bin der Vetter.

Die Frau (*aus den Wolken fallend*)   Was sind Sie?

Der Junge Herr   Mein Name ist Shui Ta.

Die Gäste (*sich gegenseitig aufrüttelnd*)   Der Vetter! – Aber
das war doch ein Witz, sie hat ja gar keinen Vetter! – Aber
hier ist jemand, der sagt, er ist der Vetter! – Unglaublich,
so früh am Tag!

Der Neffe   Wenn Sie der Vetter der Gastgeberin sind,
Herr, dann schaffen Sie uns schleunigst etwas zum
Frühstück!

Shui Ta (*die Lampe auslöschend*)   Die ersten Kunden
kommen bald, bitte, ziehen Sie sich schnell an, daß ich
meinen Laden aufmachen kann.

Der Mann   Ihren Laden? Ich denke, das ist der Laden
unserer Freundin Shen Te? (**Shui Ta** *schüttelt den Kopf.*)
Was, das ist gar nicht ihr Laden?

Die Schwägerin   Da hat sie uns also angeschmiert! Wo
steckt sie überhaupt?

Shui Ta   Sie ist abgehalten. Sie läßt Ihnen sagen, daß sie
nunmehr, nachdem ich da bin, nichts mehr für Sie tun
kann.

2
The Tobacco Shop

People are sleeping all about. The lamp is still burning. There's a knock on the door.

The Wife (*waking, groggy*)   Shen Te! Knocking! Where is she?

The Nephew   Fetching us breakfast probably. Her cousin, Mr Shambolical,* he's buying!

The Wife *laughs and shuffles to the door. She opens it; a* **Young Man** *enters and behind him,* **The Carpenter**.

The Young Man   I'm the cousin.

The Wife (*falling out of the clouds*)   Excuse me?

The Young Man   My name is Shui Ta.

The Guests (*shaking each other awake*)   The cousin's here! – But that was a joke, she doesn't have any cousins! – But this guy says he's her cousin! – It's unbelievably rude, barging in at this hour of the morning!

The Nephew   If you're really our hostess's cousin, mister, run off and see what's happened to our breakfast.

Shui Ta (*snuffing the lamp*)   The first customers will be arriving soon, please get up and get dressed so I can open my shop.

The Husband   Your shop? Doesn't this shop in point of fact belong to our friend Shen Te?

Shui Ta *shakes his head 'no'*.

The Husband   It doesn't?

The Sister-in-Law   She lied to us! Where is she anyway?

Shui Ta   Unavoidably detained. She's asked me to say to you that now that I'm arrived there'll be nothing further she can do for you.

Die Frau (*erschüttert*)   Und wir hielten sie für einen guten Menschen!

Der Neffe   Glaubt ihm nicht! Sucht sie!

Der Mann   Ja, das wollen wir. (*Er organisiert.*) Du und du und du und du, ihr sucht sie überall. Wir und Großvater bleiben hier, die Festung zu halten. Der Junge kann inzwischen etwas zum Essen besorgen. (*Zum* **Jungen**.) Siehst du den Kuchenbäcker dort am Eck? Schleich dich hin und stopf dir die Bluse voll.

Die Schwägerin   Nimm auch ein paar von den kleinen hellen Kuchen!

Der Mann   Aber gib acht, daß der Bäcker dich nicht erwischt. Und komm dem Polizisten nicht in die Quere!

Der Junge *nickt und geht weg. Die übrigen ziehen sich vollends an.*

Shui Ta   Wird ein Kuchendiebstahl nicht diesen Laden, der Ihnen Zuflucht gewährt hat, in schlechten Ruf bringen?

Der Neffe   Kümmert euch nicht um ihn, wir werden sie schnell gefunden haben. Sie wird ihm schön heimleuchten.

Der Neffe, **Der Bruder**, **Die Schwägerin** *und* **Die Nichte** *ab.*

Die Schwägerin (*im Abgehen*)   Laßt uns etwas übrig vom Frühstück!

Shui Ta (*ruhig*)   Sie werden sie nicht finden. Meine Kusine bedauert natürlich, das Gebot der Gastfreundschaft nicht auf unbegrenzte Zeit befolgen zu können. Aber Sie sind leider zu viele! Dies hier ist ein Tabakladen, und Fräulein Shen Te lebt davon.

Der Mann   Unsere Shen Te würde so etwas überhaupt nicht über die Lippen bringen.

Shui Ta   Sie haben vielleicht recht. (*Zum* **Schreiner**.) Das Unglück besteht darin, daß die Not in dieser Stadt zu groß ist, als daß ein einzelner Mensch ihr steuern könnte.

The Wife (*shaken*)   And we thought she was a good person.

The Nephew   Don't believe him! Let's go find her!

The Husband   Yes, that's what we must do. (*He organises.*) You and you and you and you, look everywhere. Grandfather, the missus and I will wait here, hold the fort. The boy can rustle up some grub.

(*To* **The Boy**.) Did you notice that bakery on the corner? Slip in and stuff your shirt with cookies.

The Sister-in-Law   And a couple of those little lemon cakes too!

The Husband   But mind the baker. And the police!

The Boy *nods and goes out. The others finish dressing.*

Shui Ta   Won't harbouring a cake-thief bring this shop, which harboured all of you, a shady reputation?

The Nephew   Ignore him, we'll find her in no time. She'll send him back to wherever he came from.

The Sister-in-Law (*exiting*)   Save some breakfast for us!

The Nephew, **The Brother**, **The Sister-in-Law** *and* **The Niece** *exit.*

Shui Ta (*calmly*)   They won't find her. My cousin is much aggrieved, naturally, to be unable to obey full-time the commandment to be hospitable. Unfortunately there are too many of you. This is a tobacco shop, and Miss Shen Te must make her living out of it.

The Husband   Such ungenerous thoughts would perish on our Shen Te's lips.*

Shui Ta   That may be true.

(*To* **The Carpenter**.) What's ultimately unlucky is that the need in this city is so great that it lies beyond the power of any individual to remedy it. Unluckily nothing has

Darin hat sich betrüblicherweise nichts geändert in den
elfhundert Jahren, seit jemand den Vierzeiler verfaßte:
Der Gouverneur, befragt, was nötig wäre
Den Frierenden der Stadt zu helfen, antwortete:
Eine zehntausend Fuß lange Decke
Welche die ganzen Vorstädte einfach zudeckt.

Er macht sich daran, den Laden aufzuräumen.

Der Schreiner   Ich sehe, daß Sie sich bemühen, die
Angelegenheiten Ihrer Kusine zu ordnen. Da ist eine
kleine Schuld für die Stellagen zu begleichen, anerkannt
vor Zeugen. 100 Silberdollar.

Shui Ta (*die Rechnung aus der Tasche ziehend, nicht
unfreundlich*)   Glauben Sie nicht, daß 100 Silberdollar
etwas zuviel sind?

Der Schreiner   Nein. Ich kann auch nichts ablassen. Ich
habe Frau und Kinder zu ernähren.

Shui Ta (*hart*)   Wie viele Kinder?

Der Schreiner   Vier.

Shui Ta   Dann biete ich Ihnen 20 Silberdollar.

Der Mann *lacht.*

Der Schreiner   Sind Sie verrückt? Diese Stellagen sind
aus Nußbaum!

Shui Ta   Dann nehmen Sie sie weg.

Der Schreiner   Was heißt das?

Shui Ta   Sie sind zu teuer für mich. Ich ersuche Sie, die
Nußbaumstellagen wegzunehmen.

Die Frau   Das ist gut gegeben! *Sie lacht ebenfalls.*

Der Schreiner (*unsicher*)   Ich verlange, daß Fräulein
Shen Te geholt wird. Sie ist anscheinend ein besserer
Mensch als Sie.

Shui Ta   Gewiß. Sie ist ruiniert.

Der Schreiner (*nimmt resolut eine Stellage und trägt sie zur
Tür*)   Da können Sie Ihre Rauchwaren ja auf dem Boden
aufstapeln! Mir kann es recht sein.

changed here since eleven hundred years ago someone
indicted this quatrain:

When the Governor was asked what would be needed
To help the freezing poor of the city, he replied:
Get a 10,000-foot-long tarpaulin
And just spread it over the slums.

Shui Ta *begins to clean up the shop.*

The Carpenter   I see you're putting your cousin's affairs
in order. There's an outstanding bill for the shelves, there
are witnesses. 100 silver dollars.

Shui Ta (*taking the bill from his pocket*)   Don't you think
100 silver dollars is a mite steep?

The Carpenter   No. I can't settle for less. I have a wife
and children to feed.

Shui Ta (*hard*)   How many children?

The Carpenter   Four.

Shui Ta   In that case, four silver dollars.

The Husband *laughs.*

The Carpenter   Are you crazy? These are walnut!

Shui Ta   Then take them back.

The Carpenter   What do you mean?

Shui Ta   Walnut shelves are too pricey for me. I'm
asking you to remove them.

The Wife   You tell him! (*She laughs too.*)

The Carpenter (*uncertain*)   I want to see Miss Shen Te.
She's a better person than you.

Shui Ta   I know. It's ruined her.

The Carpenter (*resolutely picking up a shelf and carrying it to
the door*)   Fine! Pile the tobacco in heaps on the floor.

Shui Ta (*zu dem* **Mann**)   Helfen Sie ihm!

Der Mann (*packt ebenfalls eine Stellage und trägt sie grinsend zur Tür*)   Also hinaus mit den Stellagen!

Der Schreiner   Du Hund! Soll meine Familie verhungern?

Shui Ta   Ich biete Ihnen noch einmal 20 Silberdollar, da ich meine Rauchwaren nicht auf dem Boden aufstapeln will.

Der Schreiner   100!

Shui Ta *schaut gleichmütig zum Fenster hinaus.* **Der Mann** *schickt sich an, die Stellage hinauszutragen.*

Der Schreiner   Zerbrich sie wenigstens nicht am Türbalken, Idiot! (*Verzweifelt*). Aber sie sind doch nach Maß gearbeitet! Sie passen in dieses Loch und sonst nirgends hin. Die Bretter sind verschnitten, Herr!

Shui Ta   Eben. Darum biete ich Ihnen auch nur 20 Silberdollar. Weil die Bretter verschnitten sind.

Die Frau *quietscht vor Vergnügen.*

Der Schreiner (*plötzlich müde*)   Da kann ich nicht mehr mit. Behalten Sie die Stellagen und bezahlen Sie, was Sie wollen.

Shui Ta   20 Silberdollar.

Er legt zwei große Münzen auf den Tisch. **Der Schreiner** *nimmt sie.*

Der Mann (*die Stellagen zurücktragend*)   Genug für einen Haufen verschnittener Bretter!

Der Schreiner   Ja, genug vielleicht, mich zu betrinken! (*Ab.*)

Der Mann   Den haben wir draußen!

Die Frau (*sich die Lachtränen trocknend*)   'Sie sind aus Nußbaum!' – 'Nehmen Sie sie weg!' – '100 Silberdollar! Ich habe vier Kinder!' – 'Dann zahle ich 20!' – 'Aber sie sind doch verschnitten!' – 'Eben! 20 Silberdollar!' So muß man diese Typen behandeln!

Shui Ta (*to* **The Husband**) Lend him a hand!

The Husband (*picking up a shelf and carrying it to the door, grinning*) Out with the shelves!

The Carpenter You bastard! You want my family to starve?

Shui Ta I'd rather not pile my tobacco in heaps on the floor. That's why I offered you two silver dollars.

The Carpenter You said four!

Shui Ta *looks indifferently out the window.* **The Husband** *proceeds to carry a shelf out the door.*

The Carpenter Don't bang the wood against the doorjamb, you idiot.

(*In despair.*) But these shelves were custom built! They fit this dump, they're useless anyplace else. The lumber's been cut, mister.

Shui Ta Exactly. That's why I offer you two silver dollars. The lumber's cut up.

The Wife *squeals with delight.*

The Carpenter (*suddenly tired*) I can't do this any more. Keep the shelves and pay whatever you want.

Shui Ta Two silver dollars.

He lays two large coins on the counter. **The Carpenter** *takes them.*

The Husband (*bringing the shelf back in*) That's plenty for cut-up lumber.

The Carpenter Maybe it's enough to get myself drunk. (*Exits.*)

The Husband We turned him inside-out!

The Wife (*drying tears of laughter*) 'They're walnut!' 'Take them back!' '100 silver dollars! I have four kids!' 'Then here's four!' 'But it's been cut to pieces.' 'Exactly! Two silver dollars!' Now that's the way you handle a no-class guy like that.

Shui Ta   Ja. (*Ernst.*) Geht schnell weg.

Der Mann   Wir?

Shui Ta   Ja, ihr. Ihr seid Diebe und Schmarotzer. Wenn ihr schnell geht, ohne Zeit mit Widerrede zu vergeuden, könnt ihr euch noch retten.

Der Mann   Es ist am besten, ihm gar nicht zu antworten. Nur nicht schreien mit nüchternem Magen. Ich möcht wissen, wo bleibt der Junge?

Shui Ta   Ja, wo bleibt der Junge? Ich sagte euch vorhin, daß ich ihn nicht mit gestohlenem Kuchen in meinem Laden haben will. (*Plötzlich schreiend.*) Noch einmal: geht!

Sie bleiben sitzen.

Shui Ta (*wieder ganz ruhig*)   Wie ihr wollt.

Er geht zur Tür und grüßt tief hinaus. In der Tür taucht ein **Polizist** *auf.*

Shui Ta   Ich vermute, ich habe den Beamten vor mir, der dieses Viertel betreut?

Der Polizist   Jawohl, Herr ...

Shui Ta   Shui Ta. (*Sie lächeln einander an.*) Angenehmes Wetter heute!

Der Polizist   Nur ein wenig warm vielleicht.

Shui Ta   Vielleicht ein wenig warm.

Der Mann (*leise zu seiner Frau*)   Wenn er quatscht, bis der Junge zurückkommt, sind wir geschnappt. (*Er versucht,* **Shui Ta** *heimlich ein Zeichen zu geben.*)

Shui Ta (*ohne es zu beachten*)   Es macht einen Unterschied, ob man das Wetter in einem kühlen Lokal beurteilt oder auf der staubigen Straße.

Der Polizist   Einen großen Unterschied.

Die Frau (*zum* **Mann**)   Sei ganz ruhig! Der Junge kommt nicht, wenn er den Polizisten in der Tür stehen sieht.

Shui Ta Yes.

(*Seriously.*) Now leave immediately.

The Husband Us?

Shui Ta Yes, you. You're crooks and parasites. If you leave instantly without insolence you won't waste my time and you can make a clean getaway.

The Husband (*to his wife*) Don't take the bait. I never quarrel on an empty stomach. I wonder where that boy is?

Shui Ta Yes, where is he? I already told you I don't want him skulking about with stolen pastry.

(*He screams, suddenly.*) Again: Go!

They remain sitting.

Shui Ta (*calm again*) As you wish.

Shui Ta goes to the door and calls out a greeting. A **Policeman** *appears in the doorway.*

Shui Ta I'm correct in assuming I speak to the gendarme for this precinct?

The Policeman Yes sir, Mr . . . ?

Shui Ta Shui Ta.

They smile at one another.

Shui Ta Beautiful weather today.

The Policeman Maybe just a little warm.

Shui Ta Maybe just a little.

The Husband (*softly, to his wife*) If they keep chatting, the boy'll show up, we'll get pinched. (*He tries to make secret signals to* **Shui Ta**.)

Shui Ta (*ignoring him*) When assessing the weather, it makes a difference whether you're in cool shade or out on some dusty street.

The Policeman It makes a considerable difference.

The Wife Stay calm! The boy won't come near the place with a cop in the doorway.

Shui Ta   Treten Sie doch ein. Es ist wirklich kühler hier. Meine Kusine und ich haben einen Laden eröffnet. Lassen Sie mich Ihnen sagen, daß wir den größten Wert darauf legen, mit der Behörde auf gutem Fuß zu stehen.

Der Polizist (*tritt ein*)   Sie sind sehr gütig, Herr Shui Ta. Ja, hier ist es wirklich kühl.

Der Mann (*leise*)   Er nimmt ihn extra herein, damit der Junge ihn nicht stehen sieht.

Shui Ta   Gäste! Entfernte Bekannte meiner Kusine, wie ich höre. Sie sind auf einer Reise begriffen. (*Man verbeugt sich.*) Wir waren eben dabei, uns zu verabschieden.

Der Mann (*heiser*)   Ja, da gehen wir also.

Shui Ta   Ich werde meiner Kusine bestellen, daß Sie ihr für das Nachtquartier danken, aber keine Zeit hatten, auf ihre Rückkehr zu warten.

Von der Straße Lärm und Rufe 'Haltet den Dieb!'

Der Polizist   Was ist das?

In der Tür steht **Der Junge**. *Aus der Bluse fallen ihm Fladen und kleine Kuchen.* **Die Frau** *winkt ihm verzweifelt, er solle hinaus. Er wendet sich und will weg.*

Der Polizist   Halt du! (*Er faßt ihn.*) Woher hast du die Kuchen?

Der Junge   Von da drüben.

Der Polizist   Oh. Diebstahl, wie?

Die Frau   Wir wußten nichts davon. Der Junge hat es auf eigene Faust gemacht. Du Nichtsnutz!

Der Polizist   Herr Shui Ta, können Sie den Vorfall aufklären?

Shui Ta *schweigt.*

Shui Ta Please, it's much cooler in here. My cousin and I are proprietors of this shop. And may I say we set great store in starting off on the right foot with the authorities.

The Policeman (*entering*) You're too kind, Mr Shui Ta. You're right, it's really cool in here.

The Husband (*softly*) He did that just so the boy won't see the cop.

Shui Ta Guests! Casual acquaintances of my cousin, or so they say. They're off on a trip.

The Husband *bows.*

Shui Ta We were just saying our goodbyes.

The Husband (*hoarsely*) Yes, well, we'll be going then.

Shui Ta I'll let my cousin know how grateful you were for the use of her bedding; too bad you can't wait for her return.

From the street, noise and shouting: 'Stop, thief!'

The Policeman What was that?

The Boy *stands in the doorway. Cookies and cakes fall out from under his shirt.* **The Wife** *waves at him desperately to run. He turns and tries to escape.*

The Policeman Stop!

The Policeman *nabs* **The Boy**.

The Policeman Where did you get the pastries?

The Boy Over there.

The Policeman Uh huh. Shoplifting?

The Wife We didn't know! The boy's incorrigible! You knucklehead!

The Policeman Mr Shui Ta, can you help clear this up?

Shui Ta *is silent.*

Der Polizist   Aha. Ihr kommt alle mit auf die Wache.

Shui Ta   Ich bin außer mir, daß in meinem Lokal so etwas passieren konnte.

Die Frau   Er hat zugesehen, als der Junge wegging!

Shui Ta   Ich kann Ihnen versichern, Herr Polizist, daß ich Sie kaum hereingebeten hätte, wenn ich einen Diebstahl hätte decken wollen.

Der Polizist   Das ist klar. Sie werden also auch verstehen, Herr Shui Ta, daß es meine Pflicht ist, diese Leute abzuführen. (**Shui Ta** *verbeugt sich.*) Vorwärts mit euch! (*Er treibt sie hinaus.*)

Der Grossvater (*friedlich unter der Tür*)   Guten Tag.

Alle außer **Shui Ta** *ab.* **Shui Ta** *räumt weiter auf. Eintritt* **Die Hausbesitzerin**.

Die Hausbesitzerin   So, Sie sind dieser Herr Vetter! Was bedeutet das, daß die Polizei aus diesem meinem Haus Leute abführt? Wie kommt Ihre Kusine dazu, hier ein Absteigequartier aufzumachen? Das hat man davon, wenn man Leute ins Haus nimmt, die gestern noch in Fünfkäschkämmerchen gehaust und vom Bäcker an der Ecke Hirsefladen erbettelt haben! Sie sehen, ich weiß Bescheid.

Shui Ta   Das sehe ich. Man hat Ihnen Übles von meiner Kusine erzählt. Man hat sie beschuldigt, gehungert zu haben! Es ist notorisch, daß sie in Armut lebte. Ihr Leumund ist der allerschlechteste: es ging ihr elend!

Die Hausbesitzerin   Sie war eine ganz gewöhnliche ...

Shui Ta   Unbemittelte, sprechen wir das harte Wort aus!

Die Hausbesitzerin   Ach, bitte, keine Gefühlsduseleien! Ich spreche von ihrem Lebenswandel, nicht von ihren Einkünften. Ich bezweifle nicht, daß es da gewisse Einkünfte gegeben hat, sonst gäbe es diesen Laden nicht. Einige ältere Herren werden schon gesorgt haben. Woher bekommt man einen Laden? Herr, dies ist ein respektables Haus! Die Leute, die hier Miete zahlen, wünschen nicht, mit einer solchen Person unter einem

The Policeman   Aha. You're all coming down to the station.

Shui Ta   I'm horrified to find such people in my shop.

The Wife   He knew all about it!

Shui Ta   Obviously, officer, I wouldn't have asked you in if had anything larcenous to hide.

The Policeman   Obviously. I'm sorry, Mr Shui Ta, but it's my duty to take these people in.

Shui Ta *bows.*

The Policeman   Come on, you.

He drives the others out.

The Grandfather (*pleasantly, at the doorway*)   Good evening.

*Everyone except **Shui Ta** exits. **Shui Ta** resumes cleaning. **The Landlady** enters.*

The Landlady   So you're this Mr Cousin person. Why is that policeman escorting those people off my property? I've seen them before, pestering the baker for stale millet cakes! If your cousin thinks she can turn this shop into a night-time flophouse for a little extra cash, boarding paupers from the city shelters, she has another think coming! I wasn't born yesterday.

Shui Ta   I see that. People have told you bad things about my cousin.* How she went hungry. How poor she was. How miserable.

The Landlady   People say she was a cheap little —

Shui Ta   Mendicant, let's say the ugly word.

The Landlady   Oh spare me! I'm talking about her reputation, not her income level! She got money from somewhere. A number of older gentlemen provided for her. How else did she get the lease for this shop? Mister, this is a respectable property. Other people who pay rent

Dach zu wohnen, jawohl. (*Pause.*) Ich bin kein
Unmensch, aber ich muß Rücksichten nehmen.

Shui Ta (*kalt*)   Frau Mi Tzü, ich bin beschäftigt. Sagen
Sie mir einfach, was es uns kosten wird, in diesem
respektablen Haus zu wohnen.

Die Hausbesitzerin   Ich muß sagen, Sie sind jedenfalls
kaltblütig!

Shui Ta (*zieht aus dem Ladentisch den Mietskontrakt*)   Die
Miete ist sehr hoch. Ich entnehme diesem Kontrakt, daß
sie monatlich zu entrichten ist.

Die Hausbesitzerin (*schnell*)   Aber nicht für Leute wie
Ihre Kusine!

Shui Ta   Was heißt das?

Die Hausbesitzerin   Es heißt, daß Leute wie Ihre Kusine
die Halbjahresmiete von 200 Silberdollar im voraus zu
bezahlen haben.

Shui Ta   200 Silberdollar! Das ist halsabschneiderisch!
Wie soll ich das aufbringen? Ich kann hier nicht auf
großen Umsatz rechnen. Ich setze meine einzige
Hoffnung darauf, daß die Sacknäherinnen von der
Zementfabrik viel rauchen, da die Arbeit, wie man mir
gesagt hat, sie sehr erschöpft. Aber sie verdienen schlecht.

Die Hausbesitzerin   Das hätten Sie vorher bedenken
müssen.

Shui Ta   Frau Mi Tzü, haben Sie ein Herz! Es ist wahr,
meine Kusine hat den unverzeihlichen Fehler begangen,
Unglücklichen Obdach zu gewähren. Aber sie kann sich
bessern, ich werde sorgen, daß sie sich bessert.
Andrerseits, wie könnten Sie einen besseren Mieter
finden als einen, der die Tiefe kennt, weil er aus ihr
kommt? Er wird sich die Haut von den Fingern arbeiten,
Ihnen die Miete pünktlichst zu bezahlen, er wird alles
tun, alles opfern, alles verkaufen, vor nichts
zurückschrecken und dabei wie ein Mäuschen sein, still
wie eine Fliege, sich Ihnen in allem unterwerfen, ehe er
zurückgeht dorthin. Solch ein Mieter ist nicht mit Gold
aufzuwiegen.

here don't want to share their roof with alley trash like that. (*Pause.*) I'm not a monster, but I have to be careful.

Shui Ta (*coldly*) Mrs Mi Tzu, I'm busy. Just tell me what it'll cost to lease this respectable property.

The Landlady Well aren't you a cold-blooded —

Shui Ta (*taking the lease from underneath the counter*) The rent's already exorbitant. This is a monthly lease.

The Landlady (*quickly*) Not for people like your cousin!

Shui Ta People like my cousin —

The Landlady — pay half the year's rent of 200 silver dollars in advance.

Shui Ta 200 silver dollars! You're cutting my throat! How'm I supposed to come up with that? We don't move a lot of merchandise here. I'm counting on the sack-stitching girls from the cement factory, I figure they'll take to smoking, something to pep them up after all day hunched over sacking. But what do they make? Not much.

The Landlady You should have thought this out before.

Shui Ta Have a heart, Mrs Mi Tzu! It's true my cousin committed the unpardonable mistake of sheltering unfortunates. But she'll do better from now on, I'll see that she does. And you'll never find more reliable tenants than people who've lived at the bottom of the barrel, who know what it's like, life at the bottom, desperate people who'll work the skin off their fingers to pay you on time, sell anything, sacrifice everything, stop at nothing and yet they're timid as mice, flies on the wall, they'd grovel before you every chance they get so long as they don't have to go back to life like that. A desperate tenant's cash in the bank! Good as gold.

Die Hausbesitzerin   200 Silberdollar im voraus oder sie geht zurück auf die Straße, woher sie kommt.

Herein **Der Polizist**.

Der Polizist   Lassen Sie sich nicht stören, Herr Shui Ta!

Die Hausbesitzerin   Die Polizei zeigt wirklich ein ganz besonderes Interesse für diesen Laden.

Der Polizist   Frau Mi Tzü, ich hoffe, Sie haben keinen falschen Eindruck bekommen. Herr Shui Ta hat uns einen Dienst erwiesen, und ich komme lediglich, ihm dafür im Namen der Polizei zu danken.

Die Hausbesitzerin   Nun, das geht mich nichts an. Ich hoffe, Herr Shui Ta, mein Vorschlag sagt Ihrer Kusine zu. Ich liebe es, mit meinen Mietern in gutem Einvernehmen zu sein. Guten Tag, meine Herren. (*Ab.*)

Shui Ta   Guten Tag, Frau Mi Tzü.

Der Polizist   Haben Sie Schwierigkeiten mit Frau Mi Tzü?

Shui Ta   Sie verlangt Vorausbezahlung der Miete, da meine Kusine ihr nicht respektabel erscheint.

Der Polizist   Und Sie haben das Geld nicht? *Shui Ta schweigt.* Aber jemand wie Sie, Herr Shui Ta, muß doch Kredit finden?

Shui Ta   Vielleicht. Aber wie sollte jemand wie Shen Te Kredit finden?

Der Polizist   Bleiben Sie denn nicht?

Shui Ta   Nein. Und ich kann auch nicht wiederkommen. Nur auf der Durchreise konnte ich ihr eine Hand reichen, nur das Schlimmste konnte ich abwehren. Bald wird sie wieder auf sich selber angewiesen sein. Ich frage mich besorgt, was dann werden soll.

Der Polizist   Herr Shui Ta, es tut mir leid, daß Sie Schwierigkeiten mit der Miete haben. Ich muß zugeben, daß wir diesen Laden zuerst mit gemischten Gefühlen betrachteten, aber Ihr entschlossenes Auftreten vorhin hat uns gezeigt, wer Sie sind. Wir von der Behörde haben es schnell heraus, wen wir als Stütze der Ordnung ansehen können.

The Landlady   200 silver dollars advance or she'll be walking the streets again.

The Policeman *enters.*

The Policeman   Sorry about all that, Mr Shui Ta.

The Landlady   This cop really feels at home here.

The Policeman   Mrs Mi Tzu, I hope I'm not importuning or causing you concern. Mr Shui Ta has done his civic duty, and I'm here as a representative of the Force to say thank you.

The Landlady   I don't want to know and I don't need to know, I only hope your cousin can meet my terms, Mr Shui Ta. I like it when I'm getting on with tenants. (*Exits.*)

Shui Ta   Good day, Mrs Mi Tzu.

The Policeman   Is there some problem with Mrs Mi Tzu?

Shui Ta   She wants half the year's rent up front, since my cousin by her lights isn't respectable.

The Policeman   Don't you have the money?

Shui Ta *is silent.*

The Policeman   A gentleman such as yourself, Mr Shui Ta, can surely obtain a loan.

Shui Ta   I might. But could someone like Shen Te obtain one?

The Policeman   You aren't staying?

Shui Ta   No. Nor returning. I stopped over on a trip to forestall disaster. She'll have to rely on herself after this. I'm afraid for her.

The Policeman   It's really too bad you can't make the rent, Mr Shui Ta. I must tell you that at first we cast a gimlet eye at the doings in this shop, beggars in and out, but your rectitude's corrected that. The Force is eager to recognise upstanding orderly citizens.

Shui Ta (*bitter*)   Herr, um diesen kleinen Laden zu retten, den meine Kusine als ein Geschenk der Götter betrachtet, bin ich bereit, bis an die äußerste Grenze des gesetzlich Erlaubten zu gehen. Aber Härte und Verschlagenheit helfen nur gegen die Unteren, denn die Grenzen sind klug gezogen. Mir geht es wie dem Mann, der mit den Ratten fertig geworden ist, aber dann kam der Fluß!

(*Nach einer kleinen Pause.*) Rauchen Sie?

Der Polizist (*zwei Zigarren einsteckend*)   Wir von der Station verlören Sie höchst ungern hier, Herr Shui Ta. Aber Sie müssen Frau Mi Tzü verstehen. Die Shen Te hat, da wollen wir uns nichts vormachen, davon gelebt, daß sie sich an Männer verkaufte. Sie können mir einwenden: was sollte sie machen? Wovon sollte sie zum Beispiel ihre Miete zahlen? Aber der Tatbestand bleibt: es ist nicht respektabel. Warum? Erstens: Liebe verkauft man nicht, sonst ist es käufliche Liebe. Zweitens: respektabel ist, nicht mit dem, der einen bezahlt, sondern mit dem, den man liebt. Drittens: nicht für eine Handvoll Reis, sondern aus Liebe. Schön, antworten Sie mir, was hilft alle Weisheit, wenn die Milch schon verschüttet ist? Was soll sie machen? Sie muß eine Halbjahresmiete auftreiben? Herr Shui Ta, ich muß Ihnen sagen, ich weiß es nicht. (*Er denkt eifrig nach.*) Herr Shui Ta, ich hab's! Suchen Sie doch einfach einen Mann für sie!

Herein eine kleine alte Frau.

Die Alte   Eine gute billige Zigarre für meinen Mann. Wir sind nämlich morgen vierzig Jahre verheiratet und da machen wir eine kleine Feier.

Shui Ta (*höflich*)   Vierzig Jahre und noch immer eine Feier!

Die Alte   Soweit unsere Mittel es gestatten! Wir haben den Teppichladen gegenüber. Ich hoffe, wir halten gute Nachbarschaft, das sollte man, die Zeiten sind schlecht.

Shui Ta (*legt ihr verschiedene Kistchen vor*)   Ein sehr alter Satz, fürchte ich.

Der Polizist   Herr Shui Ta, wir brauchen Kapital. Nun, ich schlage eine Heirat vor.

Shui Ta (*bitter*)   Officer, my cousin regards this shop as a gift from the Gods, and to save it I'd go to the furthest limits of the law. But driving hard bargains only helps you drive off the underdogs, the ones above you are cleverer and better protected. I'm the man who smoked the rats out of his cellar just in time for the floods.

(*After a small pause.*) Do you smoke?

The Policeman (*pocketing two cigars*)   Everyone at the precinct house would hate to see you go, Mr Shui Ta. But Mrs Mi Tzu has her point. Shen Te sold herself to men. It's no good to argue that she had to. True, she'd never have made rent if she hadn't. But still, it isn't respectable. Why? First: because nobody should sell love,* because then love's just merchandise. Two: what's respectable is not doing it with the guy who has the money but with the guy you love. And C and lastly: not for a handful of rice, but for love. OK, you answer, but what's the use of all this philosophy when the milk's already spilt? What's the girl to do? She's got to raise half a year's rent? Mr Shui Ta, I'll tell you: I have no idea.

(*He gives it some hard thought.*) Mr Shui Ta, I've got it! Just find her a husband!

A little old woman enters.

The Old Woman   A good cheap cigar for my husband. Tomorrow we're having a little celebrating for our fortieth anniversary.

Shui Ta (*politely*)   Forty years and still celebrating!

The Old Woman   As much as we can afford! Ours is the rug shop across the way. I hope we'll be good neighbours, one should try, these being such very hard times.

Shui Ta (*placing various boxes of cigars before her*)   The only kind of times we ever get.

The Policeman   We need capital, Mr Shui Ta. I'm proposing a wedding.

Shui Ta (*entschuldigend zu der Alten*) Ich habe mich dazu
verleiten lassen, den Herrn Polizisten mit meinen
privaten Bekümmernissen zu behelligen.

Der Polizist Wir haben die Halbjahresmiete nicht.
Schön, wir heiraten ein wenig Geld.

Shui Ta Das wird nicht so leicht sein.

Der Polizist Wieso? Sie ist eine Partie. Sie hat ein
kleines, aufstrebendes Geschäft. (*Zu der Alten.*) Was
denken Sie darüber?

Die Alte (*unschlüssig*) Ja ...

Der Polizist Eine Annonce in der Zeitung.

Die Alte (*zurückhaltend*) Wenn das Fräulein
einverstanden ist ...

Der Polizist Was soll sie dagegen haben? Ich setze
Ihnen das auf. Ein Dienst ist des andern wert. Denken Sie
nicht, daß die Behörde kein Herz für den
hartkämpfenden kleinen Geschäftsmann hat. Sie gehen
uns an die Hand, und wir setzen Ihnen dafür Ihre
Heiratsannonce auf! Hahaha! *Er zieht eifrig sein Notizbuch
hervor, befeuchtet den Bleistiftstummel und schreibt los.*

Shui Ta (*langsam*) Das ist keine schlechte Idee.

Der Polizist 'Welcher ... ordentliche ... Mann mit
kleinem Kapital ... Witwer nicht ausgeschlossen ...
wünscht Einheirat ... in aufblühendes Tabakgeschäft?'
Und dann fügen wir noch hinzu: 'Bin hübsche
sympathische Erscheinung.' Wie?

Shui Ta Wenn Sie meinen, daß das keine Übertreibung
wäre.

Die Alte (*freundlich*) Durchaus nicht. Ich habe sie
gesehen.

Der Polizist *reißt aus seinem Buch das Blatt und überreicht es*
Shui Ta.

Shui Ta Mit Entsetzen sehe ich, wieviel Glück nötig ist,
damit man nicht unter die Räder kommt! Wie viele
Einfälle! Wie viele Freunde! (*Zum* **Polizisten**.) Trotz aller
Entschlossenheit war ich zum Beispiel am Ende meines
Witzes, was die Ladenmiete betraf. Und jetzt kamen Sie
und halfen mir mit einem guten Rat. Ich sehe tatsächlich
einen Ausweg.

Shui Ta (*apologetically, to* **The Old Woman**) I've been confiding my woes to this officer.

The Policeman So we don't have the rent? So what! We'll marry some money!

Shui Ta Easier said than done.

The Policeman Why? She's a tasty dish. She's got a growing concern.

(*To* **The Old Woman**.) What's your opinion?

The Old Woman (*undecided*) Well ...

The Policeman We could take out a personals ad.

The Old Woman (*reluctantly*) If the young Miss agrees ...

The Policeman Why shouldn't she? I'll make one up for you. Just to show that the authorities aren't heartlessly disinterested in the struggling entrepreneur. You did us a favour, and in turn we will now compose your personals ad. Hahahaha!

He eagerly pulls out his notebook, licks his pencil-tip, and starts to write.

Shui Ta (*slowly*) It's an idea.

The Policeman Seeking ... upstanding ... gentleman with a little capital ... open paren, widowers considered, close paren ... interested in marrying into ... up and coming tobacco business? And then we can add: She has a, um, she's got a ... A sympathetic face!

Shui Ta Sympathetic? Don't overdo it.

The Old Woman (*friendly*) Not in the least. I've seen her.

The Policeman *rips the page from the notebook and gives it to* **Shui Ta**.

Shui Ta With dismay I see how lucky you must be to escape being crushed under the wheels! How much you must scheme! How many friends you need! (*To* **The Policeman**.) For instance, despite my iron will I was at the end of my wits over the rent. And then you made a very good suggestion. And now I actually see a way out.

3
Abend im Stadtpark

Ein junger Mann in abgerissenen Kleidern verfolgt mit den Augen ein Flugzeug, das anscheinend in einem hohen Bogen über den Park geht. Er zieht einen Strick aus der Tasche und schaut sich suchend um. Als er auf eine große Weide zugeht, kommen zwei Prostituierte des Weges. Die eine ist schon alt, die andere ist **Die Nichte** *aus der achtköpfigen Familie.*

Die Junge Guten Abend, junger Herr. Kommst du mit, Süßer?

Sun Möglich, meine Damen, wenn ihr mir was zum Essen kauft.

Die Alte Du bist wohl übergeschnappt? (*Zur* **Jungen**.) Gehen wir weiter. Wir verlieren nur unsere Zeit mit ihm. Das ist ja der stellungslose Flieger.

Die Junge Aber es wird niemand mehr im Park sein, es regnet gleich.

Die Alte Vielleicht doch.

Sie gehen weiter. Sun zieht, sich umschauend, seinen Strick hervor und wirft ihn um einen Weidenast. Er wird aber wieder gestört. Die beiden Prostituierten kommen schnell zurück. Sie sehen ihn nicht.

Die Junge Es wird ein Platzregen.

Shen Te *kommt des Weges spaziert.*

Die Alte Schau, da kommt das Untier! Dich und die Deinen hat sie ins Unglück gebracht!

Die Junge Nicht sie. Ihr Vetter war es. Sie hatte uns ja aufgenommen, und später hat sie uns angeboten, die Kuchen zu zahlen. Gegen sie habe ich nichts.

Die Alte Aber ich! (*Laut.*) Ach, da ist ja unsere feine Schwester mit dem Goldhafen! Sie hat einen Laden, aber sie will uns immer noch Freier wegfischen.

3
Evening in the City Park

A young man in torn clothing watches a plane, which is apparently flying in high curves above the park. He pulls a rope from his pocket and looks about. As he approaches a big willow tree, two prostitutes enter. One is turning old, the other is **The Niece** *from the family of eight.*

The Niece, *who is now* **The Young Prostitute**   Nice evening, huh, scout?

Sun   Ladies.

The Young Prostitute   Wanna walk with me, sweetheart?

Sun   I might, if you buy me dinner.

The Old Prostitute   You must be nuts. (*To* **The Young Prostitute**.) Let's go. He's a waste of time. He's an out-of-work pilot.

The Young Prostitute   But there's no one else, the park's empty, it's going to rain.

The Old Prostitute   It's never empty. Someone'll come by.

They walk on. **Sun** *throws the rope over a branch of the willow. He's tying a noose when he's interrupted: the two prostitutes hurry back quickly. They don't see him under the willow.*

The Young Prostitute   I told you, the sky's about to burst.

(**Shen Te** *comes walking down the path.*)

The Old Prostitute   Lookie that, it's the animal who wrecked your whole family.

The Young Prostitute   She didn't, her cousin. She took us in, and afterwards when she came home, she offered to pay the baker for the cakes we swiped. I have no problem with her.

The Old Prostitute   Good for you! I got a problem! (*loudly*) Oh look at that, jingling her gold, our elegant sister with her own shop now, still out walking, fishing for our customers.

Shen Te   Friß mich doch nicht gleich auf! Ich gehe ins Teehaus am Teich.

Die Junge   Ist es wahr, daß du einen Witwer mit drei Kindern heiraten wirst?

Shen Te   Ja, ich treffe ihn dort.

Sun (*ungeduldig*)   Schert euch endlich weiter, ihr Schnepfen! Kann man nicht einmal hier seine Ruhe haben?

Die Alte   Halt das Maul!

Die beiden Prostituierten ab.

Sun (*ruft ihnen nach*)   Aasgeier! (*Zum Publikum.*) Selbst an diesem abgelegenen Platz fischen sie unermüdlich nach Opfern, selbst im Gebüsch, selbst bei Regen suchen sie verzweifelt nach Käufern.

Shen Te (*zornig*)   Warum beschimpfen Sie sie? *Sie erblickt den Strick.* Oh.

Sun   Was glotzt du?

Shen Te   Wozu ist der Strick?

Sun   Geh weiter, Schwester, geh weiter! Ich habe kein Geld, nichts, nicht eine Kupfermünze. Und wenn ich eine hätte, würde ich nicht dich, sondern einen Becher Wasser kaufen vorher.

Es fängt an zu regnen.

Shen Te   Wozu ist der Strick? Das dürfen Sie nicht!

Sun   Was geht dich das an? Scher dich weg!

Shen Te   Es regnet.

Sun   Versuch nicht, dich unter diesen Baum zu stellen.

Shen Te (*bleibt unbeweglich im Regen stehen*)   Nein.

Sun   Schwester, laß ab, es hilft dir nichts. Mit mir ist kein Geschäft zu machen. Du bist mir auch zu häßlich. Krumme Beine.

Shen Te   Das ist nicht wahr.

Shen Te Fish away, don't bark at me. I'm going to meet someone. At the tea house by the pond.

The Young Prostitute So it's true? You're marrying a widower? With three kids?

Shen Te Yes.

Sun (*impatient*) Beat it already, you hens. Can't I get peace and quiet anywhere?

The Old Prostitute Up yours!

The two prostitutes exit.

Sun (*calling after them*) Buzzards! (*To the audience.*) Even in this wasteland of a park they're circling, red eyes peeled for corpses and carrion, not even a storm'll scare them off, not when there's rotten flesh to peck at.

Shen Te (*angrily*) Why are you picking on them?

(*She sees the rope.*) Oh.

Sun Oh what? What do you want?

Shen Te What's the rope for?

Sun Get lost, sister, get lost! I don't have money, nothing, not a copper coin. And if I did have any, I'd buy a glass of water before I'd buy you.

It starts to rain.

Shen Te What's the rope for? Please, don't.

Sun What's it to you? Beat it!

Shen Te It's raining.

Sun Don't think about coming under this tree.

Shen Te (*motionless in the rain*) No.

Sun It's useless, lady. You and me aren't making any deals. You're way too ugly for me. Bandy-legs.

Shen Te That's not true.

Sun   Zeig sie nicht! Komm schon, zum Teufel, unter den Baum, wenn es regnet!

Sie geht langsam hin und setzt sich unter den Baum.

Shen Te   Warum wollen Sie das tun?

Sun   Willst du es wissen? Dann werde ich es dir sagen, damit ich dich loswerde. (*Pause.*) Weißt du, was ein Flieger ist?

Shen Te   Ja, in einem Teehaus habe ich Flieger gesehen.

Sun   Nein, du hast keine gesehen. Vielleicht ein paar windige Dummköpfe mit Lederhelmen, Burschen ohne Gehör für Motore und ohne Gefühl für eine Maschine. Das kommt nur in eine Kiste, weil es den Hangarverwalter schmieren kann. Sag so einem: Laß deine Kiste aus 2000 Fuß Höhe durch die Wolken hinunter abfallen und dann fang sie auf, mit einem Hebeldruck, dann sagt er: Das steht nicht im Kontrakt. Wer nicht fliegt, daß er seine Kiste auf den Boden aufsetzt, als wäre es sein Hintern, der ist kein Flieger, sondern ein Dummkopf. Ich aber bin ein Flieger. Und doch bin ich der größte Dummkopf, denn ich habe alle Bücher über die Fliegerei gelesen auf der Schule in Peking. Aber eine Seite eines Buchs habe ich nicht gelesen und auf dieser Seite stand, daß keine Flieger mehr gebraucht werden. Und so bin ich ein Flieger ohne Flugzeug geworden, ein Postflieger ohne Post. Aber was das bedeutet, das kannst du nicht verstehen.

Shen Te   Ich glaube, ich verstehe es doch.

Sun   Nein, ich sage dir ja, du kannst es nicht verstehen, also kannst du es nicht verstehen.

Shen Te (*halb lachend, halb weinend*)   Als Kinder hatten wir einen Kranich mit einem lahmen Flügel. Er war freundlich zu uns und trug uns keinen Spaß nach und stolzierte hinter uns drein, schreiend, daß wir nicht zu schnell für ihn liefen. Aber im Herbst und im Frühjahr, wenn die großen Schwärme über das Dorf zogen, wurde er sehr unruhig, und ich verstand ihn gut.

Sun   Don't show me. Alright already, to hell with you, come out of the rain, under the tree.

She walks slowly under the tree and sits.

Shen Te   Why do you want to do that?

Sun   You really want to know? If I tell you will you leave me alone?

Pause.

You know what a pilot is?

Shen Te   Yes, I've seen pilots drinking, in the tea houses.

Sun   You have not. What you saw were dumbass windbags with leather helmets, boys with tin ears for the sound of engines and no sensitivity for machines. They have to grease the airfield manager's palm just to get into a plane. Tell them: You're going to let your plane fall through the clouds from a height of 2,000 feet and then jolt her back up with a flick of the joystick, and they'll say: That's not in the contract. If you can't land a plane easy as settling your ass on a barstool, you're not a pilot, you're a jerk. But I'm a pilot. And I'm the biggest jerk, because I read every single page of every textbook in the pilot school in Peking. Except one page: and that's the page where they told you they don't need any more pilots. And so I'm a pilot without a plane, a mail carrier with no mail. But you'd never understand what that's like.

Shen Te   I think I do understand.

Sun   No, I said you couldn't understand so you can't understand.

Shen Te (*half-laughing, half-crying*)   When we were children we had a crane with a crippled wing. He was friendly, he didn't mind our teasing and he strutted behind us, squawking if we ran too fast. But in the fall and in the spring the great flocks would fly over the village, and he became discontented, and I understood.

Sun   Heul nicht.

Shen Te   Nein.

Sun   Es schadet dem Teint.

Shen Te   Ich höre schon auf.

Sie trocknet sich mit dem Ärmel die Tränen ab. An den Baum gelehnt, langt er, ohne sich ihr zuzuwenden, nach ihrem Gesicht.

Sun   Du kannst dir nicht einmal richtig das Gesicht abwischen. (*Er wischt es ihr mit einem Sacktuch ab. Pause.*)

Sun   Wenn du schon sitzen bleiben mußtest, damit ich mich nicht aufhänge, dann mach wenigstens den Mund auf.

Shen Te   Ich weiß nichts.

Sun   Warum willst du mich eigentlich vom Ast schneiden, Schwester?

Shen Te   Ich bin erschrocken. Sicher wollten Sie es nur tun, weil der Abend so trüb ist.

(*Zum Publikum.*) In unserem Lande
Dürfte es trübe Abende nicht geben
Auch hohe Brücken über die Flüsse
Selbst die Stunde zwischen Nacht und Morgen
Und die ganze Winterzeit dazu, das ist gefährlich.
Denn angesichts des Elends
Genügt ein Weniges
Und die Menschen werfen
Das unerträgliche Leben fort.

Sun   Sprich von dir.

Shen Te   Wovon? Ich habe einen kleinen Laden.

Sun (*spöttisch*)   Ach, du gehst nicht auf den Strich, du hast einen Laden!

Shen Te (*fest*)   Ich habe einen Laden, aber zuvor bin ich auf die Straße gegangen.

Sun   Und den Laden, den haben dir wohl die Götter geschenkt?

Sun Stop blubbering.

Shen Te No.

Sun It's bad for your skin.

Shen Te I've stopped. See?

She dries her tears with her sleeve. Leaning against the tree, he reaches for her face without turning towards her.

Sun You can't even dry your face.

He wipes her face with his handkerchief. Pause.

If you're going to remain an obstacle to my suicide, you could at least talk.

Shen Te I don't know what to say.

Sun Why'd you want to cut me down from this tree, sister?

Shen Te I'm shocked. Surely it's only because the evening is so gloomy that you'd think of doing that.

(*To the audience.*)
  In our country
  They shouldn't allow gloomy evenings,
  Or high bridges over the rivers,
  Or even the hours between night and morning,
  Nor wintertime; even that's dangerous.
  Given how miserable people are here,
  A little more misery is more than enough
  And people throw
  The unbearable life away.

Sun Who are you? Tell me something.

Shen Te Like what? I have a small shop.

Sun (*mocking*) Oh, I see, you're not a hooker, you're a shopkeeper.

Shen Te (*firm*) Now I have a shop. Before that, I walked the streets.

Sun And your shop fell out of the sky from heaven?

Shen Te   Ja.

Sun   Eines schönes Abends standen sie da und sagten:
Hier hast du Geld.

Shen Te (*leise lachend*)   Eines Morgens.

Sun   Unterhaltsam bist du nicht gerade.

Shen Te (*nach einer Pause*)   Ich kann Zither spielen, ein
wenig, und Leute nachmachen. (*Sie macht mit tiefer Stimme
einen würdigen Mann nach.*) 'Nein, so etwas, ich muß
meinen Geldbeutel vergessen haben!' Aber dann kriegte
ich den Laden. Da habe ich als erstes die Zither
weggeschenkt. Jetzt, sagte ich mir, kann ich ein Stockfisch
sein, und es macht nichts.

Ich bin eine Reiche, sagte ich.
Ich gehe allein. Ich schlafe allein.
Ein ganzes Jahr, sagte ich
Mache ich nichts mehr mit einem Mann.

Sun   Aber jetzt heiratest du einen? Den im Teehaus am
Teich.

Shen Te *schweigt.*

Sun   Was weißt du eigentlich von Liebe?

Shen Te   Alles.

Sun   Nichts, Schwester. Oder war es etwa angenehm?

Shen Te   Nein.

Sun (*streicht ihr mit der Hand über das Gesicht, ohne sich ihr
zuzuwenden*)   Ist das angenehm?

Shen Te   Ja.

Sun   Genügsam, das bist du. Was für eine Stadt!

Shen Te   Haben Sie keinen Freund?

Sun   Einen ganzen Haufen, aber keinen, der hören will,
daß ich immer noch ohne eine Stelle bin. Sie machen ein
Gesicht, als ob sie einen sich darüber beklagen hören, daß
im Meer noch Wasser ist. Hast etwa du einen Freund?

Shen Te (*zögernd*)   Einen Vetter.

Shen Te   Yes.

Sun   One enchanted evening the Gods walked up and handed you the money.

Shen Te (*laughing softly*)   It was at dawn.

Sun   Any other talents? Besides lying?*

Shen Te (*after a pause*)   I can play the zither, sort of, and I can imitate people. (*Deepening her voice, she imitates a bigwig.*) 'No, how about that, I forgot my money bag!' But then I got the shop. The first thing I did was give the zither away. Now I can be as dumb as a mackerel, and it won't matter.

I am rich, I told myself.
I live alone. I sleep alone.
A whole year, I told myself,
I'm not doing anything with a man.

Sun   But now you're marrying one. In the tea house by the pond.

Shen Te *is silent.*

What do you think you know about love?

Shen Te   Everything.

Sun   You know nothing, sister. You ever enjoy it?

Shen Te   No.

Without looking at her he strokes her face with his hand.

Sun   Enjoy this?

Shen Te   Yes.

Sun   Easy to please. This hick town!

Shen Te   Don't you have friends here?

Sun   Houses full, but they don't want to hear about how I don't have work. They flinch, it's like I'm whining that the ocean's wet. You have a friend?

Shen Te (*hesitant*)   A cousin.

Sun Dann nimm dich nur in acht vor ihm.

Shen Te Er war bloß ein einziges Mal da. Jetzt ist er weggegangen und kommt nie wieder. Aber warum reden Sie so hoffnungslos? Man sagt: Ohne Hoffnung sprechen heißt ohne Güte sprechen.

Sun Red nur weiter! Eine Stimme ist immerhin eine Stimme.

Shen Te (*eifrig*) Es gibt noch freundliche Menschen, trotz des großen Elends. Als ich klein war, fiel ich einmal mit einer Last Reisig hin. Ein alter Mann hob mich auf und gab mir sogar einen Käsch. Daran habe ich mich oft erinnert. Besonders die wenig zu essen haben, geben gern ab. Wahrscheinlich zeigen die Menschen einfach gern, was sie können, und womit könnten sie es besser zeigen, als indem sie freundlich sind? Bosheit ist bloß eine Art Ungeschicklichkeit. Wenn jemand ein Lied singt oder eine Maschine baut oder Reis pflanzt, das ist eigentlich Freundlichkeit. Auch Sie sind freundlich.

Sun Da gehört nicht viel dazu bei dir, scheint es.

Shen Te Ja. Und jetzt habe ich einen Regentropfen gespürt.

Sun Wo?

Shen Te Zwischen den Augen.

Sun Mehr am rechten oder mehr am linken?

Shen Te Mehr am linken.

Sun Gut. (*Nach einer Weile, schläfrig.*) Und mit den Männern bist du fertig?

Shen Te (*lächelnd*) Aber meine Beine sind nicht krumm.

Sun Vielleicht nicht.

Shen Te Bestimmt nicht.

Sun (*sich müde an den Baum zurücklehnend*) Aber da ich seit zwei Tagen nichts gegessen habe und nichts getrunken seit einem, könnte ich dich nicht lieben, Schwester, auch wenn ich wollte.

Shen Te Es ist schön im Regen.

Sun Beware cousins.

Shen Te He visited once. He's gone now and he's never coming back. But why do you sound so hopeless? They say: If you can't talk about hope you can't talk about goodness.

Sun Keep talking. Even your stupid chatter beats no sound at all.

Shen Te (*eagerly*) There are still friendly people, even though the poverty's great. When I was little I was carrying a load of wood and I fell. An old man helped me up and he even gave me a coin. I often think of that. Those who have little to eat, give the most. People like to show what they do well, and how better to show that than by being friendly? Badness is simply awkwardness. If someone sings or builds a machine or plants rice, that's actually friendliness. Even you are friendly.

Sun To hear you tell it, who isn't?

Shen Te True. And just now I was struck by a raindrop.

Sun Where?

Shen Te Between the eyes.

Sun More to the right, or more to the left.

Shen Te To the left.

Sun Good. (*After a while, sleepily.*) And you're sure you're through with men?

Shen Te (*smiling*) But I don't have bandy-legs.

Sun Maybe you don't.

Shen Te Definitely not.

Sun (*leaning against the tree, tired*) I haven't had food in two days or water in one, I couldn't make love to you even if I wanted to, sister.

Shen Te It's beautiful in the rain.

Wang, *der Wasserverkäufer, kommt. Er singt das* Lied des
Wasserverkäufers im Regen.

Ich hab Wasser zu verkaufen
Und nun steh ich hier im Regen
Und ich bin weithin gelaufen
Meines bißchen Wassers wegen.
Und jetzt schrei ich mein: Kauft Wasser!
Und keiner kauft es
Verschmachtend und gierig
Und zahlt es und sauft es.
Kauft Wasser, ihr Hunde!

Könnt ich doch dies Loch verstopfen!
Träumte jüngst, es wäre sieben
Jahr der Regen ausgeblieben:
Wasser maß ich ab nach Tropfen!
Ach, wie schrieen sie: Gib Wasser!
Jeden, der nach meinem Eimer faßte
Sah ich mir erst an daraufhin
Ob mir seine Nase paßte.
Da lechzten die Hunde!

Lachend.

Ja, jetzt sauft ihr kleinen Kräuter
Auf dem Rücken mit Behagen
Aus dem großen Wolkeneuter
Ohne nach dem Preis zu fragen
Und ich schreie mein: Kauft Wasser!
Und keiner kauft es
Verschmachtend und gierig
Und zahlt es und sauft es.
Kauft Wasser, ihr Hunde!

Der Regen hat aufgehört. **Shen Te** *sieht* **Wang** *und läuft auf
ihn zu.*

Shen Te   Ach, Wang, bist du wieder zurück? Ich habe
dein Traggerät bei mir untergestellt.

Wang   Besten Dank für die Aufbewahrung! Wie geht es
dir, Shen Te?

Wang *the waterseller enters. He sings* The Song of the
Waterseller in the Rain.

Wang (*sings*)

I've got water here for sale,
But my labours are in vain;
Shouldering my heavy pail,
While I'm drowning in the rain.
And still I'm shouting: Buy Water!
Nobody will buy.
No one fishes out his money.
No one's thirsty, no one's dry.
(Buy water, you bastards!)

Someday all the rain will stop!
Everywhere there'll be a drought!
Then you'll have to do without!
I'll sell water, drop by drop,
And hear them beg me: Give us water!
All their gullets gone bone dry.
If I like your face, then maybe
I might let you buy.
(The rest of you bastards: go suck stones!)

Laughing.

Go on, soak it up, you flowers,
Drink your fill until the frost,
You don't ask the thundershowers
How much does this water cost?
Meanwhile, I'm shrieking: Buy Water!
Nobody will buy.
No need for a waterseller
When nobody's dry.
(Buy my goddamn water, you worthless bastards!)

The rain stops. **Shen Te** *sees* **Wang** *and runs to him.*

Shen Te   Oh, Wang, you've come back. I've kept your
carrying pole and cup for you.

Wang   Thanks so much for looking after it, Shen Te.
How's it going?

Shen Te   Gut. Ich habe einen sehr klugen und kühnen
Menschen kennengelernt. Und ich möchte einen Becher
von deinem Wasser kaufen.

Wang   Leg doch den Kopf zurück und mach den Mund
auf, dann hast du Wasser, soviel du willst. Dort die Weide
tropft noch immer.

Shen Te   Aber ich will dein Wasser, Wang.
  Das weither getragene
  Das müde gemacht hat
  Und das schwer verkauft wird, weil es heute regnet.
  Und ich brauche es für den Herrn dort drüben.
  Er ist ein Flieger. Ein Flieger
  Ist kühner als andere Menschen. In der Gesellschaft
    der Wolken
  Den großen Stürmen trotzend
  Fliegt er durch die Himmel und bringt
  Den Freunden im fernen Land
  Die freundliche Post.

Sie bezahlt und läuft mit dem Becher zu Sun hinüber.

Shen Te (*ruft lachend zu* **Wang** *zurück*)   Er ist
eingeschlafen. Die Hoffnungslosigkeit und der Regen
und ich haben ihn müde gemacht.

ZWISCHENSPIEL
WANGS NACHTLAGER IN EINEM KANALROHR

*Der Wasserverkäufer schläft. Musik. Das Kanalrohr wird
durchsichtig, und dem Träumenden erscheinen die Götter.*

Wang (*strahlend*)   Ich habe sie gesehen, Erleuchtete! Sie
ist ganz die alte!

Der Erste Gott   Das freut uns.

Wang   Sie liebt! Sie hat mir ihren Freund gezeigt. Es
geht ihr wirklich gut.

Der Erste Gott   Das hört man gern. Hoffentlich bestärkt
sie das in ihrem Streben nach Gutem.

Wang   Unbedingt! Sie tut soviel Wohltaten, als sie kann.

Shen Te   Good. I've just met a smart and courageous person. And I'd like to buy him a cup of your water.

Wang   Tell him: 'Rear your head back and open wide, the willow's still dripping, drink your fill, it's free.'

Shen Te   But I would like your water, Wang.
 Which you've carried far.
 Which made you tired.
 Which is hard to sell, because it's raining today.
 And I need it for that gentleman there.
 He's a pilot. A pilot
 Is more courageous than other people,
 In the company of clouds
 Braving great storms
 He flies through heaven bringing
 Friends in far-off places
 The friendly mail.

She pays and brings the cup to **Sun**.

Shen Te (*Calling back to* **Wang**, *laughing*.)   He's fallen asleep. Hopelessness and the rain and I have knocked him out.

INTERLUDE
WANG'S NIGHT-LODGING IN A DRAIN PIPE

Wang *the waterseller is sleeping. Music. The drain pipe becomes transparent, and* **the Gods** *appear to the dreamer.*

Wang (*radiant*)   I saw her, Awakened Ones! She's the same as she ever was!

The First God   That pleases us.

Wang   She's in love! She showed me her boyfriend. Really, everything's going good with her.

The First God   Glad to hear it. Hopefully her desire to be good will grow even stronger.

Wang   Absolutely! She's always doing good deeds.

Der Erste Gott   Was für Wohltaten? Erzähl uns davon,
lieber Wang!

Wang   Sie hat ein freundliches Wort für jeden.

Der Erste Gott (*eifrig*)   Ja, und?

Wang   Selten geht einer aus ihrem kleinen Laden ohne
Tabak, nur weil er etwa kein Geld hat.

Der Erste Gott   Das klingt nicht schlecht. Noch anderes?

Wang   Eine achtköpfige Familie hat sie bei sich
beherbergt!

Der Erste Gott (*triumphierend zum zweiten*)   Achtköpfig!
(*Zu* **Wang**.) Und womöglich noch was?

Wang   Mir hat sie, obwohl es regnete, einen Becher von
meinem Wasser abgekauft.

Der Erste Gott   Natürlich, diese kleineren Wohltaten
alle. Das versteht sich.

Wang   Aber sie laufen ins Geld. So viel gibt ein kleiner
Laden nicht her.

Der Erste Gott   Freilich, freilich! Aber ein umsichtiger
Gärtner tut auch mit einem winzigen Fleck wahre
Wunder.

Wang   Das tut sie wahrhaftig! Jeden Morgen teilt sie Reis
aus, dafür geht mehr als die Hälfte des Verdienstes drauf,
das könnt ihr glauben!

Der Erste Gott (*etwas enttäuscht*)   Ich sage auch nichts.
Ich bin nicht unzufrieden mit dem Anfang.

Wang   Bedenkt, die Zeiten sind nicht die besten! Sie
mußte einmal einen Vetter zu Hilfe rufen, da ihr Laden
in Schwierigkeiten geriet.

Kaum war da eine windgeschützte Stelle
Kam des ganzen winterlichen Himmels
Zerzaustes Gevögel geflogen und
Raufte um den Platz und der hungrige Fuchs durchbiß

The First God   What good deeds has she done? Tell us, dear Wang.

Wang   She's got a friendly word for everyone.

The First God (*eagerly*)   Yes, and ...?

Wang   Only very seldom do people leave her little shop without tobacco simply because they can't pay for it.

The First God   That's certainly not bad. Anything else?

Wang   She took in a family of eight!

The First God (*triumphant, to* **The Second God**)   A family of eight!

(*To* **Wang**.) And possibly there's more?

Wang   Even though it was raining, she bought a cup of my water.

The First God   Of course she did. These many small kindnesses are only what we would have expected.

Wang   But they cost a lot of money. A little shop like that doesn't bring in very much.

The First God   Very true, very true. But a circumspect gardener can work wonders on even the tiniest patch of land.

Wang   Which is what she's doing, believe you me! She gives out rice every morning: that eats up more than half her profits.

The First God (*slightly disappointed*)   Free rice is – well it's not exactly a wonder, but it's a beginning.*

Wang   Think about how hard times are! She even had to call in her cousin to help, once the shop got into difficulties.

A shelter from the winter wind was found
And instantly every ragged bird in the sky flew in
Fighting for a place, and the hungry fox bit through

Die dünne Wand und der einbeinige Wolf
Stieß den kleinen Eßnapf um.

Kurz, sie konnte alle die Geschäfte allein nicht mehr
überblicken. Aber alle sind sich einig, daß sie ein gutes
Mädchen ist. Sie heißt schon überall: Der Engel der
Vorstädte. So viel Gutes geht von ihrem Laden aus. Was
immer der Schreiner Lin To sagen mag!

Der Erste Gott Was heißt das? Spricht der Schreiner Lin
To denn schlecht von ihr?

Wang Ach, er sagt nur, die Stellagen im Laden seien
nicht voll bezahlt worden.

Der Zweite Gott Was sagst du da? Ein Schreiner wurde
nicht bezahlt? In Shen Tes Laden? Wie konnte sie das
zulassen?

Wang Sie hatte wohl das Geld nicht.

Der Zweite Gott Ganz gleich, man bezahlt, was man
schuldig ist. Schon der bloße Anschein von Unbilligkeit
muß vermieden werden. Erstens muß der Buchstabe der
Gebote erfüllt werden, zweitens ihr Geist.

Wang Aber es war nur der Vetter, Erleuchtete, nicht sie
selber!

Der Zweite Gott Dann übertritt dieser Vetter nicht
mehr ihre Schwelle!

Wang (*niedergeschlagen*) Ich verstehe, Erleuchteter! Zu
Shen Tes Verteidigung laß mich vielleicht nur noch
geltend machen, daß der Vetter als durchaus achtbarer
Geschäftsmann gilt. Sogar die Polizei schätzt ihn.

Der Erste Gott Nun, wir wollen diesen Herrn Vetter ja
auch nicht ungehört verdammen. Ich gebe zu, ich
verstehe nichts von Geschäften, vielleicht muß man sich
da erkundigen, was das Übliche ist. Aber überhaupt
Geschäfte! Ist das denn so nötig? Immer machen sie jetzt
Geschäfte! Machten die sieben guten Könige Geschäfte?
Verkaufte der gerechte Kung Fische? Was haben
Geschäfte mit einem rechtschaffenen und würdigen
Leben zu tun?

The thin walls and the one-legged wolf
Knocked over the little supper bowl.

In other words she couldn't make it entirely on her own.
But everyone agrees she's a good girl. They call her: the
Angel of the Outskirts. That's how much good she does
in her shop. No matter what the carpenter Lin To says!

The First God Does the carpenter Lin To say bad things
about her?

Wang Not much, he claims her shop shelving wasn't
paid for.

The Second God She failed to pay the carpenter?

Wang She probably couldn't afford to.

The Second God But she has to! Pay as you go! Without
exception! First obey the law, then worry about
everything else.

Wang And the carpenter doesn't complain about her,
Awakened Ones, it was her cousin who gypped him!

The Second God Then this cousin must never darken
her door again.

Wang (*knocked down*) I understand, Awakened Ones.
But let me say in Shen Te's defence that her cousin is a
highly esteemed businessman. Even the police are
impressed with him.

The First God Well, and we would not want to condemn
this cousin person without having heard his case. I have
to confess I don't understand the first thing about
business, perhaps we should try to understand it, you
know, inquire about what constitutes standard business
practice. But it's all we ever hear about these days,
business, money, must it be so inescapable? Everyone
nowadays, eternally transacting! Did the Seven Good
Kings do business? Did Kung the Righteous peddle fish?
What's business got to do with leading an honest decent
life?

Der Zweite Gott (*sehr verschnupft*)   Jedenfalls darf so etwas nicht mehr vorkommen.

Er wendet sich zum Gehen. Die beiden anderen Götter wenden sich auch.

Der Dritte Gott (*als letzter, verlegen*)   Entschuldige den etwas harten Ton heute! Wir sind übermüdet und nicht ausgeschlafen. Das Nachtlager! Die Wohlhabenden geben uns die allerbesten Empfehlungen an die Armen, aber die Armen haben nicht Zimmer genug.

Die Götter (*sich entfernend, schimpfen*)   Schwach, die beste von ihnen! Nichts Durchschlagendes! Wenig, wenig! Alles natürlich von Herzen, aber es sieht nach nichts aus! Sie müßte doch zumindest ...

Man hört sie nicht mehr.

Wang (*ruft ihnen nach*)   Ach, seid nicht ungnädig, Erleuchtete! Verlangt nicht zu viel für den Anfang!

The Second God (*irritatedly*)   At any rate, she should take care in the future to avoid this dodgy kind of thing.

He turns to leave. The other **Gods** *follow.*

The Third God (*embarrassed*)   Please excuse our irritability today. We're very tired and haven't slept much. The places we've lodged in! The rich graciously pass us on to the poor, and the poor have no room.

The Gods (*exiting, complaining*)   The best of them are weaklings! Inconclusive results! They have good intentions, but not much to show for them! She could at least have ... (*They become inaudible.*)

Wang (*calling after them*)   Oh don't be intemperate with her, Awakened Ones! It's only a beginning! Don't expect so much!

4
Platz vor Shen Tes Tabakladen

Eine Barbierstube, ein Teppichgeschäft und **Shen Tes**
Tabakladen. Es ist Montag. Vor **Shen Tes** *Laden warten zwei
Überbleibsel der achtköpfigen Familie,* **Der Großvater** *und* **Die
Schwägerin**, *sowie* **Der Arbeitslose** *und* **Die Shin**.

Die Schwägerin Sie war nicht zu Hause gestern nacht!

Die Shin Ein unglaubliches Benehmen! Endlich ist
dieser rabiate Herr Vetter weg, und man bequemt sich,
wenigstens ab und zu etwas Reis von seinem Überfluß
abzugeben, und schon bleibt man nächtelang fort und
treibt sich, die Götter wissen wo, herum!

Aus der Barbierstube hört man laute Stimmen. Heraus stolpert
Wang, *ihm folgt der dicke Barbier,* **Herr Shu Fu**, *eine schwere
Brennschere in der Hand.*

Herr Shu Fu Ich werde dir geben, meine Kunden zu
belästigen mit deinem verstunkenen Wasser! Nimm
deinen Becher und scher dich fort!

Wang *greift nach dem Becher, den* **Herr Shu Fu** *ihm hinhält,
und der schlägt ihm mit der Brennschere auf die Hand, daß*
Wang *laut aufschreit.*

Herr Shu Fu Da hast du es! Laß dir das eine Lektion
sein! (*Er schnauft in seine Barbierstube zurück.*)

Der Arbeitslose (*hebt den Becher auf und reicht ihn* **Wang**)
Für den Schlag kannst du ihn anzeigen.

Wang Die Hand ist kaputt.

Der Arbeitslose Ist etwas zerbrochen drin?

Wang Ich kann sie nicht mehr bewegen.

Der Arbeitslose Setz dich hin und gib ein wenig Wasser
drüber!

4

The Square in Front of Shen Te's Tobacco Shop

A barber's shop, a rug shop and **Shen Te***'s tobacco shop. It is Monday. Two members of the family of eight,* **The Grandfather** *and* **The Sister-in-Law***, are loitering outside* **Shen Te***'s shop, as well as* **The Unemployed Man** *and* **Mrs Shin***.*

The Sister-in-Law She didn't come home last night!

Mrs Shin It's appalling behaviour! Her rabid cousin finally departs, so every now and again she condescends to give away a few spoons of rice out of the bushels she's got, and then she takes to roaming around at night, Lord only knows where.

(*Loud voices from the barber shop.* **Wang** *stumbles out, followed by the fat barber,* **Mr Shu Fu***, wielding a heavy curling iron.*)

Shu Fu I warned you about bothering my customers with your stinking water! Take your cup and scram!

(**Wang** *reaches for the cup* **Shu Fu** *is holding out, and* **Shu Fu** *hits him on the hand with the curling iron.* **Wang** *screams.*)

Shu Fu There! And don't forget it!

He goes wheezing back into his barbershop.

The Unemployed Man *picks up the cup and hands it to* **Wang***.*

The Unemployed Man You could bring charges against him for assault.

Wang My hand's a mess.

The Unemployed Man It's broken?

Wang I can't move my fingers.

The Unemployed Man Sit down and pour water on it.

Wang *setzt sich.*

Die Shin   Jedenfalls hast du das Wasser billig.

Die Schwägerin   Nicht einmal einen Fetzen Leinen kann man hier bekommen früh um acht. Sie muß auf Abenteuer ausgehen! Skandal!

Die Shin (*düster*)   Vergessen hat sie uns!

Die Gasse herunter kommt **Shen Te**, *einen Topf mit Reis tragend.*

Shen Te (*zum Publikum*)   In der Frühe habe ich die Stadt nie gesehen. In diesen Stunden lag ich immer noch mit der schmutzigen Decke über der Stirn, in Furcht vor dem Erwachen. Heute bin ich zwischen den Zeitungsjungen gegangen, den Männern, die den Asphalt mit Wasser überspülen, und den Ochsenkarren mit dem frischen Gemüse vom Land. Ich bin einen langen Weg von Suns Viertel bis hierher gegangen, aber mit jedem Schritt wurde ich lustiger. Ich habe immer gehört, wenn man liebt, geht man auf Wolken, aber das Schöne ist, daß man auf der Erde geht, dem Asphalt. Ich sage euch, die Häusermassen sind in der Frühe wie Schutthaufen, in denen Lichter angezündet werden, wenn der Himmel schon rosa und noch durchsichtig, weil ohne Staub ist. Ich sage euch, es entgeht euch viel, wenn ihr nicht liebt und eure Stadt seht in der Stunde, wo sie sich vom Lager erhebt wie ein nüchterner alter Handwerker, der seine Lungen mit frischer Luft vollpumpt und nach seinem Handwerkzeug greift, wie die Dichter singen. (*Zu den Wartenden.*) Guten Morgen! Da ist der Reis! (*Sie teilt aus, dann erblickt sie* **Wang**.) Guten Morgen, Wang. Ich bin leichtsinnig heute. Auf dem Weg habe ich mich in jedem Schaufenster betrachtet und jetzt habe ich Lust, mir einen Shawl zu kaufen. (*Nach kurzem Zögern.*) Ich würde so gern schön aussehen. (*Sie geht schnell in den Teppichladen.*)

Herr Shu Fu (*der wieder in die Tür getreten ist, zum Publikum*)   Ich bin betroffen, wie schön heute Fräulein Shen Te aussieht, die Besitzerin des Tabakladens von Visavis, die mir bisher gar nicht aufgefallen ist. Drei

Wang *sits.*

Mrs Shin   Pour generously, you only pay wholesale.

The Sister-in-Law   It's eight in the morning, it's an emergency, and we can't get rags off her for bandages. Gallivanting around town. It's a scandal!

Mrs Shin (*gloomy*)   She's forgotten us!

Shen Te *enters carrying a pot of rice.*

Shen Te (*to the audience*)   I'm not used to seeing the city at dawn. I'd lay awake with my dirty blanket pulled over my head, afraid to get out of bed. Early today I went out among the newspaper boys, the men who wash the sidewalks down, and the oxcarts bringing fresh vegetables from the country. It's a long walk from Sun's neighbourhood to this one, but with each step I've become happier. They say when you're in love you walk on clouds but in fact what's really wonderful is that you walk on the earth, on sidewalks. I'm telling you, in the morning the houses are one big pile of rubble with little lights inside, and the sky's pink and clear because there's no dust. I'm telling you you don't know what you're missing if you aren't in love and haven't seen your city when she rises from her bed like an old master craftsman who fills his lungs deep with fresh city air as he reaches for his tools, like in the songs of the poets.

(*To the waiting people.*) Good morning! Here's the rice!

She starts to hand out the rice, when she sees **Wang**.

Shen Te   Good morning, Wang! I'm dizzy today. I saw my reflection in every shop window on the way and now I want to buy myself a shawl. (*After a moment's hesitation.*) I'd love to look beautiful. (*She goes quickly into the rug shop.*)

Shu Fu (*at his doorway, to the audience*)   I am stunned at how lovely Miss Shen Te, the tobacconist across the way to whom I never gave a second glance, is looking today. I've been glancing for the past three minutes and I feel like I've fallen in love. An unbelievably sympathetic person!

Minuten sehe ich sie, und ich glaube, ich bin schon
verliebt in sie. Eine unglaublich sympathische Person!
(*Zu* **Wang**.) Scher dich weg, Halunke! (*Er geht in die
Barbierstube zurück.*)

Shen Te *und ein sehr altes Paar,* **Der Teppichhändler** *und
seine Frau, treten aus dem Teppichladen.* **Shen Te** *trägt einen
Shawl,* **Der Teppichhändler** *einen Spiegel.*

Die Alte   Er ist sehr hübsch und auch nicht teuer, da er
ein Löchlein unten hat.

Shen Te (*auf den Shawl am Arm der Alten schauend*)   Der
grüne ist auch schön.

Die Alte (*lächelnd*)   Aber er ist leider nicht ein bißchen
beschädigt.

Shen Te   Ja, das ist ein Jammer. Ich kann keine großen
Sprünge machen mit meinem Laden. Ich habe noch
wenig Einnahmen und doch viele Ausgaben.

Die Alte   Für Wohltaten. Tun Sie nicht zu viel. Am
Anfang spielt ja jede Schale Reis eine Rolle, nicht?

Shen Te (*probiert den durchlöcherten Shawl an*)   Nur, das
muß sein, aber jetzt bin ich leichtsinnig. Ob mir diese
Farbe steht?

Die Alte   Das müssen Sie unbedingt einen Mann fragen.

Shen Te (*zum Alten gewendet*)   Steht sie mir?

Der Alte   Fragen Sie doch lieber ...

Shen Te (*sehr höflich*)   Nein, ich frage Sie.

Der Alte (*ebenfalls höflich*)   Der Shawl steht Ihnen. Aber
nehmen Sie die matte Seite nach außen.

Shen Te *bezahlt.*

Die Alte   Wenn er nicht gefällt, tauschen Sie ihn ruhig
um. (*Zieht sie beiseite.*) Hat er ein wenig Kapital?

Shen Te (*lachend*)   O nein.

Die Alte   Können Sie denn dann die Halbjahresmiete
bezahlen?

(*To* **Wang**.) Lose yourself, garbage!

He goes back into his barbershop. **Shen Te** *and the old couple, the rug merchant and his wife, come out of the rug shop.* **Shen Te** *is wearing a shawl, and the rug merchant is holding a mirror.*

The Old Woman   It's very pretty and it's a bargain, because it's got a small hole in one corner.

Shen Te *looks at another shawl draped over the rug merchant's arm.*

Shen Te   The green one is nice too.

The Old Woman (*smiling*)   But unfortunately not damaged.

Shen Te   Too bad. I can't be a big spender with my shop. There isn't much income and the overhead's sky high.

The Old Woman   Your overhead's all your charity. Don't give everything away. When you're starting out you have to watch every bowl of rice. Right?

Shen Te (*trying on the shawl with holes*)   I should, but right now I'm feeling a bit foolish. Is this a good colour for me?

The Old Woman   Ask a man.

Shen Te (*to the rug merchant*)   Does it look good on me?

The Old Man   You should ask your —

Shen Te (*very politely*)   No, I want your opinion.

The Old Man (*also politely*)   The shawl looks good on you. But wear it dull-side-out.

Shen Te *pays.*

The Old Woman   If it fails to please, you can exchange it.

She takes **Shen Te** *aside.*

The Old Woman   Does your sweetheart have any savings?

Shen Te   Die Halbjahresmiete! Das habe ich ganz vergessen!

Die Alte   Das dachte ich mir! Und nächsten Montag ist schon der Erste. Ich möchte etwas mit Ihnen besprechen. Wissen Sie, mein Mann und ich waren ein wenig zweiflerisch in bezug auf die Heiratsannonce, nachdem wir Sie kennengelernt haben. Wir haben beschlossen, Ihnen im Notfall unter die Arme zu greifen. Wir haben uns Geld zurückgelegt und können Ihnen die 200 Silberdollar leihen. Wenn Sie wollen, können Sie uns Ihre Vorräte an Tabak verpfänden. Schriftliches ist aber zwischen uns natürlich nicht nötig.

Shen Te   Wollen Sie wirklich einer so leichtsinnigen Person Geld leihen?

Die Alte   Offen gestanden, Ihrem Herrn Vetter, der bestimmt nicht leichtsinnig ist, würden wir es vielleicht nicht leihen, aber Ihnen leihen wir es ruhig.

Der Alte (*tritt hinzu*)   Abgemacht?

Shen Te   Ich wünschte, die Götter hätten Ihrer Frau eben zugehört, Herr Deng. Sie suchen gute Menschen, die glücklich sind. Und Sie müssen wohl glücklich sein, daß Sie mir helfen, weil ich durch Liebe in Ungelegenheiten gekommen bin.

Die beiden Alten lächeln sich an.

Der Alte   Hier ist das Geld.

Er übergibt ihr ein Kuvert. Shen Te nimmt es entgegen und verbeugt sich. Auch die Alten verbeugen sich. Sie gehen zurück in ihren Laden.

Shen Te (*zu Wang, ihr Kuvert hochhebend*)   Das ist die Miete für ein halbes Jahr! Ist das nicht wie ein Wunder? Und was sagst du zu meinem neuen Shawl, Wang?

Wang   Hast du den für ihn gekauft, den ich im Stadtpark gesehen habe?

Shen Te *nickt.*

Shen Te (*smiling*)   Oh, no.

The Old Woman   Then how are you going to get the half-year's rent?

Shen Te   I completely forgot about that!

The Old Woman   I suspected as much. And it's due next Monday. I'd like to speak with you about something. After we'd gotten to know you my husband and I became sceptical about the wisdom of your personals ad. We've decided to take you under our wing, if you need that. We've got savings and we'll lend you the 200 silver dollars. If you want you can pledge us your tobacco stock as collateral. But nothing has to be in writing.

Shen Te   Do you really want to lend money to somebody as foolish as me?

The Old Woman   To tell you the truth, we'd never offer it to your extremely unfoolish cousin, but we have no worries lending it to you.

The Old Man (*joining them*)   Done deal?

Shen Te   I wish the Gods could have heard your wife, Mr Deng. They're looking for good people who are happy. And you must be happy, because you're helping one who has gotten herself in a fix on account of love.

The husband and wife smile at each other.

The Old Man   Here's the money, then.

He gives her an envelope. **Shen Te** *takes it and bows. The man and woman also bow. They go back into their shop.*

Shen Te (*to* **Wang**, *holding the envelope high*)   The rent! It's like a miracle, isn't it? And this shawl, Wang, how about that?

Wang   You bought it to wear for the man in the Park?

Shen Te *nods.*

Die Shin   Vielleicht sehen Sie sich lieber seine kaputte Hand an, als ihm Ihre zweifelhaften Abenteuer zu erzählen!

Shen Te (*erschrocken*)   Was ist mit deiner Hand?

Die Shin   Der Barbier hat sie vor unseren Augen mit der Brennschere zerschlagen.

Shen Te (*über ihre Achtlosigkeit entsetzt*)   Und ich habe gar nichts bemerkt! Du mußt sofort zum Arzt gehen, sonst wird deine Hand steif und du kannst nie mehr richtig arbeiten. Das ist ein großes Unglück. Schnell, steh auf! Geh schnell!

Der Arbeitslose   Er muß nicht zum Arzt, sondern zum Richter! Er kann vom Barbier, der reich ist, Schadenersatz verlangen.

Wang   Meinst du, da ist eine Aussicht?

Die Shin   Wenn sie wirklich kaputt ist. Aber ist sie kaputt?

Wang   Ich glaube. Sie ist schon ganz dick. Wäre es eine Lebensrente?

Die Shin   Du mußt allerdings einen Zeugen haben.

Wang   Aber ihr alle habt es ja gesehen! Ihr alle könnt es bezeugen.

Er blickt um sich. **Der Arbeitslose**, **Der Großvater** *und* **Die Schwägerin** *sitzen an der Hauswand und essen. Niemand sieht auf.*

Shen Te (*zur* **Shin**)   Sie selber haben es doch gesehen!

Die Shin   Ich will nichts mit der Polizei zu tun haben.

Shen Te (*zur* **Schwägerin**)   Dann Sie!

Die Schwägerin   Ich? Ich habe nicht hingesehen!

Die Shin   Natürlich haben Sie hingesehen. Ich habe gesehen, daß Sie hingesehen haben! Sie haben nur Furcht, weil der Barbier zu mächtig ist.

Mrs Shin Maybe you'll want to look at his broken hand before you tell him more about your peccadilloes.

Shen Te (*alarmed*) What's wrong with your hand?

Mrs Shin The barber smashed it with his curling iron, right in front of us.

Shen Te (*disgusted with her own insensitivity and inattentiveness*) And I didn't even notice! You have to go to a doctor or the bones will knit badly, and you won't be able to work. This is very unfortunate. Get up, now! Quick!

The Unemployed Man He doesn't need a doctor, he needs a judge. Sue the barber, he's loaded.

Wang You think I'd win?

Mrs Shin If it's really broken. Is it?

Wang I think so. It's puffed up fat. A large enough settlement to live off of, like a pension?

Mrs Shin You'll need a witness.

Wang But everyone saw it! You're all witnesses.

He looks around. **The Grandfather**, **The Sister-in-Law**, *and* **The Unemployed Man** *sit against the wall of the shop and eat their rice. No one looks up.*

Shen Te (*to* **Mrs Shin**) You saw it!

Mrs Shin I'm not getting mixed up with the police.

Shen Te (*to* **The Sister-in-Law**) Then you!

The Sister-in-Law I wasn't looking.

Mrs Shin Oh yes you were. I saw you looking. You're afraid because the barber's a powerful man.

Shen Te (*zum* **Großvater**)   Ich bin sicher, Sie bezeugen den Vorfall.

Die Schwägerin   Sein Zeugnis wird nicht angenommen. Er ist gaga.

Shen Te (*zum* **Arbeitslosen**)   Es handelt sich vielleicht um eine Lebensrente.

Der Arbeitslose   Ich bin schon zweimal wegen Bettelei aufgeschrieben worden. Mein Zeugnis würde ihm eher schaden.

Shen Te (*ungläubig*)   So will keines von euch sagen, was ist? Am hellen Tage wurde ihm die Hand zerbrochen, ihr habt alle zugeschaut, und keines will reden?
(*Zornig.*) Oh, ihr Unglücklichen!
Euerm Bruder wird Gewalt angetan, und ihr kneift die
    Augen zu!
Der Getroffene schreit laut auf, und ihr schweigt?
Der Gewalttätige geht herum und wählt sein Opfer
Und ihr sagt: uns verschont er, denn wir zeigen kein
    Mißfallen.
Was ist das für eine Stadt, was seid ihr für Menschen!
Wenn in einer Stadt ein Unrecht geschieht, muß ein
    Aufruhr sein
Und wo kein Aufruhr ist, da ist es besser, daß die Stadt
    untergeht
Durch ein Feuer, bevor es Nacht wird!
Wang, wenn niemand deinen Zeugen macht, der dabei war, dann will ich deinen Zeugen machen und sagen, daß ich es gesehen habe.

Die Shin   Das wird Meineid sein.

Wang   Ich weiß nicht, ob ich das annehmen kann. Aber vielleicht muß ich es annehmen. (*Auf seine Hand blikkend, besorgt.*) Meint ihr, sie ist auch dick genug? Es kommt mir vor, als sei sie schon wieder abgeschwollen?

Der Arbeitslose (*beruhigt ihn*)   Nein, sie ist bestimmt nicht abgeschwollen.

Shen Te (*to* **The Grandfather**)   Surely you'll be a witness to this.

The Sister-in-Law   His testimony's inadmissable. He's gaga.

Shen Te (*to* **The Unemployed Man**)   It could set him up for life.

The Unemployed Man   I've gotten two citations for begging. My testimony would be more hindrance than help.

Shen Te (*incredulous*)   No one will say what happened? His hand's shattered right before you, in the plain light of day, but you're not going to speak?

(*Angrily.*) Oh you miserable people!
Your brother's hurt, and you close your eyes!
He screams in pain, and you're silent?
The violent man seeks his victim,
And you say: he'll spare us if we don't disapprove.
What kind of city is this, what kind of people are you?
If there's an injustice committed in a city, there must be
    outrage,
And if there's no outrage, then the city ought to perish
In flames, before the night falls!
Wang, if none of these witnesses will be your witness, then
I'll say I was.

Mrs Shin   That would be perjury.

Wang   I'm not sure I could go along with that. But maybe I'll have to. (*Looking worriedly at his hand.*) Is it swollen enough? The swelling seems to be going down.

The Unemployed Man (*reassuring him*)   No, it's definitely alarmingly swollen.

Wang   Wirklich nicht? Ja, ich glaube auch, sie schwillt sogar ein wenig mehr an. Vielleicht ist doch das Gelenk gebrochen! Ich laufe besser gleich zum Richter. *Seine Hand sorgsam haltend, den Blick immer darauf gerichtet, läuft er weg.*

Die Shin *läuft in die Barbierstube.*

Der Arbeitslose   Sie läuft zum Barbier sich einschmeicheln.

Die Schwägerin   Wir können die Welt nicht ändern.

Shen Te (*entmutigt*)   Ich habe euch nicht beschimpfen wollen. Ich bin nur erschrocken. Nein, ich wollte euch beschimpfen. Geht mir aus den Augen!

Der Arbeitslose, **Die Schwägerin** *und* **Der Großvater** *gehen essend und maulend ab.*

Shen Te (*zum Publikum*)

Sie antworten nicht mehr. Wo man sie hinstellt
Bleiben sie stehen, und wenn man sie wegweist
Machen sie schnell Platz!
Nichts bewegt sie mehr. Nur
Der Geruch des Essens macht sie aufschauen.

Eine alte Frau kommt gelaufen. Es ist **Suns** *Mutter,* **Frau Yang**.

Frau Yang (*atemlos*)   Sind Sie Fräulein Shen Te? Mein Sohn hat mir alles erzählt. Ich bin Suns Mutter, Frau Yang. Denken Sie, er hat jetzt die Aussicht, eine Fliegerstelle zu bekommen! Heute morgen, eben vorhin, ist ein Brief gekommen, aus Peking. Von einem Hangarverwalter beim Postflug.

Shen Te   Daß er wieder fliegen kann? Oh, Frau Yang!

Frau Yang   Aber die Stelle kostet schreckliches Geld: 500 Silberdollar.

Shen Te   Das ist viel, aber am Geld darf so etwas nicht scheitern. Ich habe doch den Laden.

Wang   You think? You're right, and it's gotten purpler. Maybe he broke my wrist. I'd better go to the judge immediately.

Holding his hand gingerly, watching it carefully, **Wang** *exits.* **Mrs Shin** *goes into the barber shop.*

The Unemployed Man   She's going to suck up to the barber.

The Sister-in-Law   We can't change the world.

Shen Te (*discouraged*)   I didn't mean to insult you. But you shock me. No, I did mean to insult you. Get out of my sight!

The Sister-in-Law, **The Grandfather**, *and* **The Unemployed Man** *exit, eating and grumbling.*

Shen Te (*to the audience*)

They don't talk back now. They stay
Where you put them, when you dismiss them
They go quickly!
Nothing moves them anymore. Only
The smell of food makes them look up.

An old lady enters running. It's **Sun**'s *mother,* **Mrs Yang**.

Mrs Yang (*breathless*)   Are you Miss Shen Te? My son told me all about you. I'm Sun's mother Mrs Yang. Guess what, he has a shot at a pilot's job! This morning, just now, a letter from Peking. From the airfield manager at the airmail station.

Shen Te   He can fly again! Oh, Mrs Yang!

Mrs Yang   But the job will cost him a horrible sum: 500 silver dollars.

Shen Te   That's a lot, but an opportunity as good as this one mustn't founder over money. I still have the shop.

Frau Yang   Wenn Sie da etwas tun könnten!

Shen Te (*umarmt sie*)   Wenn ich ihm helfen könnte!

Frau Yang   Sie würden einem begabten Menschen eine Chance geben!

Shen Te   Wie dürfen sie einen hindern, sich nützlich zu machen! (*Nach einer Pause.*) Nur, für den Laden werde ich zu wenig bekommen, und die 200 Silberdollar Bargeld hier sind bloß ausgeliehen. Die freilich können Sie gleich mitnehmen. Ich werde meine Tabakvorräte verkaufen und sie davon zurückzahlen. (*Sie gibt ihr das Geld der beiden Alten.*)

Frau Yang   Ach, Fräulein Shen Te, das ist Hilfe am rechten Ort. Und sie nannten ihn schon den toten Flieger hier in der Stadt, weil sie alle überzeugt waren, daß er so wenig wie ein Toter je wieder fliegen würde.

Shen Te   Aber 300 Silberdollar brauchen wir noch für die Fliegerstelle. Wir müssen nachdenken, Frau Yang. (*Langsam.*) Ich kenne jemand, der mir da vielleicht helfen könnte. Einen, der schon einmal Rat geschaffen hat. Ich wollte ihn eigentlich nicht mehr rufen, da er zu hart und zu schlau ist. Es müßte wirklich das letzte Mal sein. Aber ein Flieger muß fliegen, das ist klar.

Fernes Motorengeräusch.

Frau Yang   Wenn der, von dem Sie sprechen, das Geld beschaffen könnte! Sehen Sie, das ist das morgendliche Postflugzeug, das nach Peking geht!

Shen Te (*entschlossen*)   Winken Sie, Frau Yang! Der Flieger kann uns bestimmt sehen! (*Sie winkt mit ihrem Shawl.*) Winken Sie auch!

Frau Yang (*winkend*)   Kennen Sie den, der da fliegt?

Shen Te   Nein. Einen, der fliegen wird. Denn der Hoffnungslose soll fliegen, Frau Yang. Einer wenigstens soll über all dies Elend, einer soll über uns alle sich erheben können!

Mrs Yang   If only you could manage something!

Shen Te (*embracing her*)   If only I can help him!

Mrs Yang   You'd be giving a talented man the break he needs.

Shen Te   How can they stop a man from using his talents?

(*After a pause.*) But I'll never get enough from the shop, and this 200 silver dollars cash is a loan. Of course you can have that right now. I'll sell my tobacco stock and pay them back from that.

Shen Te *gives* **Mrs Yang** *the old couple's money.*

Mrs Yang   Oh Miss Shen Te, your heart's in the right place. Everywhere I go, I hear them calling him the better-off-dead pilot, because they said a cadaver's got more hope of getting a plane to fly.

Shen Te   But we still need 300 silver dollars more. We must think of something, Mrs Yang. (*Slowly.*) There's someone who'd be able to help, he advised me once before. I didn't want to call him back because he's tough and crafty. One last time. A pilot has to fly, that's all there is to it.

The distant sound of a motor, above.

Mrs Yang   I pray the one of whom you speak will find the cash. Look, there's the morning mailplane to Peking.

Shen Te (*resolved*)   Wave, Mrs Yang! I know the pilot sees us! (*She waves with her shawl.*) Wave!

Mrs Yang (*waving*)   Do you know the pilot flying that plane?

Shen Te   No. But I know one who will fly. Because the hopeless should fly, Mrs Yang. One of us at least should rise above this misery, above us all!

Zum Publikum.

Yang Sun, mein Geliebter, in der Gesellschaft der
   Wolken!
Den großen Stürmen trotzend
Fliegend durch die Himmel und bringend
Den Freunden im fernen Land
Die freundliche Post.

ZWISCHENSPIEL
VOR DEM VORHANG

Shen Te *tritt, in den Händen die Maske und den Anzug des*
Shui Ta, *auf und singt* Das Lied von der Wehrlosigkeit der
Götter und Guten.

In unserem Lande
Braucht der Nützliche Glück. Nur
Wenn er starke Helfer findet
Kann er sich nützlich erweisen.
Die Guten
Können sich nicht helfen und die Götter sind machtlos.
   Warum haben die Götter nicht Tanks und Kanonen
   Schlachtschiffe und Bombenflugzeuge und Minen
   Die Bösen zu fällen, die Guten zu schonen?
   Es stünde wohl besser mit uns und mit ihnen.

Sie legt den Anzug des **Shui Ta** *an und macht einige Schritte in*
seiner Gangart.

Die Guten
Können in unserem Lande nicht lang gut bleiben.
Wo die Teller leer sind, raufen sich die Esser.
Ach, die Gebote der Götter
Helfen nicht gegen den Mangel.
   Warum erscheinen die Götter nicht auf unsern
      Märkten
   Und verteilen lächelnd die Fülle der Waren
   Und gestatten den vom Brot und vom Weine
      Gestärkten
   Miteinander nun freundlich und gut zu verfahren?

(*To the audience.*) Yang Sun, my lover, keeping company
  with the clouds!
Braving great storms,
Flying through heaven bringing
Friends in far-off places
The friendly mail.

INTERLUDE
IN FRONT OF THE CURTAIN

Shen Te *comes out with the mask and suit of* **Shui Ta** *in her hands and sings* The Song of the Defencelessness of the Gods and the Good.

Shen Te
  In our land,
  A helpful person must be lucky. Only
  If he finds strong help
  Can he prove himself helpful.
  The Good Ones
  Can't help themselves, and the Gods are powerless.
    Why don't the Gods command armies with guns?
    With guns they could help the Good carry the day.
    We could scourge humankind of the inhuman ones.
    If we learned to fight battles, instead of to pray.

She puts on **Shui Ta***'s suit and tries out his walk.*

Shen Te
  The Good
  Can't stay good in our country.
  The hungry fight each other over empty plates.
  Ah, the Gods' Holy Commandments!
  You can't eat 'em ...
    Why don't the Gods invent clouds that rain honey?
    Why not make miracles? Burden our shelves
    With piles of food, so we never need money,
    So we no longer need to sell goods, or ourselves.

Sie setzt die Maske des **Shui Ta** *auf und fährt mit seiner Stimme zu singen fort.*

Um zu einem Mittagessen zu kommen
Braucht es der Härte, mit der sonst Reiche gegründet
   werden.
Ohne zwölf zu zertreten
Hilft keiner einem Elenden.
   Warum sagen die Götter nicht laut in den obern
      Regionen
   Daß sie den Guten nun einmal die gute Welt schulden?
   Warum stehn sie den Guten nicht bei mit Tanks und
      Kanonen
   Und befehlen: Gebt Feuer! und dulden kein Dulden?

She puts on **Shui Ta**'s *mask and sings in his voice.*

Shui Ta
   Just to buy lunch for yourself
   You need the kind of grit that builds empires.
   Unless you're willing to walk across twelve throats
   You'll never reach anyone who needs your help.
      Oh almighty Gods in your heaven above us:
      Give the Good a good world, and repair what's
         repairable;
      What's wicked, destroy it, oh Gods, if you love us!
      And no longer ask us to bear what's unbearable.

5
Der Tabakladen

Hinter dem Ladentisch sitzt **Shui Ta** *und liest die Zeitung. Er beachtet nicht im geringsten* **Die Shin***, die aufwischt und dabei redet.*

Die Shin   So ein kleiner Laden ist schnell ruiniert, wenn einmal gewisse Gerüchte sich im Viertel verbreiten, das können Sie mir glauben. Es wäre hohe Zeit, daß Sie als ordentlicher Mann in die dunkle Affäre zwischen dem Fräulein und diesem Yang Sun aus der Gelben Gasse hineinleuchteten. Vergessen Sie nicht, daß Herr Shu Fu, der Barbier von nebenan, ein Mann, der zwölf Häuser besitzt und nur eine einzige und dazu alte Frau hat, mir gegenüber erst gestern ein schmeichelhaftes Interesse für das Fräulein angedeutet hat. Er hatte sich sogar schon nach ihren Vermögensverhältnissen erkundigt. Das beweist wohl echte Neigung, möchte ich meinen. (*Da sie keine Antwort erhält, geht sie endlich mit dem Eimer hinaus.*)

Suns Stimme (*von draußen*)   Ist das Fräulein Shen Tes Laden?

Stimme Der Shin   Ja, das ist er. Aber heute ist der Vetter da.

Shui Ta *läuft mit den leichten Schritten der* **Shen Te** *zu einem Spiegel und will eben beginnen, sich das Haar zu richten, als er im Spiegel den Irrtum bemerkt. Er wendet sich leise lachend ab. Eintritt* **Yang Sun***. Hinter ihm kommt neugierig* **Die Shin***. Sie geht an ihm vorüber ins Gelaß.*

Sun   Ich bin Yang Sun. *Shui Ta verbeugt sich.* Ist Shen Te da?

Shui Ta   Nein, sie ist nicht da.

Sun   Aber Sie sind wohl im Bild, wie wir zueinander stehen. (*Er beginnt den Laden in Augenschein zu nehmen.*) Ein leibhaftiger Laden! Ich dachte immer, sie nimmt da den Mund etwas voll. (*Er schaut befriedigt in die Kistchen*

5
The Tobacco Shop

Shui Ta *sits behind the counter, reading a newspaper. He pays no attention to* **Mrs Shin**, *who is tidying and talking.*

Mrs Shin A small shop like this can be ruined by neighbourhood gossips, believe you me. It's high time you looked into these nocturnal carryings-on between the young Miss and that Yang Sun of Yellow Lane. As I believe I've mentioned, Mr Shu Fu, the barber, your neighbour with twelve houses and only one wife, and an old wife to boot, indicated to me only yesterday a flattering interest in the young Miss. He even asked about her finances. If you ask me, that's serious.

Getting no response, she exits with her bucket.

Sun's Voice (*from outside*) Is this Miss Shen Te's shop?

Mrs Shin's Voice It is. But her cousin's in today.

Shui Ta *runs with* **Shen Te**'s *light step to a mirror and starts to arrange his hair when he sees his error in a mirror. He turns away, laughing softly.* **Sun** *enters.* **Mrs Shin** *is right behind him, curious. She goes around him and into the room.*

Sun I'm Yang Sun.

Shui Ta *bows.*

Sun Is Shen Te here?

Shui Ta No, she isn't.

Sun But she's painted the picture for you, how it stands between her and me. (*He looks around the shop.*) The shop for real! I always thought she was talking big. (*He looks with satisfaction in the boxes and porcelain pots.*) Man, I'm going to fly again.

und Porzellantöpfchen.) Mann, ich werde wieder fliegen!
(*Er nimmt sich eine Zigarre und Shui Ta reicht ihm Feuer.*)
Glauben Sie, wir können noch 300 Silberdollar aus dem
Laden herausschlagen?

Shui Ta   Darf ich fragen: haben Sie die Absicht, ihn auf
der Stelle zu verkaufen?

Sun   Haben wir denn die 300 bar? (**Shui Ta** *schüttelt den
Kopf.*) Es war anständig von ihr, daß sie die 200 sofort
herausrückte. Aber ohne die 300, die noch fehlen,
bringen sie mich nicht weiter.

Shui Ta   Vielleicht war es ein bißchen schnell, daß sie
Ihnen das Geld zusagte. Es kann sie den Laden kosten.
Man sagt: Eile heißt der Wind, der das Baugerüst
umwirft.

Sun   Ich brauche das Geld schnell oder gar nicht. Und
das Mädchen gehört nicht zu denen, die lang zaudern,
wenn es gilt, etwas zu geben. Unter uns Männern: Es hat
bisher mit nichts gezaudert.

Shui Ta   So.

Sun   Was nur für sie spricht.

Shui Ta   Darf ich wissen, wozu die 500 Silberdollar
dienen würden?

Sun   Sicher. Ich sehe, es soll mir auf den Zahn gefühlt
werden. Der Hangarverwalter in Peking, ein Freund von
mir aus der Flugschule, kann mir die Stelle verschaffen,
wenn ich ihm 500 Silberdollar ausspucke.

Shui Ta   Ist die Summe nicht außergewöhnlich hoch?

Sun   Nein. Er muß eine Nachlässigkeit bei einem Flieger
entdecken, der eine große Familie hat und deshalb sehr
pflichteifrig ist. Sie verstehen. Das ist übrigens im
Vertrauen gesagt, und Shen Te braucht es nicht zu wissen.

Shui Ta   Vielleicht nicht. Nur eines: wird der
Hangarverwalter dann nicht im nächsten Monat Sie
verkaufen?

He takes a cigar and **Shui Ta** *gives him a light.*

Sun You really think we can get 300 silver dollars out of this place?

Shui Ta May I ask: Are you planning to sell it immediately?

Sun Do you have 300 cash-in-hand?

Shui Ta *shakes his head 'no'.*

Sun I appreciate how she forked over the 200 straight away. But I've got to get the remaining 300 or I'm screwed.

Shui Ta She may have been a bit hasty to promise you the money. It could mean she loses the shop. They say: Impetuosity is the wind that tears down the scaffolding.

Sun I need the money now or not at all. And this isn't a girl who holds out. Between you and me, pal: she hasn't held out anything yet.

Shui Ta Aha.

Sun Which I think is entirely to her credit.*

Shui Ta May I know to what purpose the 500 silver dollars will be put?

Sun Sure. I get it, you're checking me out. The airfield manager in Peking, a guy I knew from school, he can get me a job if I make him a 500 silver dollar contribution.

Shui Ta That's rather a large sum.

Sun Not if you think about it. The manager's going to have to prove that another pilot's been negligent, and this particular pilot has a large family, so he's always extremely careful. Follow me? This is between you and me, by the way, there's no need for Shen Te to know about it.

Shui Ta Perhaps not. However: Won't the airfield manager sell you out next month?

Sun   Nicht mich. Bei mir wird es keine Nachlässigkeit geben. Ich bin lange genug ohne Stelle gewesen.

Shui Ta (*nickt*)   Der hungrige Hund zieht den Karren schneller nach Hause. (*Er betrachtet ihn eine Zeitlang prüfend.*) Die Verantwortung ist sehr groß. Herr Yang Sun, Sie verlangen von meiner Kusine, daß sie ihr kleines Besitztum und alle ihre Freunde in dieser Stadt aufgibt und ihr Schicksal ganz in Ihre Hände legt. Ich nehme an, daß Sie die Absicht haben, Shen Te zu heiraten?

Sun   Dazu wäre ich bereit.

Shui Ta   Aber ist es dann nicht schade, den Laden für ein paar Silberdollar wegzuhökern? Man wird wenig dafür bekommen, wenn man schnell verkaufen muß. Mit den 200 Silberdollar, die Sie in den Händen haben, wäre die Miete für ein halbes Jahr gesichert. Würde es Sie nicht auch locken, das Tabakgeschäft weiterzuführen?

Sun   Mich? Soll man Yang Sun, den Flieger, hinter einem Ladentisch stehen sehen: 'Wünschen Sie eine starke Zigarre oder eine milde, geehrter Herr?' Das ist kein Geschäft für die Yang Suns, nicht in diesem Jahrhundert!

Shui Ta   Gestatten Sie mir die Frage, ob die Fliegerei ein Geschäft ist?

Sun (*zieht einen Brief aus der Tasche*)   Herr, ich bekomme 250 Silberdollar im Monat! Sehen Sie selber den Brief. Hier ist die Briefmarke und der Stempel Peking.

Shui Ta   250 Silberdollar? Das ist viel.

Sun   Meinen Sie, ich fliege umsonst?

Shui Ta   Die Stelle ist anscheinend gut. Herr Yang Sun, meine Kusine hat mich beauftragt, Ihnen zu dieser Stelle als Flieger zu verhelfen, die Ihnen alles bedeutet. Vom Standpunkt meiner Kusine aus sehe ich keinen triftigen Einwand dagegen, daß sie dem Zug ihres Herzens folgt. Sie ist vollkommen berechtigt, der Freuden der Liebe teilhaftig zu werden. Ich bin bereit, alles hier zu Geld zu machen. Da kommt die Hausbesitzerin, Frau Mi Tzü, die ich wegen des Verkaufs um Rat fragen will.

Sun No way. I'll never be negligent. I've been unemployed too long.

Shui Ta (*nodding*) The hungry dog pulls the cart home faster.

Shui Ta *observes* **Sun** *for a while, searchingly.*

It's a great responsibility. Mr Yang Sun, you're asking my cousin to give up the small security she has and all her friends in this city and entrust her fate to your hands. You do intend to marry Shen Te?

Sun I'm prepared to do that.

Shui Ta But isn't it a waste to lose the shop for a few dollars? You get little when you sell fast. You could apply the 200 silver dollars you've already got to half the year's rent. Does running a tobacco business have no appeal for you?

Sun For me? Can you see Yang Sun the pilot standing behind a counter: 'Would you like a strong cigar or something milder, worthy Sir?' Not for the Yang Suns of this world, not in this century!

Shui Ta But permit me to ask if flying's a reliably remunerative venture?

Sun (*pulling a letter out of his pocket*) Mister, it pays 250 silver dollars a month! See for yourself. Here's the postmark and the stamp. Peking.

Shui Ta 250 silver dollars. That's a lot.

Sun You think I fly for free?

Shui Ta This appears to be a good job. Mr Yang Sun, my cousin wants me to help you secure this pilot's position which means the world to you. I see nothing inimical to my cousin's interests in her following her heart's desire. She's as entitled to be in love as anyone. I'm ready to liquidate the shop. Here's Mrs Mi Tzu, whom I want to consult on the details of the sale.

Die Hausbesitzerin (*herein*) Guten Tag, Herr Shui Ta. Es handelt sich wohl um die Ladenmiete, die übermorgen fällig ist.

Shui Ta Frau Mi Tzü, es sind Umstände eingetreten, die es zweifelhaft gemacht haben, ob meine Kusine den Laden weiterführen wird. Sie gedenkt zu heiraten, und ihr zukünftiger Mann (*er stellt* **Yang Sun** *vor*), Herr Yang Sun, nimmt sie mit sich nach Peking, wo sie eine neue Existenz gründen wollen. Wenn ich für meinen Tabak genug bekomme, verkaufe ich.

Die Hausbesitzerin Wieviel brauchen Sie denn?

Sun 300 auf den Tisch.

Shui Ta (*schnell*) Nein, 500!

Die Hausbesitzerin (*zu* **Sun**) Vielleicht kann ich Ihnen unter die Arme greifen. Was hat Ihr Tabak gekostet?

Shui Ta Meine Kusine hat einmal 1,000 Silberdollar dafür bezahlt, und es ist sehr wenig verkauft worden.

Die Hausbesitzerin 1,000 Silberdollar! Sie ist natürlich hereingelegt worden. Ich will Ihnen etwas sagen: ich zahle Ihnen 300 Silberdollar für den ganzen Laden, wenn Sie übermorgen ausziehen.

Sun Das tun wir. Es geht, Alter!

Shui Ta Es ist zu wenig!

Sun Es ist genug!

Shui Ta Ich muß wenigstens 500 haben.

Sun Wozu?

Shui Ta Gestatten Sie, daß ich mit dem Verlobten meiner Kusine etwas bespreche. (*Beiseite zu* **Sun**.) Der ganze Tabak hier ist verpfändet an zwei alte Leute für die 200 Silberdollar, die Ihnen gestern ausgehändigt wurden.

Sun (*zögernd*) Ist etwas Schriftliches darüber vorhanden?

Shui Ta Nein.

The Landlady (*entering*)   Good day Mr Shui Ta. This is probably about the rent? It's due, day after tomorrow.

Shui Ta   Mrs Mi Tzu, circumstances have arisen which mitigate against my cousin's continuing in business. She's marrying, and her intended (*he gestures towards* **Sun**), Mr Yang Sun, will be taking her with him to Peking, where she'll start a new life. A decent offer for my tobacco could induce me to sell.

The Landlady   How much?

Sun   300 over the counter.

Shui Ta (*quickly*)   No, 500!

The Landlady (*to* **Sun**)   I might be able to help. What did the tobacco cost?

Shui Ta   My cousin paid 1,000 silver dollars for it, and she's sold nearly nothing.

The Landlady   1,000 silver dollars! She was swindled, naturally. How's this: 300 silver dollars for everything if you move out the day after tomorrow.

Sun   Deal! It's plenty, grandma!

Shui Ta   It's not enough!

Sun   Yes it is!

Shui Ta   I must have at least 500.

Sun   What for?

Shui Ta   Allow me a little talk with my cousin's fiancé.

(*Aside, to* **Sun**.) The tobacco's collateral for a loan from two old people. She owes them 200 silver dollars, which she gave to you yesterday.

Sun (*cautiously*)   Anything in writing?

Shui Ta   No.

Sun (*zur* **Hausbesitzerin** *nach einer kleinen Pause*)   Wir können es machen mit den 300.

Die Hausbesitzerin   Aber ich müßte noch wissen, ob der Laden schuldenfrei ist.

Sun   Antworten Sie.

Shui Ta   Der Laden ist schuldenfrei.

Sun   Wann wären die 300 zu bekommen?

Die Hausbesitzerin   Übermorgen, und Sie können es sich ja überlegen. Wenn Sie einen Monat Zeit haben mit dem Verkaufen, werden Sie mehr herausholen. Ich zahle 300 und das nur, weil ich gern das Meine tun will, wo es sich anscheinend um ein junges Liebesglück handelt. (*Ab.*)

Sun (*nachrufend*)   Wir machen das Geschäft! Kistchen, Töpfchen und Säcklein, alles für 300, und der Schmerz ist zu Ende. (*Zu* **Shui Ta.**) Vielleicht bekommen wir bis übermorgen woanders mehr? Dann könnten wir sogar die 200 zurückzahlen.

Shui Ta   Nicht in der kurzen Zeit. Wir werden keinen Silberdollar mehr haben als die 300 der Mi Tzü. Das Geld für die Reise zu zweit und die erste Zeit haben Sie?

Sun   Sicher.

Shui Ta   Wieviel ist das?

Sun   Jedenfalls werde ich es auftreiben, und wenn ich es stehlen müßte!

Shui Ta   Ach so, auch diese Summe müßte erst aufgetrieben werden?

Sun   Kipp nicht aus den Schuhen, Alter. Ich komme schon nach Peking.

Shui Ta   Aber für zwei Leute kann es nicht so billig sein.

Sun   Zwei Leute? Das Mädchen lasse ich doch hier. Sie wäre mir in der ersten Zeit nur ein Klotz am Bein.

Shui Ta   Ich verstehe.

Sun (*A short pause, then, to* **The Landlady**.)   300 is fine.

The Landlady   I'll need proof that the shop is debt free.

Sun   Answer her!

Shui Ta   The shop is debt free.

Sun   When can we have the 300?

The Landlady   The day after tomorrow, and I suggest you think it over in the meantime. Wait a month and you can do better. 300 is the most I can do, and I'm only doing that because I like to support young love. (*Exits.*)

Sun (*calling after her*)   It's a deal! Bags, pots and boxes for 300 and it'll only hurt a minute. (*To* **Shui Ta**.) Maybe we'll get a better offer before she comes back. Then we could pay back the 200.

Shui Ta   Not with time so tight. 300 from Mrs Mi Tzu and not a silver dollar more. You have enough of your own money to get to Peking? And something to live on?

Sun   You bet.

Shui Ta   How much have you got?

Sun   Stop worrying, I'll get it even if I have to mug somebody.

Shui Ta   Aha. So even the price of the tickets has to be grubbed up.

Sun   Keep your hat on, grandma. Nothing's keeping me from Peking.

Shui Ta   No doubt, but two people – that'll be expensive.

Sun   What two people? The girl stays behind. She'd just be a drag at first.

Shui Ta   I see.

Sun Warum schauen Sie mich an wie einen undichten Ölbehälter? Man muß sich nach der Decke strecken.

Shui Ta Und wovon soll meine Kusine leben?

Sun Können Sie nicht etwas für sie tun?

Shui Ta Ich werde mich bemühen. (*Pause.*) Ich wollte, Sie händigten mir die 200 Silberdollar wieder aus, Herr Yang Sun, und ließen sie hier, bis Sie imstande sind, mir zwei Billetts nach Peking zu zeigen.

Sun Lieber Schwager, ich wollte, du mischtest dich nicht hinein.

Shui Ta Fräulein Shen Te …

Sun Überlassen Sie das Mädchen ruhig mir.

Shui Ta Wird vielleicht ihren Laden nicht mehr verkaufen wollen, wenn sie erfährt …

Sun Sie wird auch dann.

Shui Ta Und von meinem Einspruch befürchten Sie nichts?

Sun Lieber Herr!

Shui Ta Sie scheinen zu vergessen, daß sie ein Mensch ist und eine Vernunft hat.

Sun (*belustigt*) Was gewisse Leute von ihren weiblichen Verwandten und der Wirkung vernünftigen Zuredens denken, hat mich immer gewundert. Haben Sie schon einmal von der Macht der Liebe oder dem Kitzel des Fleisches gehört? Sie wollen an ihre Vernunft appellieren? Sie hat keine Vernunft! Dagegen ist sie zeitlebens mißhandelt worden, armes Tier! Wenn ich ihr die Hand auf die Schulter lege und ihr sage 'Du gehst mit mir', hört sie Glocken und kennt ihre Mutter nicht mehr.

Shui Ta (*mühsam*) Herr Yang Sun!

Sun Herr … wie Sie auch heißen mögen!

Shui Ta Meine Kusine ist Ihnen ergeben, weil …

Sun Stop looking at me like I'm a leaky oil filter. Everybody'll have to make sacrifices.

Shui Ta And how should my cousin live?

Sun Can't you help her?

Shui Ta I can try. (*Pause.*) I would like you to hand over the 200 silver dollars here, Mr Yang Sun, and leave it here, until you're able to show me two tickets to Peking.

Sun Dear brother-in-law, I would like you to butt out of business that's not your concern.

Shui Ta Miss Shen Te —

Sun Let me take care of the girl.

Shui Ta — might choose not to sell her shop when she learns —

Sun Trust me, she will.

Shui Ta You seem to forget that she's a rational person.

Sun (*amused*) I love it that people think their female relations respond to rational persuasion. Don't you know about the force of love and getting goosebumps? Rational? She isn't rational! Considering her whole life's been getting knocked around, poor mutt!* If I put my hand on her shoulder and say 'you'll be with me, baby, someday,' she'll hear bells and she wouldn't recognise her own mother.

Shui Ta (*anguished*) Mr Yang Sun!

Sun Mr ... whatever your name is!

Shui Ta My cousin gave herself to you because —

Sun   Wollen wir sagen, weil ich die Hand am Busen habe? Stopf's in deine Pfeife und rauch's! (*Er nimmt sich noch eine Zigarre, dann steckt er ein paar in die Tasche, und am Ende nimmt er die Kiste unter den Arm.*) Du kommst zu ihr nicht mit leeren Händen: bei der Heirat bleibt's. Und da bringt sie die 300, oder du bringst sie, oder sie, oder du! (*Ab.*)

Die Shin (*steckt den Kopf aus dem Gelaß*)   Keine angenehme Erscheinung! Und die ganze Gelbe Gasse weiß, daß er das Mädchen vollständig in der Hand hat.

Shui Ta (*aufschreiend*)   Der Laden ist weg! Er liebt nicht! Das ist der Ruin. Ich bin verloren! (*Er beginnt herumzulaufen wie ein gefangenes Tier, immerzu wiederholend 'Der Laden ist weg!', bis er plötzlich stehenbleibt und* **Die Shin** *anredet.*) Shin, Sie sind am Rinnstein aufgewachsen, und so bin ich es. Sind wir leichtfertig? Nein. Lassen wir es an der nötigen Brutalität fehlen? Nein. Ich bin bereit, Sie am Hals zu nehmen und Sie solang zu schütteln, bis Sie den Käsch ausspucken, den sie mir gestohlen haben, Sie wissen es. Die Zeiten sind furchtbar, diese Stadt ist eine Hölle, aber wir krallen uns an der glatten Mauer hoch. Dann ereilt einen von uns das Unglück: er liebt. Das genügt, er ist verloren. Eine Schwäche und man ist abserviert. Wie soll man sich von allen Schwächen freimachen, vor allem von der tödlichsten, der Liebe? Sie ist ganz unmöglich! Sie ist zu teuer! Freilich, sagen Sie selbst, kann man leben, immer auf der Hut? Was ist das für eine Welt? Die Liebkosungen gehen in Würgungen über. Der Liebesseufzer verwandelt sich in den Angstschrei. Warum kreisen die Geier dort? Dort geht eine zum Stelldichein!

Die Shin   Ich denke, ich hole lieber gleich den Barbier. Sie müssen mit dem Barbier reden. Das ist ein Ehrenmann. Der Barbier, das ist der Richtige für Ihre Kusine. (*Da sie keine Antwort erhält, läuft sie weg.*)

Shui Ta *läuft wieder herum, bis* **Herr Shu Fu** *eintritt, gefolgt von der* **Shin***, die sich jedoch auf einen Wink* **Herrn Shu Fus** *zurückziehen muß.*

Sun Because I squeezed her tits. So you tell her to be
rational, but remember: I. Squeeze. Her. Tits.*

*He takes another cigar, then puts a couple in his pocket, and
finally takes the whole box under his arm.*

You're not going back to her empty-handed: we're
engaged to be married. And she should bring the 300
with her, or you should, however you get it, bring it to the
wedding! (*Exits.*)

Mrs Shin (*sticking her head out from the back room*)
Charming! Everyone on Yellow Street says she's dangling
from his finger.

Shui Ta (*screaming*)   The shop is lost! He's not in love!
I'm ruined. I'm lost!

*He paces a circle like a captive animal, repeating 'The shop is
lost!', then suddenly stops and speaks to* **Mrs Shin**.

Shui Ta   Shin, you're from the gutter and so am I. Are
we fools? No. Do we lack the necessary brutality? No. I'll
grab you by the throat and shake you till you spit out the
penny you stole from me, and you know I will. Times are
horrendous, this city is a Hell, but nevertheless we
clamber up the glass wall. Then one of us slips
calamitously: he loves. That's enough, he's finished. One
little weakness and you're doomed. How can you
extirpate every weakness, especially the most fatal – Love?
It's absolutely impossible! It costs too much! Of course
you tell yourself no one can live that way, always on
guard, what kind of world is that?

Mrs Shin   I think the best thing to do is fetch the barber.
Talk to the barber. He's a real gentleman. The barber's
the perfect match for your cousin.

Getting no answer from **Shui Ta**, **Mrs Shin** *exits.* **Shui Ta** *paces
again.*

Shui Ta (*eilt ihm entgegen*)   Lieber Herr, vom Hörensagen
weiß ich, daß Sie für meine Kusine einiges Interesse
angedeutet haben. Lassen Sie mich alle Gebote der
Schicklichkeit, die Zurückhaltung fordern, beiseite
setzen, denn das Fräulein ist im Augenblick in größter
Gefahr.

Herr Shu Fu   Oh!

Shui Ta   Noch vor wenigen Stunden im Besitz eines
eigenen Ladens, ist meine Kusine jetzt wenig mehr als
eine Bettlerin. Herr Shu Fu, dieser Laden ist ruiniert.

Herr Shu Fu   Herr Shui Ta, der Zauber Fräulein Shen
Tes besteht kaum in der Güte ihres Ladens, sondern in
der Güte ihres Herzens. Der Name, den dieses Viertel
dem Fräulein verlieh, sagt alles: Der Engel der Vorstädte!

Shui Ta   Lieber Herr, diese Güte hat meine Kusine an
einem einzigen Tage 200 Silberdollar gekostet! Da muß
ein Riegel vorgeschoben werden.

Herr Shu Fu   Gestatten Sie, daß ich eine abweichende
Meinung äußere: dieser Güte muß der Riegel erst recht
eigentlich geöffnet werden: Es ist die Natur des Fräuleins,
Gutes zu tun. Was bedeutet da die Speisung von vier
Menschen, die ich sie jeden Morgen mit Rührung
vornehmen sehe! Warum darf sie nicht vierhundert
speisen? Ich höre, sie zerbricht sich zum Beispiel den
Kopf, wie ein paar Obdachlose unterbringen. Meine
Häuser hinter dem Viehhof stehen leer. Sie sind zu ihrer
Verfügung und so weiter und so weiter. Herr Shui Ta,
dürfte ich hoffen, daß solche Ideen, die mir in den
letzten Tagen gekommen sind, bei Fräulein Shen Te
Gehör finden könnten?

Shui Ta   Herr Shu Fu, sie wird so hohe Gedanken mit
Bewunderung anhören.

Herein **Wang** *mit dem* **Polizisten.** **Herr Shu Fu** *wendet sich
um und studiert die Stellagen.*

Wang   Ist Fräulein Shen Te hier?

Shui Ta   He caresses your neck then he strangles you.* Your wet panting coarsens, then you're shrieking in terror. Why are vultures circling in the sky over there? Because they know: A woman's meeting with her lover.

Shu Fu *enters, followed by* **Mrs Shin***, who then withdraws upon being waved out by* **Shu Fu***.*

Shui Ta (*rushing to him*)   My dear sir, I've heard it rumoured that you've expressed some interest in my cousin. Forgive me for abandoning decorum and discretion, for the young lady's in terrible danger.

Shu Fu   Oh!

Shui Ta   Only a few hours ago the owner of her own concern, my cousin is now practically empaupered. Mr Shu Fu, this shop is ruined.

Shu Fu   Mr Shui Ta, Miss Shen Te's charm lies not in the goodness of her shop but of her heart. The name they've given her in these parts says it all: The Angel of the Outskirts!

Shui Ta   My dear sir, this goodness of hers has cost my cousin 200 silver dollars in a single day! It's time to staunch the flow!

Shu Fu   Permit me a divergent opinion: the flow of her goodness should burst the floodgates. It's the young lady's nature to do good. What's the point in feeding four people, which each and every morning, with swelling emotion, I watch her doing. Why shouldn't she feed four hundred? I hear for instance that she's been beating her head against a wall trying to shelter a pair of homeless people. My buildings behind the cattleyard are empty. They could be placed at her disposal. Etcetera. Mr Shui Ta, might I hope that Miss Shen Te would grant audience to these ideas, which have recently struck me.

Shui Ta   Mr Shu Fu, she would hear such fine ideas with complete admiration.

Wang *enters with* **The Policeman***.* **Shu Fu** *turns and studies the shelves.*

Wang   Is Miss Shen Te here?

Shui Ta Nein.

Wang Ich bin Wang, der Wasserverkäufer. Sie sind wohl Herr Shui Ta?

Shui Ta Ganz richtig. Guten Tag, Wang.

Wang Ich bin befreundet mit Shen Te.

Shui Ta Ich weiß, daß Sie einer ihrer ältesten Freunde sind.

Wang (*zum* **Polizisten**) Sehen Sie? (*Zu* **Shui Ta**.) Ich komme wegen meiner Hand.

Der Polizist Kaputt ist sie, das ist nicht zu leugnen.

Shui Ta (*schnell*) Ich sehe, Sie brauchen eine Schlinge für den Arm. (*Er holt aus dem Gelaß einen Shawl und wirft ihn* **Wang** *zu.*)

Wang Aber das ist doch der neue Shawl.

Shui Ta Sie braucht ihn nicht mehr.

Wang Aber sie hat ihn gekauft, um jemand Bestimmtem zu gefallen.

Shui Ta Das ist nicht mehr nötig, wie es sich herausgestellt hat.

Wang (*macht sich eine Schlinge aus dem Shawl*) Sie ist meine einzige Zeugin.

Der Polizist Ihre Kusine soll gesehen haben, wie der Barbier Shu Fu mit der Brennschere nach dem Wasserverkäufer geschlagen hat. Wissen Sie davon?

Shui Ta Ich weiß nur, daß meine Kusine selbst nicht zur Stelle war, als der kleine Vorfall sich abspielte.

Wang Das ist ein Mißverständnis! Lassen Sie Shen Te erst da sein, und alles klärt sich auf. Shen Te wird alles bezeugen. Wo ist sie?

Shui Ta (*ernst*) Herr Wang, Sie nennen sich einen Freund meiner Kusine. Meine Kusine hat eben jetzt sehr große Sorgen. Sie ist von allen Seiten erschreckend

Shui Ta   No.

Wang   I'm Wang the waterseller. Are you Mr Shui Ta?

Shui Ta   I am. Good day, Mr Wang.

Wang   I am a friend of Shen Te's.

Shui Ta   She's told me you're one of her oldest friends.

Wang (*to* **The Policeman**)   See?

(*To* **Shui Ta**.) I've come because of my hand.

The Policeman   It's broken, no denying that.

Shui Ta (*quickly*)   You should have it in a sling.

He gets the shawl from the back room and throws it to **Wang**.

Wang   But that's her new shawl!

Shui Ta   She doesn't need it anymore.

Wang   She bought it to please someone special.

Shui Ta   As things have turned out, that's become moot.*

Wang (*making a sling out of the shawl*)   She's my only witness.

The Policeman   Apparently your cousin saw the barber Shu Fu break the waterseller's hand with his curling iron. Do you know anything about this?

Shui Ta   Only that my cousin says she wasn't at the scene when the mishap occurred.

Wang   You must've misheard her! As soon as Shen Te comes home, she'll tell you, she's my witness. Where is she?

Shui Ta (*seriously*)   Mr Wang, you call yourself my cousin's friend. My cousin has terrible problems right now. Everyone's used her, badly. In the future she won't

ausgenutzt worden. Sie kann sich in Zukunft nicht mehr die allerkleinste Schwäche leisten. Ich bin überzeugt, Sie werden nicht verlangen, daß sie sich vollends um alles bringt, indem sie in Ihrem Fall anderes als die Wahrheit sagt.

Wang (*verwirrt*)   Aber ich bin auf ihren Rat zum Richter gegangen.

Shui Ta   Sollte der Richter Ihre Hand heilen?

Der Polizist   Nein. Aber er sollte den Barbier zahlen machen.

Herr Shu Fu *dreht sich um.*

Shui Ta   Herr Wang, es ist eines meiner Prinzipien, mich nicht in einen Streit zwischen meinen Freunden zu mischen.

Shui Ta *verbeugt sich vor* **Herrn Shu Fu**, *der sich zurückverbeugt.*

Wang (*die Schlinge wieder abnehmend und sie zurücklegend, traurig*)   Ich verstehe.

Der Polizist   Worauf ich wohl wieder gehen kann. Du bist mit deinem Schwindel an den Unrechten gekommen, nämlich an einen ordentlichen Mann. Sei das nächste Mal ein wenig vorsichtiger mit deinen Anklagen, Kerl. Wenn Herr Shu Fu nicht Gnade vor Recht ergehen läßt, kannst du noch wegen Ehrabschneidung ins Kittchen kommen. Ab jetzt!

Beide ab.

Shui Ta   Ich bitte, den Vorgang zu entschuldigen.

Herr Shu Fu   Er ist entschuldigt. (*Dringend.*) Und die Sache mit diesem 'bestimmten Jemand' (*er zeigt auf den Shawl*) ist wirklich vorüber? Ganz aus?

Shui Ta   Ganz. Er ist durchschaut. Freilich, es wird Zeit nehmen, bis alles verwunden ist.

Herr Shu Fu   Man wird vorsichtig sein, behutsam.

Shui Ta   Da sind frische Wunden.

be able to indulge even the smallest weakness. Surely you won't ask her to sacrifice everything by speaking anything other than the truth in your case.

Wang (*confused*)   But she's the one who told me to go to the judge, and I did.

Shui Ta   Will the judge heal your hand?

The Policeman   No, he's just supposed to make the barber pay.

Shu Fu *turns around.*

Shui Ta   Mr Wang, it's one of my principles to stay out of fights between friends.

Shui Ta *bows to* **Shu Fu**, *who bows back.*

Wang (*taking off the sling and putting it back, sadly*)   I understand.

The Policeman   So I'm not needed here. You tried your con game on an honest gentleman. Watch your step next time, boy. If Mr Shu Fu isn't feeling mercifully inclined, you're bound for the hoosegow* for slander. Got it?

Both exit.

Shui Ta   I beg your pardon for the interruption.

Shu Fu   Granted. And her 'special someone' – (*he points to the shawl*) Is that over? For good?

Shui Ta   Forever. She's come to her senses. Of course it'll take time for the wounds to heal.

Shu Fu   I'll be gentle.

Shui Ta   They're fresh wounds.

Herr Shu Fu   Sie wird aufs Land reisen.

Shui Ta   Einige Wochen. Sie wird jedoch froh sein, zuvor alles besprechen zu können mit jemand, dem sie vertrauen kann.

Herr Shu Fu   Bei einem kleinen Abendessen, in einem kleinen, aber guten Restaurant.

Shui Ta   In diskreter Weise. Ich beeile mich, meine Kusine zu verständigen. Sie wird sich vernünftig zeigen. Sie ist in großer Unruhe wegen ihres Ladens, den sie als Geschenk der Götter betrachtet. Gedulden Sie sich ein paar Minuten. (*Ab in das Gelaß.*)

Die Shin (*steckt den Kopf herein*)   Kann man gratulieren?

Herr Shu Fu   Man kann. Frau Shin, richten Sie heute noch Fräulein Shen Tes Schützlingen von mir aus, daß ich ihnen in meinen Häusern hinter dem Viehhof Unterkunft gewähre.

Sie nickt grinsend.

Herr Shu Fu (*aufstehend, zum Publikum*)   Wie finden Sie mich, meine Damen und Herren? Kann man mehr tun? Kann man selbstloser sein? Feinfühliger? Weitblickender? Ein kleines Abendessen! Was denkt man sich doch dabei gemeinhin Ordinäres und Plumpes! Und nichts wird davon geschehen, nichts. Keine Berührung, nicht einmal eine scheinbar zufällige, beim Reichen des Salznäpfchens! Nur ein Austausch von Ideen wird stattfinden. Zwei Seelen werden sich finden, über den Blumen des Tisches, weißen Chrysanthemen übrigens. (*Er notiert sich das.*) Nein, hier wird nicht eine unglückliche Lage ausgenutzt, hier wird kein Vorteil aus einer Enttäuschung gezogen. Verständnis und Hilfe wird geboten, aber beinahe lautlos. Nur mit einem Blick wird das vielleicht anerkannt werden, einem Blick, der auch mehr bedeuten kann.

Die Shin   So ist alles nach Wunsch gegangen, Herr Shu Fu?

Shu Fu   A trip to the country.

Shui Ta   Patience. A few weeks. She'll be happy to have someone she trusts to talk to. Finally.

Shu Fu   At an intimate dinner in a small but good restaurant.

Shui Ta   I'll tell my cousin immediately. She'll be reasonable. She's been terribly worried about this shop, which she considers a gift from the Gods. Please wait patiently.

He exits into the back room.

Mrs Shin (*sticking her head in*)   Are congratulations in order?

Shu Fu   They are. Mrs Shin, inform the people Miss Shen Te has been helping that I'm granting them lodging in my buildings behind the cattleyards.

She nods, grinning.

Shu Fu (*standing, to the audience*)   Ladies and gentlemen, what's your opinion of me? Can a man do more? Can a man be more selfless? Delicate? Visionary? An intimate dinner! This of course makes one think coarse and common thoughts! But nothing like that will happen. Hands off, not even accidental touching while passing the salt. The only intercourse will be intellectual.* Two kindred spirits finding each other across the flower arrangement. White chrysanthemums, if you're wondering. (*He makes a note of that.*) No, this isn't about exploiting a misfortune, this isn't about taking advantage of a broken heart. Solace and assistance will be offered, but almost wordlessly. And acquiesced to by a look, a look which might signify more to come.

Mrs Shin   So it went well, Mr Shu Fu?

Herr Shu Fu   Oh, ganz nach Wunsch! Es wird
vermutlich Veränderungen in dieser Gegend geben. Ein
gewisses Subjekt hat den Laufpaß bekommen, und einige
Anschläge auf diesen Laden werden zu Fall gebracht
werden. Gewisse Leute, die sich nicht entblöden, dem
Ruf des keuschesten Mädchens dieser Stadt zu nahe zu
treten, werden es in Zukunft mit mir zu tun bekommen.
Was wissen Sie von diesem Yang Sun?

Die Shin   Er ist der schmutzigste, faulste ...

Herr Shu Fu   Er ist nichts. Es gibt ihn nicht. Er ist nicht
vorhanden, Shin.

Herein **Sun**.

Sun   Was geht hier vor?

Die Shin   Herr Shu Fu, wünschen Sie, daß ich Herrn
Shui Ta rufe? Er wird nicht wollen, daß sich hier fremde
Leute im Laden herumtreiben.

Herr Shu Fu   Fräulein Shen Te hat eine wichtige
Besprechung mit Herrn Shui Ta, die nicht unterbrochen
werden darf.

Sun   Was, sie ist hier? Ich habe sie gar nicht
hineingehen sehen! Was ist das für eine Besprechung?
Da muß ich teilnehmen!

Herr Shu Fu (*hindert ihn, ins Gelaß zu gehen*)   Sie werden
sich zu gedulden haben, mein Herr. Ich denke, ich weiß,
wer Sie sind. Nehmen Sie zur Kenntnis, daß Fräulein
Shen Te und ich vor der Bekanntgabe unserer Verlobung
stehen.

Sun   Was?

Die Shin   Das setzt Sie in Erstaunen, wie?

Sun *ringt mit dem Barbier, um ins Gelaß zu kommen, heraus
tritt* **Shen Te**.

Herr Shu Fu   Entschuldigen Sie, liebe Shen Te.
Vielleicht erklären Sie ...

Sun   Was ist da los, Shen Te? Bist du verrückt geworden?

Shu Fu Oh yes, very well! And soon there'll be changes hereabouts, I'd imagine. A subject of considerable conversation lately will be handed his walking papers, and those who've plotted to undermine this establishment will be laid low. Tongue-wagglers who've besmirched the reputation of the most spotlessly chaste young woman in the city will answer to me. What have you heard about this Yang Sun?

Mrs Shin He's the most swinish, lazy, lying piece of —

Shu Fu He's nothing at all. He doesn't exist, Shin.

Sun *enters.*

Sun What's up?

Mrs Shin Should I call Mr Shui Ta, Mr Shu Fu? He hates strangers malingering on the premises.

Shu Fu Mr Shui Ta is having an especially private talk with Miss Shen Te and they're off-limits.

Sun I didn't see her come in. What are they meeting about? I should be in there with them.

Shu Fu *blocks him from entering the room.*

Shu Fu A moment sir. I believe I know who you are. And I feel you ought to know that Miss Shen Te and I are set to announce our engagement.

Sun What?

Mrs Shin Surprised?

Sun *fights with* **Shu Fu** *to get into the room.* **Shen Te** *comes out.*

Shu Fu I beg your pardon for fighting in front of you, dear Shen Te. Maybe you can explain to —

Sun What's going on here, Shen Te? Have you gone crazy?

Shen Te (*atemlos*)   Sun, mein Vetter und Herr Shu Fu
sind übereingekommen, daß ich Herrn Shu Fus Ideen
anhöre, wie man den Leuten in diesem Viertel helfen
könnte. (*Pause.*) Mein Vetter ist gegen unsere Beziehung.

Sun   Und du bist einverstanden?

Shen Te   Ja.

Pause.

Sun   Haben sie dir gesagt, ich bin ein schlechter
Mensch?

Shen Te *schweigt.*

Sun   Denn das bin ich vielleicht, Shen Te. Und das ist es,
warum ich dich brauche. Ich bin ein niedriger Mensch.
Ohne Kapital, ohne Manieren. Aber ich wehre mich. Sie
treiben dich in dein Unglück, Shen Te. (*Er geht zu ihr.
Gedämpft.*) Sieh ihn doch an! Hast du keine Augen im
Kopf? (*Mit der Hand auf ihrer Schulter.*) Armes Tier, wozu
wollten sie dich jetzt wieder bringen? In eine
Vernunftheirat! Ohne mich hätten sie dich einfach auf
die Schlachtbank geschleift. Sag selber, ob du ohne mich
nicht mit ihm weggegangen wärst?

Shen Te   Ja.

Sun   Einem Mann, den du nicht liebst!

Shen Te   Ja.

Sun   Hast du alles vergessen? Wie es regnete?

Shen Te   Nein.

Sun   Wie du mich vom Ast geschnitten, wie du mir ein
Glas Wasser gekauft, wie du mir das Geld versprochen
hast, daß ich wieder fliegen kann?

Shen Te (*zitternd*)   Was willst du?

Sun   Daß du mit mir weggehst.

Shen Te   Herr Shu Fu, verzeihen Sie mir, ich will mit
Sun weggehen.

Shen Te (*breathlessly*)   Sun, my cousin and Mr Shu Fu have asked me to listen to Mr Shu Fu's plans for helping the people of this neighbourhood. (*Pause.*) My cousin opposes our relationship.

Sun   And you're going along with him?

Shen Te   Yes.

Pause.

Sun   Have they told you I'm a terrible person?

Shen Te *is silent.*

Maybe I am, Shen Te. That's why I need you. I'm no good. No money and no manners. But I fight hard. They're leading you to misery, Shen Te!

He goes to her.

(*Subdued.*) Take a good look at him! Are you blind?

He puts an arm on her shoulder.

Poor chicken,* where are they taking you? To marry for money. Without me they'll drag you to the chopping block. Go on, say it: if I hadn't showed up you'd have gone off with him, wouldn't you?

Shen Te   Yes.

Sun   A man you don't love!

Shen Te   Yes.

Sun   Have you forgotten? The way it rained?

Shen Te   No.

Sun   How you cut me down from the willow, how you bought a glass of water for me, how you promised me money to fly again?

Shen Te (*trembling*)   What do you want from me?

Sun   Come with me.

Shen Te   Mr Shu Fu, forgive me, I want to go with Sun.

Sun Wir sind Liebesleute, wissen Sie. (*Er führt sie zur Tür.*) Wo hast du den Ladenschlüssel? (*Er nimmt ihn aus ihrer Tasche und gibt ihn der* **Shin**.) Legen Sie ihn auf die Türschwelle, wenn Sie fertig sind. Komm, Shen Te.

Herr Shu Fu Aber das ist ja eine Vergewaltigung! (*Schreit nach hinten.*) Herr Shui Ta!

Sun Sag ihm, er soll hier nicht herumbrüllen.

Shen Te Bitte rufen Sie meinen Vetter nicht, Herr Shu Fu. Er ist nicht einig mit mir, ich weiß es. Aber er hat nicht recht, ich fühle es.

Zum Publikum.

Ich will mit dem gehen, den ich liebe.
Ich will nicht ausrechnen, was es kostet.
Ich will nicht nachdenken, ob es gut ist.
Ich will nicht wissen, ob er mich liebt.
Ich will mit ihm gehen, den ich liebe.

Sun So ist es.

Beide gehen ab.

ZWISCHENSPIEL
VOR DEM VORHANG

Shen Te, *im Hochzeitsschmuck auf dem Weg zur Hochzeit, wendet sich an das Publikum.*

Shen Te Ich habe ein schreckliches Erlebnis gehabt. Als ich aus der Tür trat, lustig und erwartungsvoll, stand die alte Frau des Teppichhändlers auf der Straße und erzählte mir zitternd, daß ihr Mann vor Aufregung und Sorge um das Geld, das sie mir geliehen haben, krank geworden ist. Sie hielt es für das Beste, wenn ich ihr das Geld jetzt auf jeden Fall zurückgäbe. Ich versprach es natürlich. Sie war sehr erleichtert und wünschte mir

Sun Hear that? We're lovers.

Sun *leads* **Shen Te** *to the door.*

Sun Where's the key?

He takes it from her pocket and gives it to **Mrs Shin**.

Sun Leave it under the doormat when you close up.
Shen Te, let's go.

Shu Fu This is a rape!

(*Calling to the back.*) Mr Shui Ta!

Sun Tell him to stop shouting in your shop.

Shen Te Please don't call my cousin, Mr Shu Fu. He
disagrees with me.

But he's not right, I feel it.

(*To audience.*)
I want to go with him, whom I love.
I won't calculate what it's costing.
I won't think carefully, Is this good.
I don't want to know if he loves me.
I want to go with him, whom I love.

Sun And that's that.

Both exit.

INTERLUDE
IN FRONT OF THE CURTAIN

Shen Te *in her wedding dress on the way to her wedding, turns
to the audience.*

Shen Te Something awful has happened. When I came
out of my door, joyful and expectant, the old wife of the
rug merchant was standing on the street and she told me,
shaking, that her husband has become seriously sick,
fretting about the money she lent me. She thinks it best if
I return the loan now. Of course I promised I would. She

weinend alles Gute, mich um Verzeihung bittend, daß sie
meinem Vetter und leider auch Sun nicht voll vertrauen
könnten. Ich mußte mich auf die Treppe setzen, als sie
weg war, so erschrocken war ich über mich. In einem
Aufruhr der Gefühle hatte ich mich Yang Sun wieder in
die Arme geworfen. Ich konnte seiner Stimme und
seinen Liebkosungen nicht widerstehen. Das Böse, was er
Shui Ta gesagt hatte, hatte Shen Te nicht belehren
können. In seine Arme sinkend, dachte ich noch: die
Götter haben auch gewollt, daß ich zu mir gut bin.

Keinen verderben zu lassen, auch nicht sich selber
Jeden mit Glück zu erfüllen, auch sich, das
Ist gut.

Wie habe ich die beiden guten Alten einfach vergessen
können! Sun hat wie ein kleiner Hurrikan in Richtung
Peking meinen Laden einfach weggefegt und mit ihm all
meine Freunde. Aber er ist nicht schlecht, und er liebt
mich. Solang ich um ihn bin, wird er nichts Schlechtes
tun. Was ein Mann zu Männern sagt, das bedeutet nichts.
Da will er groß und mächtig erscheinen und besonders
hartgekocht. Wenn ich ihm sage, daß die beiden Alten
ihre Steuern nicht bezahlen können, wird er alles
verstehen. Lieber wird er in die Zementfabrik gehen, als
sein Fliegen einer Untat verdanken zu wollen. Freilich,
das Fliegen ist bei ihm eine große Leidenschaft. Werde
ich stark genug sein, das Gute in ihm anzurufen? Jetzt,
auf dem Weg zur Hochzeit, schwebe ich zwischen Furcht
und Freude. (*Sie geht schnell weg.*)

was so relieved she cried, and she begged me to forgive her for not being able to trust my cousin or, regrettably, Sun either. I had to sit on the steps after she'd gone, I was so appalled with myself. In an uproar of feelings I've thrown myself back into Yang Sun's arms. I could resist neither his voice nor his touch. The dreadful things he told Shui Ta taught Shen Te nothing. Sinking deep in his embrace, I thought second thoughts: The Gods want me to be good to myself as well.

Leave no one to die, including yourself.
Filling everyone with joy, yourself as well, that
Is good.

But how could I simply forget about the good old couple? Sun swept through my shop like a hurricane bound for Peking and took everything and all my friends. But he's not bad, and he loves me. So long as I stay with him he won't do bad things. What men say when they're alone with one another is meaningless. They want to impress, they want to appear huge and musclebound and hardboiled. If I tell him the old couple can't pay their taxes he'll be understanding. He'd rather go to work in the cement factory than owe his flying to dishonesty. His flying is a great passion in him. Will I be strong enough to bring out his goodness? I go to my wedding, seized between fear and joy.

She goes off quickly.

6
Nebenzimmer eines Billigen Restaurants in der Vorstadt

Ein **Kellner** *schenkt der Hochzeitsgesellschaft Wein ein. Bei* **Shen Te** *stehen* **Der Großvater, Die Schwägerin, Die Nichte, Die Shin** *und* **Der Arbeitslose**. *In der Ecke steht allein ein* **Bonze**. *Vorn spricht* **Sun** *mit seiner Mutter,* **Frau Yang**. *Er trägt einen Smoking.*

Sun Etwas Unangenehmes, Mama. Sie hat mir eben in aller Unschuld gesagt, daß sie den Laden nicht für mich verkaufen kann. Irgendwelche Leute erheben eine Forderung, weil sie ihr die 200 Silberdollar geliehen haben, die sie dir gab. Dabei sagt ihr Vetter, daß überhaupt nichts Schriftliches vorliegt.

Frau Yang Was hast du ihr geantwortet? Du kannst sie natürlich nicht heiraten.

Sun Es hat keinen Sinn, mit ihr über so etwas zu reden, sie ist zu dickköpfig. Ich habe nach ihrem Vetter geschickt.

Frau Yang Aber der will sie doch mit dem Barbier verheiraten.

Sun Diese Heirat habe ich erledigt. Der Barbier ist vor den Kopf gestoßen worden. Ihr Vetter wird schnell begreifen, daß der Laden weg ist, wenn ich die 200 nicht mehr herausrücke, weil dann die Gläubiger ihn beschlagnahmen, daß aber auch die Stelle weg ist, wenn ich die 300 nicht noch bekomme.

Frau Yang Ich werde vor dem Restaurant nach ihm ausschauen. Geh jetzt zu deiner Braut, Sun!

6
Sideroom of a Cheap Restaurant in the Suburbs

A **Waiter** *pours wine for the wedding company. With* **Shen Te** *are* **The Grandfather**, **The Sister-in-Law**, **The Niece**, **Mrs Shin** *and* **The Unemployed Man**. *A* **Bonze** *stands alone in a corner. Up in front,* **Sun** *talks to his mother,* **Mrs Yang**. *He is wearing a dinner jacket.*

Sun   Bad break, mama. She innocently drops the bombshell that she can't sell the shop for me. Some people lent her the 200 silver dollars she gave you and they're demanding repayment. Even though her cousin told me there's nothing in writing.

Mrs Yang   How did you handle it? You can't marry her then.

Sun   No point talking to her about money and stuff, she's a fat-head.* I sent for her cousin.

Mrs Yang   But he wants her married to the barber.

Sun   I scuttled that, I gave the barber a snootful of how much she's hot for me. And her cousin's been around, he knows how it works, he knows I'm not giving back the 200, so the shop's up the chimney, the old folks'll take it, and without the extra 300 I don't get the job, so there we all are. Busted.

Mrs Yang   I'll watch for him outside. Go see after your bride, Sun!

Shen Te (*beim Weineinschenken zum Publikum*)   Ich habe mich nicht in ihm geirrt. Mit keiner Miene hat er Enttäuschung gezeigt. Trotz des schweren Schlages, den für ihn der Verzicht auf das Fliegen bedeuten muß, ist er vollkommen heiter. Ich liebe ihn sehr. (*Sie winkt* **Sun** *zu sich.*) Sun, mit der Braut hast du noch nicht angestoßen!

Sun   Worauf soll es sein?

Shen Te   Es soll auf die Zukunft sein.

Sie trinken.

Sun   Wo der Smoking des Bräutigams nicht mehr nur geliehen ist!

Shen Te   Aber das Kleid der Braut noch mitunter in den Regen kommt!

Sun   Auf alles, was wir uns wünschen!

Shen Te   Daß es schnell eintrifft!

Frau Yang (*im Abgehen zu* **Shin**)   Ich bin entzückt von meinem Sohn. Ich habe ihm immer eingeschärft, daß er jede bekommen kann. Warum, er ist als Mechaniker ausgebildet und Flieger. Und was sagt er mir jetzt? Ich heirate aus Liebe, Mama, sagt er. Geld ist nicht alles. Es ist eine Liebesheirat! (*Zur* **Schwägerin.**) Einmal muß es ja sein, nicht wahr? Aber es ist schwer für eine Mutter, es ist schwer. (*Zum* **Bonzen** *zurückrufend.*) Machen Sie es nicht zu kurz. Wenn Sie sich zu der Zeremonie ebensoviel Zeit nehmen wie zum Aushandeln der Taxe, wird sie würdig sein. (*Zu* **Shen Te.**) Wir müssen allerdings noch ein wenig aufschieben, meine Liebe. Einer der teuersten Gäste ist noch nicht eingetroffen. (*Zu allen.*) Entschuldigt, bitte. (*Ab.*)

Die Schwägerin   Man geduldet sich gern, solang es Wein gibt.

Sie setzen sich.

Der Arbeitslose   Man versäumt nichts.

Shen Te (*to the audience, pouring wine*)   My faith in him wasn't misplaced. He didn't look disappointed at all. Even though giving up his flying was a heavy blow, he's perfectly cheerful. I love him very much.

She waves at **Sun** *to come over to her.*

Shen Te   You haven't raised your glass to your bride yet.

Sun   What should I toast?

Shen Te   The future.

Sun   May the groom someday own his own dinner jacket.

Shen Te   But may the bride's dress get soaked in the rain from time to time.

Sun   To everything we wish for ourselves!

Shen Te   And quickly, too!

Mrs Yang (*to* **Mrs Shin**, *as she exits*)   I'm so pleased with my son. I always told him he could get anyone he wanted. Why not, he's a trained mechanic and a pilot. And so what does he reply? I'm marrying for love, mama, he tells me. Money isn't everything. It's a love-match!

(*To* **The Sister-in-Law**.) Kids, well what are you going to do? But that's how it's got to be, right?

But it's tough being a mother, it's very tough.

(*Calling back to* **The Bonze**.) And don't rush through the service. If you spend as much time marrying them as you did haggling over your fee it'll be a very impressive ceremony.

(*To* **Shen Te**.) We'll have to delay a little, dear. One of the most important guests hasn't arrived.

(*To everyone*.) Excuse me, please. (*Exits*.)

The Sister-in-Law   Happy to wait if the wine holds out.

They sit.

The Unemployed Man   They sure didn't skimp.

Sun (*laut und spaßhaft vor den Gästen*)   Und vor der Verehelichung muß ich noch ein kleines Examen abhalten mit dir. Das ist wohl nicht unnötig, wenn so schnelle Hochzeiten beschlossen werden. (*Zu den Gästen.*) Ich weiß gar nicht, was für eine Frau ich bekomme. Das beunruhigt mich. Kannst du zum Beispiel aus drei Teeblättern fünf Tassen Tee kochen?

Shen Te   Nein.

Sun   Ich werde also keinen Tee bekommen. Kannst du auf einem Strohsack von der Größe des Buches schlafen, das der Priester liest?

Shen Te   Zu zweit?

Sun   Allein.

Shen Te   Dann nicht.

Sun   Ich bin entsetzt, was für eine Frau ich bekomme.

Alle lachen. Hinter **Shen Te** *tritt* **Frau Yang** *in die Tür. Sie bedeutet* **Sun** *durch ein Achselzucken, daß der erwartete Gast nicht zu sehen ist.*

Frau Yang (*zum* **Bonzen**, *der ihr seine Uhr zeigt*)   Haben Sie doch nicht solche Eile. Es kann sich doch nur noch um Minuten handeln. Ich sehe, man trinkt und man raucht und niemand hat Eile.

Sie setzt sich zu den Gästen.

Shen Te   Aber müssen wir nicht darüber reden, wie wir alles ordnen werden?

Frau Yang   Oh, bitte nichts von Geschäften heute! Das bringt einen so gewöhnlichen Ton in eine Feier, nicht?

Die Eingangsglocke bimmelt. Alles schaut zur Tür, aber niemand tritt ein.

Shen Te   Auf wen wartet deine Mutter, Sun?

Sun   Das soll eine Überraschung für dich sein. Was macht übrigens dein Vetter Shui Ta? Ich habe mich gut mit ihm verstanden. Ein sehr vernünftiger Mensch! Ein Kopf! Warum sagst du nichts?

Sun (*joking loudly in front of the guests*)   Before I marry
you you have to pass a little exam. We're marrying in
haste, so take the test. (*To the guests.*) Otherwise who
knows what sort of woman I'm getting? That's been
bothering me. Question one: can you brew a cup of
strong tea from just one tea leaf?

Shen Te   No.

Sun   Okay then no tea for me. Can you sleep on a sack
of straw the size of the book the priest's reading?

Shen Te   The two us together?

Sun   Alone.

Shen Te   Then no.

Sun   I'm can't believe I'm marrying her.

Everyone laughs. **Mrs Yang** *steps through the door behind* **Shen
Te**. *She lets* **Sun** *know with a shrug of her shoulders that the
expected guest is nowhere to be seen.* **The Bonze** *sees her and
points to his watch.*

Mrs Yang (*to* **The Bonze**)   What's your rush? It'll be a
few minutes yet. I'm seeing people drinking and smoking
and no one's in a rush but you. (*She sits down with the
guests.*)

Shen Te   Perhaps we should discuss our future
arrangements?

Mrs Yang   Oh please, no business talk today! Too crude
a note for these joyful festivities, don't you think?

The doorbell rings. Everyone looks at the door but no one enters.

Shen Te   Who's your mother waiting for, Sun?

Sun   That's a surprise. But speaking of waiting, how's
your cousin Shui Ta? We really hit it off. He's a
reasonable man! A real brain! How's he doing?

Shen Te   Ich weiß nicht. Ich will nicht an ihn denken.

Sun   Warum nicht?

Shen Te   Weil du dich nicht mit ihm verstehen sollst.
Wenn du mich liebst, kannst du ihn nicht lieben.

Sun   Dann sollen ihn die drei Teufel holen: der
Bruchteufel, der Nebelteufel und der Gasmangelteufel.
Trink, Dickköpfige! (*Er nötigt sie.*)

Die Schwägerin (*zur* **Shin**)   Hier stimmt etwas nicht.

Die Shin   Haben Sie etwas anderes erwartet?

Der Bonze (*tritt resolut zu* **Frau Yang***, die Uhr in der Hand*)
Ich muß weg, Frau Yang. Ich habe noch eine zweite
Hochzeit und morgen früh ein Begräbnis.

Frau Yang   Meinen Sie, es ist mir angenehm, daß alles
hinausgeschoben wird? Wir hofften mit einem Krug Wein
auszukommen. Sehen Sie jetzt, wie er zur Neige geht.
(*Laut zu* **Shen Te**.) Ich verstehe nicht, liebe Shen Te,
warum dein Vetter so lang auf sich warten läßt!

Shen Te   Mein Vetter?

Frau Yang   Aber, meine Liebe, er ist es doch, den wir
erwarten. Ich bin altmodisch genug zu meinen, daß ein
so naher Verwandter der Braut bei der Hochzeit zugegen
sein muß.

Shen Te   Oh, Sun, ist es wegen der 300 Silberdollar?

Sun (*ohne sie anzusehen*)   Du hörst doch, warum es ist. Sie
ist altmodisch. Ich nehme da Rücksicht. Wir warten eine
kleine Viertelstunde, und wenn er dann nicht gekommen
ist, da die drei Teufel ihn im Griff haben, fangen wir an!

Frau Yang   Sie wissen wohl alle schon, daß mein Sohn
eine Stelle als Postflieger bekommt. Das ist mir sehr
angenehm. In diesen Zeiten muß man gut verdienen.

Die Schwägerin   Es soll in Peking sein, nicht wahr?

Frau Yang   Ja, in Peking.

Shen Te   I don't know. I don't want to think about him.

Sun   Why not?

Shen Te   Because I don't want you to like him. If you love me you can't love him.

Sun   Then I hope the three devils get him: the crash-devil, the fog-devil and the shit-I'm-out-of-fuel devil! Drink, ox!*

He forces her to drink.

The Sister-in-Law (*to* **Mrs Shin**)   Something's off here.

Mrs Shin   It sure is.

The Bonze *goes resolutely to* **Mrs Yang**, *his watch in hand.*

The Bonze   I'm going to have to leave, Mrs Yang. I have another marriage this evening and then up bright and early for a burial.

Mrs Yang   I paid you to marry them so you stay till they're wed!* I can't be held responsible for unavoidable delays! I wanted to get it over and done before we had to open too many bottles, well no hope of that, the way they're knocking it back, and – (*loud, to* **Shen Te**) I don't understand, dear Shen Te, what's keeping your cousin?

Shen Te   My cousin?

Mrs Yang   Of course dear, who else do you think we're waiting for? Call me old-fashioned, but I think close relatives of the bride should be at her wedding.

Shen Te   Oh, Sun, is this about the 300 silver dollars?

Sun   You heard what it's about. She's old-fashioned, and I respect that. Just fifteen more minutes, and if he doesn't show by then, well then the three devils got him and we'll start without him.

Mrs Yang   You've all probably heard that my son will be starting work as a pilot for the post office. I'm so proud of him. To be pulling such high wages, in times like these.

The Sister-in-Law   In Peking, right?

Mrs Yang   Yes, Peking.

Shen Te Sun, du mußt es deiner Mutter sagen, daß aus Peking nichts werden kann.

Sun Dein Vetter wird es ihr sagen, wenn er so denkt wie du. Unter uns: ich denke nicht so.

Shen Te (*erschrocken*) Sun!

Sun Wie ich dieses Sezuan hasse! Und was für eine Stadt! Weißt du, wie ich sie alle sehe, wenn ich die Augen halb zumache? Als Gäule. Sie drehen bekümmert die Hälse hoch: was donnert da über sie weg? Wie, sie werden nicht mehr benötigt? Was, ihre Zeit ist schon um? Sie können sich zu Tode beißen in ihrer Gäulestadt! Ach, hier herauszukommen!

Shen Te Aber ich habe den Alten ihr Geld zurückversprochen.

Sun Ja, das hast du mir gesagt. Und da du solche Dummheiten machst, ist es gut, daß dein Vetter kommt. Trink und überlaß das Geschäftliche uns! Wir erledigen das.

Shen Te (*entsetzt*) Aber mein Vetter kann nicht kommen!

Sun Was heißt das?

Shen Te Er ist nicht mehr da.

Sun Und wie denkst du dir unsere Zukunft, willst du mir das sagen?

Shen Te Ich dachte, du hast noch die 200 Silberdollar. Wir können sie morgen zurückgeben und den Tabak behalten, der viel mehr wert ist, und ihn zusammen vor der Zementfabrik verkaufen, weil wir die Halbjahresmiete ja nicht bezahlen können.

Sun Vergiß das! Vergiß das schnell, Schwester! Ich soll mich auf die Straße stellen und Tabak verramschen an die Zementarbeiter, ich, Yang Sun, der Flieger! Lieber bringe ich die 200 in einer Nacht durch, lieber schmeiße ich sie in den Fluß! Und dein Vetter kennt mich. Mit ihm habe ich ausgemacht, daß er die 300 zur Hochzeit bringt.

Shen Te Sun, you should have told your mother that we've given up on Peking.

Sun Let your cousin tell her, if he sees it the way you do. Just between you and me: I see him seeing different.

Shen Te (*shocked*) Sun!

Sun God I hate Szechwan! What kind of city is this? Want to know what I see when I see the people here? When I squint? Horses! Anxious, craning their thick necks towards the sky: Uh-oh, what's that noise like thunder way high up above them? Oh no, no one needs horses anymore? What, their time's up? Done for? Already? I hope you all bite each other to death in your shitty little horse town. I want out of here!

Shen Te But I promised the old couple their money back.

Sun You told me that already! And because you make air-headed promises we need your cousin. Drink, leave the business to us! Him and me, we'll manage things.

Shen Te (*horrified*) But my cousin can't come!

Sun What are you talking about?

Shen Te He's not there anymore. He's gone.

Sun Uh huh. And how do you imagine you'll manage without him?* How do you imagine us, our future, you thought about that? Care to tell me about that?

Shen Te You still have the 200 silver dollars. I thought, we can give it back tomorrow and keep the tobacco, which is worth much more, and since we can't pay the rent we could sell cigarettes together on the street in front of the cement factory.

Sun Forget it! Forget it, sister, in a hurry! I'm supposed to stand on the street selling cheap cigarettes to cement workers, me, Yang Sun, the pilot? I'd rather blow the 200 in one night of drinking, I'd rather throw it in the river. Your cousin knows I'd do it, too. We had a deal, he was supposed to bring the 300 to the wedding.

Shen Te Mein Vetter kann nicht kommen.

Sun Und ich dachte, er kann nicht wegbleiben.

Shen Te Wo ich bin, kann er nicht sein.

Sun Wie geheimnisvoll!

Shen Te Sun, das mußt du wissen, er ist nicht dein Freund. Ich bin es, die dich liebt. Mein Vetter Shui Ta liebt niemand. Er ist mein Freund, aber er ist keines meiner Freunde Freund. Er war damit einverstanden, daß du das Geld der beiden Alten bekamst, weil er an die Fliegerstelle in Peking dachte. Aber er wird dir die 300 Silberdollar nicht zur Hochzeit bringen.

Sun Und warum nicht?

Shen Te (*ihm in die Augen sehend*) Er sagt, du hast nur ein Billett nach Peking gekauft.

Sun Ja, das war gestern, aber sieh her, was ich ihm heute zeigen kann! (*Er zieht zwei Zettel halb aus der Brusttasche.*) Die Alte braucht es nicht zu sehen. Das sind zwei Billette nach Peking, für mich und für dich. Meinst du noch, daß dein Vetter gegen die Heirat ist?

Shen Te Nein. Die Stelle ist gut. Und meinen Laden habe ich nicht mehr.

Sun Deinetwegen habe ich die Möbel verkauft.

Shen Te Sprich nicht weiter! Zeig mir nicht die Billette! Ich spüre eine zu große Furcht, ich könnte einfach mit dir gehen. Aber, Sun, ich kann dir die 300 Silberdollar nicht geben, denn was soll aus den beiden Alten werden?

Sun Was aus mir? (*Pause.*) Trink lieber! Oder gehörst du zu den Vorsichtigen? Ich mag keine vorsichtige Frau. Wenn ich trinke, fliege ich wieder. Und du, wenn du trinkst, dann verstehst du mich vielleicht möglicherweise.

Shen Te Glaub nicht, ich verstehe dich nicht. Daß du fliegen willst, und ich kann dir nicht dazu helfen.

Sun 'Hier ein Flugzeug, Geliebter, aber es hat nur einen Flügel!'

Shen Te My cousin can't come.

Sun What, and miss the wedding of the year?

Shen Te Where I am, he can't be.

Sun Oooh, a mystery.

Mrs Shin You can say that again.*

Shen Te Sun, please understand, he isn't your friend. I am, I love you. My cousin Shui Ta loves no one. He's my friend, but he's my friends' enemy. He agreed to give you the old couple's money because you told him about the pilot's job in Peking. But he isn't bringing you 300 silver dollars. Not now.

Sun Why not?

Shen Te (*looking him in the eyes*) He says you only have one ticket to Peking.

Sun That was yesterday, this is today! (*He pulls two tickets halfway out of his breast pocket.*) My old lady doesn't need to see them. Two tickets, me and you. Now do you think your cousin will oppose our marriage?

Shen Te No. It's a very good job. And I can't keep the shop.

Sun I sold ma's furniture to get you a ticket.

Shen Te Please stop talking! Don't show me the tickets again! I'm so afraid I'll go away with you. Sun I can't give you the 300 silver dollars, if I do, what'll happen to the old people?

Sun What'll happen to me?

(*Pause.*) Drink! Or did you join a temperance league? I don't like temperate women. When I drink, it's like I'm flying again. Maybe if you get drunk you'll understand me.

Shen Te Please don't think I don't understand you. You want to fly, and I can't help you.

Sun 'Here, my love, I want to give you an airplane, tough luck it's only got one wing.'

Shen Te   Sun, zu der Stelle in Peking können wir nicht ehrlich kommen. Darum brauche ich die 200 Silberdollar wieder, die du von mir bekommen hast. Gib sie mir gleich, Sun!

Sun   'Gib sie mir gleich, Sun!' Von was redest du eigentlich? Bist du meine Frau oder nicht? Denn du verrätst mich, das weißt du doch? Zum Glück, auch zu dem deinen, kommt es nicht mehr auf dich an, da alles ausgemacht ist.

Frau Yang (*eisig*)   Sun, bist du sicher, daß der Vetter der Braut kommt? Es könnte beinahe erscheinen, er hat etwas gegen diese Heirat, da er ausbleibt.

Sun   Wo denkst du hin, Mama! Er und ich sind ein Herz und eine Seele. Ich werde die Tür weit aufmachen, damit er uns sofort findet, wenn er gelaufen kommt, seinem Freund Sun den Brautführer zu machen. (*Er geht zur Tür und stößt sie mit dem Fuß auf. Dann kehrt er, etwas schwankend, da er schon zu viel getrunken hat, zurück und setzt sich wieder zu* **Shen Te**.) Wir warten. Dein Vetter hat mehr Vernunft als du. Die Liebe, sagt er weise, gehört zur Existenz. Und, was wichtiger ist, er weiß, was es für dich bedeutet: keinen Laden mehr und auch keine Heirat!

Es wird gewartet.

Frau Yang   Jetzt!

Man hört Schritte und alle schauen nach der Tür. Aber die Schritte gehen vorüber.

Die Shin   Es wird ein Skandal. Man kann es fühlen, man kann es riechen. Die Braut wartet auf die Hochzeit, aber der Bräutigam wartet auf den Herrn Vetter.

Sun   Der Herr Vetter läßt sich Zeit.

Shen Te (*leise*)   Oh, Sun!

Sun   Hier zu sitzen mit den Billetten in der Tasche und eine Närrin daneben, die nicht rechnen kann! Und ich sehe den Tag kommen, wo du mir die Polizei ins Haus schickst, damit sie 200 Silberdollar abholt.

Shen Te Sun, we can't come by the job in Peking honourably. That's why you have to give back the 200 silver dollars. Give them to me now, Sun!

Sun 'Give them to me now, Sun!' Are you my wife or not? If you are then you're betraying me, you know that, right? Lucky for everyone, lucky for you it's not your decision, it's all been arranged.

Mrs Yang (*icily*) Sun, are you sure the bride's cousin's coming? One might conclude he opposes the marriage, one might conclude he's keeping quit of the whole shebang.

Sun Oh no, Mama! He and I we're one heart and one soul! Let me open the door wide, so he'll know we're here when he comes running to be his friend Sun's best man.

Sun *kicks the door open. Then he turns back, swaying because he's drunk too much, and sits with* **Shen Te** *again.*

We'll wait.*

They wait. Steps are heard and everyone looks towards the door.

Mrs Yang He's here!

The steps go by.

Mrs Shin This is one for the record books. Headline: The bride waited for the wedding, the groom waited for her cousin.

Sun Look at me, two tickets in my pocket, and look at you, a moron who can't add and subtract.

Shen Te (*softly*) Oh, Sun!

Sun Your cousin's got more sense than you is how I know he'll show. Love, he once wisely observed, is for the living. He totally gets what his absence'll spell out for you: you lose the shop and your husband, both. And I see the day coming when you send the police after me, just to get back your 200 silver dollars.

Shen Te (*zum Publikum*)   Er ist schlecht und er will, daß auch ich schlecht sein soll. Hier bin ich, die ihn liebt, und er wartet auf den Vetter. Aber um mich sitzen die Verletzlichen, die Greisin mit dem kranken Mann, die Armen, die am Morgen vor der Tür auf den Reis warten, und ein unbekannter Mann aus Peking, der um seine Stelle besorgt ist. Und sie alle beschützen mich, indem sie mir alle vertrauen.

Sun (*starrt auf den Glaskrug, in dem der Wein zur Neige gegangen ist*)   Der Glaskrug mit dem Wein ist unsere Uhr. Wir sind arme Leute, und wenn die Gäste den Wein getrunken haben, ist sie abgelaufen für immer.

Frau Yang *bedeutet ihm zu schweigen, denn wieder werden Schritte hörbar.*

Der Kellner (*herein*)   Befehlen Sie noch einen Krug Wein, Frau Yang?

Frau Yang   Nein, ich denke, wir haben genug. Der Wein macht einen nur warm, nicht?

Die Shin   Er ist wohl auch teuer.

Frau Yang   Ich komme immer ins Schwitzen durch das Trinken.

Der Kellner   Dürfte ich dann um die Begleichung der Rechnung bitten?

Frau Yang (*überhört ihn*)   Ich bitte die Herrschaften, sich noch ein wenig zu gedulden, der Verwandte muß ja unterwegs sein. (*Zum* **Kellner**.) Stör die Feier nicht!

Der Kellner   Ich darf Sie nicht ohne die Begleichung der Rechnung weglassen.

Frau Yang   Aber man kennt mich doch hier!

Der Kellner   Eben.

Frau Yang   Unerhört, diese Bedienung heutzutage!* Was sagst du dazu, Sun?

Der Bonze   Ich empfehle mich. (*Gewichtig ab.*)

Frau Yang (*verzweifelt*)   Bleibt alle ruhig sitzen! Der Priester kommt in wenigen Minuten zurück.

Shen Te (*to the audience*)   He is bad, and he wants me to be bad. I'm here, I love him, and he only wants the money. But all around me sit the wounded and the vulnerable, the old lady with the sick husband, the poor who will be waiting for their rice in the morning, and a pilot in Peking I've never met, who's frightened of losing his job. All these protect me, because they trust me.

Sun (*staring at the wine bottle, nearly empty*)   This wine jug here's our clock. We're poor people, we can't afford more wine, which means: when the guests have drunk this to the dregs, time's up, the clock's unwound forever.

The Waiter (*entering*)   Another jug, Mrs Yang?

Mrs Yang   No, thanks, too much wine makes you sweat.

Mrs Shin   And broke.

Mrs Yang   It makes me sweat.

The Waiter   I'll bring the bill then?

Mrs Yang (*ignoring him*)   I beg the company's kind indulgence, her relative must be close by now. Round the corner. (*To* **The Waiter**.) You're wrecking the party! Go.

The Waiter   They told me to watch so you don't skip out without paying.

Mrs Yang   They did not! I'm a regular here! They know me!

The Waiter   Exactly.

The Bonze   I take my leave. (*He exits ponderously.*)

Mrs Yang (*in despair*)   Everyone sit! Nobody move! The priest's only visiting the toilet.

Sun Laß nur, Mama. Meine Herrschaften, nachdem der Priester gegangen ist, können wir Sie nicht mehr zurückhalten.

Die Schwägerin Komm, Großvater!

Der Grossvater (*leert ernst sein Glas*) Auf die Braut!

Die Nichte (*zu* **Shen Te**) Nehmen Sie es ihm nicht übel. Er meint es freundlich. Er hat Sie gern.

Die Shin Das nenne ich eine Blamage!

Alle Gäste gehen ab.

Shen Te Soll ich auch gehen, Sun?

Sun Nein, du wartest. (*Er zerrt sie an ihrem Brautschmuck, so daß er schief zu sitzen kommt.*) Ist es nicht deine Hochzeit? Ich warte noch, und die Alte wartet auch noch. Sie jedenfalls wünscht den Falken in den Wolken. Ich glaube freilich jetzt fast, das wird am Sankt Nimmerleinstag sein, wo sie vor die Tür tritt und sein Flugzeug donnert über ihr Haus. (*Nach den leeren Sitzen hin, als seien die Gäste noch da.*) Meine Damen und Herren, wo bleibt die Konversation? Gefällt es Ihnen nicht hier? Die Hochzeit ist doch nur ein wenig verschoben, des erwarteten wichtigen Verwandten wegen, und weil die Braut nicht weiß, was Liebe ist. Um Sie zu unterhalten, werde ich, der Bräutigam, Ihnen ein Lied vorsingen.

Er singt Das Lied vom Sankt Nimmerleinstag.

Eines Tags, und das hat wohl ein jeder gehört
Der in ärmlicher Wiege lag
Kommt des armen Weibs Sohn auf 'nen goldenen Thron
Und der Tag heißt Sankt Nimmerleinstag.
    Am Sankt Nimmerleinstag
    Sitzt er auf 'nem goldenen Thron.

Und an diesem Tag zahlt die Güte sich aus
Und die Schlechtigkeit kostet den Hals

Sun   It's over, mama. Ladies and gents, the priest's gone, the wine's gone, we can't hold you any longer.

The Sister-in-Law   Come, grandfather!

The Grandfather (*emptying his glass, seriously*)   To the bride!

The Niece (*to* **Shen Te**)   Don't mind him. He means well. He likes you.

Mrs Shin   One for the record books.

All the guests exit.

Shen Te   Should I go too, Sun?

Sun   No, don't go, let me –

He pulls at her veil and jewelry, making a mess of it.

Sun   I'm waiting, so's my old mother, she's my true helpmeet, waiting alongside me. She wants her eagle to soar through the clouds again. But I'm very much afraid, mama, it'll be the feast day of St Never-To-Be before you step out of your front door to see me up there, up against the blue, my plane swooping and diving over your unfurnished house.* (*To the empty seats, as if the guests were there.*) Ladies and gents, what's happened to the table talk? Aren't you having fun? The wedding delayed, because the bride doesn't know what love is. Meanwhile, to entertain you, I, the bridegroom, will sing you a song.

He sings The Song of the Day of St Never-To-Be.

Sun (*sings*)
In your rickety cradle the stories they tell you,
How someday, when everything's free,
The poor boy shall be shown to his very own throne,
On the day of St Never-To-Be.
    On St Never-To-Be Day,
    He'll sit on a golden throne.

And on this day losers can eat till they burst,
As much as their bellies permit,

Und Verdienst und Verdienen, die machen gute Mienen
Und tauschen Brot und Salz.
   Am Sankt Nimmerleinstag
   Da tauschen sie Brot und Salz.

Und das Gras sieht auf den Himmel hinab
Und den Fluß hinauf rollt der Kies
Und der Mensch ist nur gut. Ohne daß er mehr tut
Wird die Erde zum Paradies.
   Am Sankt Nimmerleinstag
   Wird die Erde zum Paradies.

Und an diesem Tag werd ich Flieger sein
Und ein General bist du
Und du Mann mit zuviel Zeit kriegst endlich Arbeit
Und du armes Weib kriegst Ruh.
   Am Sankt Nimmerleinstag
   Kriegst armes Weib du Ruh.

Und weil wir gar nicht mehr warten können
Heißt es, alles dies sei
Nicht erst auf die Nacht um halb acht oder acht
Sondern schon beim Hahnenschrei
   Am Sankt Nimmerleinstag
   Beim ersten Hahnenschrei.

Frau Yang   Er kommt nicht mehr.

Die drei sitzen, und zwei von ihnen schauen nach der Tür.

ZWISCHENSPIEL
WANGS NACHTLAGER

*Wieder erscheinen dem Wasserverkäufer im Traum die Götter. Er
ist über einem großen Buch eingeschlafen. Musik.*

Wang   Gut, daß ihr kommt, Erleuchtete! Gestattet eine
Frage, die mich tief beunruhigt. In der zerfallenen Hütte
eines Priesters, der weggezogen und Hilfsarbeiter in der
Zementfabrik geworden ist, fand ich ein Buch, und darin
entdeckte ich eine merkwürdige Stelle. Ich möchte sie
unbedingt vorlesen. Hier ist sie (*er blättert mit der Linken in*

And beggars are able to dine at the king's table
While the king and his cronies eat shit.
    On the Day of St Never-To-Be
    The winners'll eat shit. And learn to like it.

And the grass will shine down on the heavens below,
And China trades places with Sweden,*
And the people are good, just keep knocking on wood,
And the earth is the Garden of Eden.
    On the Day of St Never-To-Be
    We'll be back in the Garden again.

And on this day I will be flying again,
While you will be drilling the troops,
And those they call shirkers will get wages like workers,
And our mothers just relax on their stoops!
    On St Never-To-Be Day,
    Women get to rest.

They tell you to wait for that day, so you wait,
While you suffer, but never despair.
And you try to survive till that Great Day arrives!
If it does, you'll be too old to care.
    The Day of St Never-To-Be!
    At cock's-crow it'll be here.

Mrs Yang   He's not coming anymore.

The three sit. Two look at the door.

INTERLUDE
WANG'S NIGHT LODGINGS

*Once again **the Gods** appear to **Wang** the waterseller in a dream. He has fallen asleep over a big book. Music.*

Wang   Thank God you've come, Awakened Ones! Please answer a question that has me deeply disturbed. In the ruins of a hut of a hermit priest who'd given up and become a worker in the cement factory I found this book, and in the book a remarkable passage. I would like to read it aloud. Here:

einem imaginären Buch über dem Buch, das er im Schoß hat,
und hebt dieses imaginäre Buch zum Lesen hoch, während das
richtige liegenbleibt)

Wang   'In Sung ist ein Platz namens Dornhain. Dort
gedeihen Katalpen, Zypressen und Maulbeerbäume. Die
Bäume nun, die ein oder zwei Spannen im Umfang
haben, die werden abgehauen von den Leuten, die Stäbe
für ihre Hundekäfige wollen. Die drei, vier Fuß im
Umfang haben, werden abgehauen von den vornehmen
und reichen Familien, die Bretter suchen für ihre Särge.
Die mit sieben, acht Fuß Umfang werden abgehauen von
denen, die nach Balken suchen für ihre Luxusvillen. So
erreichen sie alle nicht ihrer Jahre Zahl, sondern gehen
auf halbem Wege zugrunde durch Säge und Axt. Das ist
das Leiden der Brauchbarkeit.'

Der Dritte Gott   Aber da wäre ja der Unnützeste der
Beste.

Wang   Nein, nur der Glücklichste. Der Schlechteste ist
der Glücklichste.

Der Erste Gott   Was doch alles geschrieben wird!

Der Zweite Gott   Warum bewegt dich dieses Gleichnis so
tief, Wasserverkäufer?

Wang   Shen Tes wegen, Erleuchteter! Sie ist in ihrer
Liebe gescheitert, weil sie die Gebote der Nächstenliebe
befolgte. Vielleicht ist sie wirklich zu gut für diese Welt,
Erleuchtete!

Der Erste Gott   Unsinn! Du schwacher, elender Mensch!
Die Läuse und die Zweifel haben dich halb aufgefressen,
scheint es.

Wang   Sicher, Erleuchteter! Entschuldige! Ich dachte
nur, ihr könntet vielleicht eingreifen.

Der Erste Gott   Ganz unmöglich. Unser Freund hier (*er
zeigt auf den* **Dritten Gott**, *der ein blau geschlagenes Auge hat*)
hat erst gestern in einen Streit eingegriffen, du siehst die
Folgen.

He leafs with his left hand through an imaginary book which he holds above the real book in his lap, then holds the imaginary book high to read it, while leaving the real one lying.

Wang 'In Sung there's a place named Dornhain. Catalpas, cypresses and mulberry trees. Now the trees which are a couple of hand-spans in diameter, these the people who want posts for their dog cages cut down. Those trees which are three or four hand-spans are cut down by rich and distinguished families who want broad boards for their coffins. Trees of seven or eight hand-spans are cut down by those who need balconies on their luxury villas. In this manner no tree ever reaches the full number of its years, but rather is felled by saw and axe halfway through its journey. This is the catastrophe that is usefulness.'

The Third God But that means useless is best.

Wang Not best, only happiest. The least good is the happiest.

The First God The trash people write!

The Second God Why are you so disturbed by this parable, waterseller?

Wang Shen Te, Awakened Ones! She has failed in love because she obeyed the commandment to love her neighbours. Maybe she's actually too good for this world, Awakened Ones!

The First God Nonsense! Weak, wretched man! Devoured by lice and doubts.

Wang You're right, Awakened One! Forgive me! I was only hoping you might consider intervening.

The First God Out of the question. Look at our friend:

He points to **The Third God**, *who has a black eye.*

The First God Yesterday he intervened in a fight; behold the results.

Wang   Aber der Vetter mußte schon wieder gerufen werden. Er ist ein ungemein geschickter Mensch, ich habe es am eigenen Leib erfahren, jedoch auch er konnte nichts ausrichten. Der Laden scheint schon verloren.

Der Dritte Gott (*beunruhigt*)   Vielleicht sollten wir doch helfen?

Der Erste Gott   Ich bin der Ansicht, daß sie sich selber helfen muß.

Der Zweite Gott (*streng*)   Je schlimmer seine Lage ist, als desto besser zeigt sich der gute Mensch. Leid läutert!

Der Erste Gott   Wir setzen unsere ganze Hoffnung auf sie.

Der Dritte Gott   Es steht nicht zum besten mit unserer Suche. Wir finden hier und da gute Anläufe, erfreuliche Vorsätze, viele hohe Prinzipien, aber das alles macht ja kaum einen guten Menschen aus. Wenn wir halbwegs gute Menschen treffen, leben sie nicht menschenwürdig. (*Vertraulich.*) Mit dem Nachtlager steht es besonders schlimm. Du kannst an den Strohhalmen, die an uns kleben, sehen, wo wir unsere Nächte zubringen.

Wang   Nur eines, könntet ihr dann nicht wenigstens …

Die Götter   Nichts. Wir sind nur Betrachtende. Wir glauben fest, daß unser guter Mensch sich zurechtfinden wird auf der dunklen Erde. Seine Kraft wird wachsen mit der Bürde. Warte nur ab, Wasserverkäufer, und du wirst erleben, alles nimmt ein gutes …

Die Gestalten der Götter sind immer blasser, ihre Stimmen immer leiser geworden. Nun entschwinden sie, und die Stimmen hören auf.

Wang   But the cousin was summoned again. He's an unyieldingly competent man, I know from personal experience, yet not even he could set things straight. It appears the shop's already forfeit.

The Third God (*disturbed*)   Perhaps we should help?

The First God   In my opinion she must help herself.

The Second God (*stern*)   The more arduous the circumstances, the stronger grows a truly good person. Suffering purifies!

The First God   We're all banking on her.*

The Third God   Our search isn't going particularly well. Here and there promising beginnings, best intentions, noble principles galore, but all these don't add up to one good person. And when we find even a partially good person, invariably they're so wretched they're not living lives worthy of human beings. (*Confidentially.*) The sleeping situation is especially trying. You may deduce from the straw which clings to us where we've been spending nights.

Wang   But couldn't you just —

The Gods   Nothing. – We are only to observe. – We remain strong in our faith that our good person will find her way through this dark world. – Her strength will grow with her burdens. – Wait, waterseller, and you will see, everything comes to a good ...

The shapes of **the Gods** *have become more and more pale, their voices fainter. Now they disappear, and the voices stop.*

7

Hof Hinter Shen Tes Tabakladen

Auf einem Wagen ein wenig Hausrat. Von der Wäscheleine nehmen **Shen Te** *und* **Die Shin** *Wäsche.*

Die Shin Ich verstehe nicht, warum Sie nicht mit Messern und Zähnen um Ihren Laden kämpfen.

Shen Te Wie? Ich habe ja nicht einmal die Miete. Denn die 200 Silberdollar der alten Leute muß ich heute zurückgeben, aber da ich sie jemand anderem gegeben habe, muß ich meinen Tabak an Frau Mi Tzü verkaufen.

Die Shin Also alles hin! Kein Mann, kein Tabak, keine Bleibe! So kommt es, wenn man etwas Besseres sein will als unsereins. Wovon wollen Sie jetzt leben?

Shen Te Ich weiß nicht. Vielleicht kann ich mit Tabaksortieren ein wenig verdienen.

Die Shin Wie kommt Herrn Shui Tas Hose hierher? Er muß nackig von hier weggegangen sein.

Shen Te Er hat noch eine andere Hose.

Die Shin Ich dachte, Sie sagten, er sei für immer weggereist? Warum läßt er da seine Hose zurück?

Shen Te Vielleicht braucht er sie nicht mehr.

Die Shin So soll sie nicht eingepackt werden?

Shen Te Nein.

Herein stürzt **Herr Shu Fu**.

Herr Shu Fu Sagen Sie nichts. Ich weiß alles. Sie haben Ihr Liebesglück geopfert, damit zwei alte Leute, die auf Sie vertrauten, nicht ruiniert sind. Nicht umsonst gibt Ihnen dieses Viertel, dieses mißtrauische und böswillige,

7

The Courtyard Behind Shen Te's Tobacco Shop

A few household items on a cart. **Shen Te** *and* **Mrs Shin** *take the laundry down from the line.*

Mrs Shin   I don't understand why you aren't fighting knife and tooth for your shop.

Shen Te   How? I don't have the rent. To pay the old couple back today for the money they lent me, which I gave away, I have to raise 200 silver dollars, and to do that I must sell my tobacco to Mrs Mi Tzu.

Mrs Shin   And that's that. No man, no tobacco, no home. That's what comes of wanting to be better than the rest of us. How'll you keep body and soul together?

Shen Te   I don't know. I might be able to earn something sorting tobacco.

Mrs Shin   Why are Mr Shui Ta's pants hanging on the line? Did he leave here naked?

Shen Te   He's got two pairs.

Mrs Shin   But you said he left forever. Why would he leave his pants?

Shen Te   Maybe he outgrew those.

Mrs Shin   They look capacious to me. Shouldn't you send them to him?

Shen Te   No.

Shu Fu *rushes violently in.*

Shu Fu   Say nothing. I know it all. You sacrificed your wedded bliss to spare two old people who trusted you from ruination. It's not for nothing that the neighbourhood, this mean, mistrusting neighbourhood,

den Namen 'Engel der Vorstädte'. Ihr Herr Verlobter
konnte sich nicht zu Ihrer sittlichen Höhe
emporarbeiten, Sie haben ihn verlassen. Und jetzt
schließen Sie Ihren Laden, diese kleine Insel der
Zuflucht für so viele! Ich kann es nicht mit ansehen. Von
meiner Ladentür aus habe ich Morgen für Morgen das
Häuflein Elende vor Ihrem Geschäft gesehen und Sie
selbst, Reis austeilend. Soll das für immer vorbei sein?
Soll jetzt das Gute untergehen? Ach, wenn Sie mir
gestatten, Ihnen bei Ihrem guten Werk behilflich zu sein!
Nein, sagen Sie nichts! Ich will keine Zusicherung.
Keinerlei Versprechungen, daß Sie meine Hilfe
annehmen wollen! Aber hier *er zieht ein Scheckbuch heraus
und zeichnet einen Scheck, den er ihr auf den Wagen legt* fertige
ich Ihnen einen Blankoscheck aus, den Sie nach
Belieben in jeder Höhe ausfüllen können, und dann
gehe ich, still und bescheiden, ohne Gegenforderung,
auf den Fußzehen, voll Verehrung, selbstlos. (*Ab.*)

Die Shin (*untersucht den Scheck*)   Sie sind gerettet! Solche
wie Sie haben Glück! Sie finden immer einen Dummen.
Jetzt aber zugegriffen! Schreiben Sie 1,000 Silberdollar
hinein, und ich laufe damit zur Bank, bevor er wieder zur
Besinnung kommt.

Shen Te   Stellen Sie den Wäschekorb auf den Wagen.
Die Wäscherechnung kann ich auch ohne den Scheck
bezahlen.

Die Shin   Was? Sie wollen den Scheck nicht annehmen?
Das ist ein Verbrechen! Ist es nur, weil Sie meinen, daß
Sie ihn dann heiraten müssen? Das wäre hellichter
Wahnsinn. So einer will doch an der Nase herumgeführt
werden! Das bereitet so einem geradezu Wollust. Wollen
Sie etwa immer noch an Ihrem Flieger festhalten, von
dem die ganze Gelbe Gasse und auch das Viertel hier
herum weiß, wie schlecht er gegen Sie gewesen ist?

Shen Te   Es kommt alles von der Not.

(*Zum Publikum.*) Ich habe ihn nachts die Backen
    aufblasen sehn im Schlaf: sie waren böse.

has christened you 'Angel of the Outskirts'. Your fiancé wasn't compatible with your towering moral stature. You left him. And you're closing your shop, for so many a small port in the storm! I can't stand silently, passively by. Every morning I linger for a glimpse of you doling out your rice to the gaggle of paupers queued up for it. Should that be gone forever? Should the good always go under? Oh, if only you'd let me help you with your good work! Please, say nothing. I need no promises. No pledging how you want my help! Here:

He takes out a chequebook, writes a cheque and lays it on her cart.

Shu Fu   A blank cheque, it's yours, fill it out at your discretion for any amount you like, and now I am going: tender, unpretentious, demanding nothing as recompense, on tip-toe, devoted, selfless.

He exits.

Mrs Shin (*looking at the cheque*)   You're saved! People like you are born lucky, you come up with a dummy, every time. So, carpe diem! Write down 1,000 silver dollars, and I'll hike over to the bank before he realises what he's done.

Shen Te   Put the laundry basket on the cart. I can pay you for the washing without his cheque.

Mrs Shin   You're not refusing the cheque? But that's criminal! Why? Are you worried you'll have to marry him? You'll never! Open your eyes: A man like that lives to be led around by the nose! It gets him hot. Or are you still keeping yourself for that pilot, no matter that everyone from this end of town to that one from Easy Street* to Yellow Street knows how he's abused you?

Shen Te   Need causes it all:

To the audience.

At night I've watched as he puffed his cheeks in his sleep:
    He looked like a demon.

Und in der Frühe hielt ich seinen Rock gegen das Licht,
   da sah ich die Wand durch.
Wenn ich sein schlaues Lachen sah, bekam ich Furcht, aber
Wenn ich seine löchrigen Schuhe sah, liebte ich ihn sehr.

Die Shin   Sie verteidigen ihn also noch? So etwas
Verrücktes habe ich nie gesehen. (*Zornig.*) Ich werde
aufatmen, wenn wir Sie aus dem Viertel haben.

Shen Te (*schwankt beim Abnehmen der Wäsche*)   Mir
schwindelt ein wenig.

Die Shin (*nimmt ihr die Wäsche ab*)   Wird Ihnen öfter
schwindlig, wenn Sie sich strecken oder bücken? Wenn
da nur nicht was Kleines unterwegs ist! (*Lacht.*) Der hat
Sie schön hereingelegt! Wenn das passiert sein sollte, ist
es mit dem großen Scheck Essig! Für solche Gelegenheit
war der nicht gedacht. (*Sie geht mit einem Korb nach
hinten.*)

Shen Te *schaut ihr bewegungslos nach. Dann betrachtet sie
ihren Leib, betastet ihn, und eine große Freude zeigt sich auf
ihrem Gesicht.*

Shen Te (*leise*)   O Freude! Ein kleiner Mensch entsteht in
meinem Leibe. Man sieht noch nichts. Er ist aber schon
da. Die Welt erwartet ihn im geheimen. In den Städten
heißt es schon: Jetzt kommt einer, mit dem man rechnen
muß. (*Sie stellt ihren kleinen Sohn dem Publikum vor.*)

Ein Flieger!
Begrüßt einen neuen Eroberer
Der unbekannten Gebirge und unerreichbaren
   Gegenden! Einen
Der die Post von Mensch zu Mensch
Über die unwegsamen Wüsten bringt!

(*Sie beginnt auf und ab zu gehen und ihren kleinen Sohn an der
Hand zu nehmen.*) Komm, Sohn, betrachte dir die Welt.
Hier, das ist ein Baum. Verbeuge dich, begrüße ihn. (*Sie
macht die Verbeugung vor.*) So, jetzt kennt ihr euch. Horch,
dort kommt der Wasserverkäufer. Ein Freund, gib ihm
die Hand. Sei unbesorgt. 'Bitte, ein Glas frisches Wasser
für meinen Sohn. Es ist warm.' (*Sie gibt ihm das Glas.*)

And in the morning I held his coat to the light: I saw the
wall through it.
When I see his sly smile, I become afraid, but
When I see the holes in his shoes, I love him very much.

Mrs Shin You're defending him? Still? That's the
craziest thing I ever saw. (*Angry.*) I'll be able to breathe
better when you finally leave this neighbourhood.

Shen Te (*faltering while picking up the laundry basket*) I
feel a little nauseous.

Mrs Shin *takes the basket from her.*

Mrs Shin Does that happen often, like when you stretch
or bend over? Let's hope you don't have a bundle on the
way! (*She laughs.*) He really fixed you! If you're knocked
up, forget about the blank cheque! It wasn't intended for
that eventuality.

She takes the basket to the back. **Shen Te** *watches her go,
motionless. Then she looks at her body, touches it, and a great joy
shows on her face.*

Shen Te (*softly*) Oh joy! A small person is coming into
being in my body. The world is secretly waiting for this
person. In the cities they're already saying it: Someone is
coming with whom we'll have to reckon!

(*She introduces her child to the audience.*) A pilot!

Greet the new conqueror
Of unknown mountains and unmapped terrain! Who'll
Bring the mail from one person to the other
Across impassable deserts!

She begins to walk back and forth holding her child's hand.

Come out, child, and see the world! This is a tree. Bow to
the tree. (*She bows.*) Now you know each other. Look, it's
the waterseller. A friend, so extend your hand. Don't be
afraid. 'Please, a glass of water for my child, who's hot.'
(*She gives the child the glass.*) Oops, the cops! Steer clear.
Maybe we'll pick some of rich Mr Feh Pung's cherries.

Ach, der Polizist! Da machen wir einen Bogen. Vielleicht holen wir uns ein paar Kirschen dort, im Garten des reichen Herrn Feh Pung. Da heißt es, nicht gesehen werden. Komm, Vaterloser! Auch du willst Kirschen! Sachte, sachte, Sohn! (*Sie gehen vorsichtig, sich umblickend.*) Nein, hier herum, da verbirgt uns das Gesträuch. Nein, so gleich los drauf zu, das kannst du nicht machen, in diesem Fall. (*Er scheint sie wegzuziehen, sie widerstrebt.*) Wir müssen vernünftig sein. (*Plötzlich gibt sie nach.*) Schön, wenn du nur gradezu drauflosgehen willst ... (*Sie hebt ihn hoch.*) Kannst du die Kirschen erreichen? Schieb in den Mund, dort sind sie gut aufgehoben. (*Sie verspeist selber eine, die er ihr in den Mund steckt.*) Schmeckt fein. Zum Teufel, der Polizist. Jetzt heißt es, laufen. (*Sie fliehen.*) Da ist die Straße. Ruhig jetzt, langsam gegangen, damit wir nicht auffallen. Als ob nicht das Geringste geschehn wäre ... (*Sie singt, mit dem Kind spazierend.*)

Eine Pflaume ohne Grund
Überfiel 'nen Vagabund
Doch der Mann war äußerst quick
Biß die Pflaume ins Genick.

Hereingekommen ist **Wang**, *der Wasserverkäufer, ein Kind an der Hand führend. Er sieht* **Shen Te** *erstaunt zu.*

Shen Te (*auf ein Husten Wangs*)   Ach, Wang! Guten Tag.

Wang   Shen Te, ich habe gehört, daß es dir nicht gut geht, daß du sogar deinen Laden verkaufen mußt, um Schulden zu bezahlen. Aber da ist dieses Kind, das kein Obdach hat. Es lief auf dem Schlachthof herum. Anscheinend gehört es dem Schreiner Lin To, der vor einigen Wochen seine Werkstatt verloren hat und seitdem trinkt. Seine Kinder treiben sich hungernd herum. Was soll man mit ihnen machen?

Shen Te (*nimmt ihm das Kind ab*)   Komm, kleiner Mann!
Zum Publikum.
He, ihr! Da bittet einer um Obdach.
Einer von morgen bittet euch um ein Heute!
Sein Freund, der Eroberer, den ihr kennt
Ist der Fürsprecher.

But we can't let him see us! Come on, fatherless boy!
You'll adore the taste of cherries! Careful, careful! (*They
look cautiously around.*) Over here, hide in the bushes. You
can't just go for them, not in a private garden. (*The child
pulls on her, she resists.*) Be reasonable now. (*She gives in.*)
Alright, now! (*She holds the child high.*) Can you reach
them? Shove them all in your mouth, they'll be safe
there. (*The child puts one in her mouth, she eats it.*) Tastes
fine. Damn, the cop! Now run!

(*They run.*) OK slow down, don't call attention. Act
casual.

She sings, walking with the child.

A very stupid plum
Fell on the head of a bum.
The bum quick hit the plum right back,
And ate it for a snack.

Wang *the waterseller, leading a child by the hand, is watching*
Shen Te *with astonishment. He coughs, and* **Shen Te** *sees him.*

Shen Te   Oh, Wang! Good day!

Wang   I heard that you were having a bad time, Shen Te,
that you've had to sell your shop. But this child's
homeless. I found him running around by the
slaughterhouse. I think he belongs to the carpenter Lin
To, who lost the lease on his workshop a few weeks back
and now drinks all day. His kids wander hungry. What
should we do with him?

Shen Te *takes the child from him.*

Shen Te   Come here, little man!

To the audience.

Hey you! Here's someone asking for shelter.
Someone from tomorrow is asking for today!
His friend, the conqueror, who you've met,
Can vouch for him.

(*Zu* **Wang**.) Er kann gut in den Baracken des Herrn Shu Fu wohnen, wohin vielleicht auch ich gehe. Ich soll selber ein Kind bekommen. Aber sag es nicht weiter, sonst erfährt es Yang Sun, und er kann uns nicht brauchen. Such Herrn Lin To in der unteren Stadt und sag ihm, er soll hierherkommen.

Wang   Vielen Dank, Shen Te. Ich wußte, du wirst etwas finden. (*Zum Kind.*) Siehst du, ein guter Mensch weiß immer einen Ausweg. Schnell laufe ich und hole deinen Vater. (*Er will gehen.*)

Shen Te   O Wang, jetzt fällt mir wieder ein: Was ist mit deiner Hand? Ich wollte doch den Eid für dich leisten, aber mein Vetter ...

Wang   Kümmere dich nicht um die Hand. Schau, ich habe schon gelernt, ohne meine rechte Hand auszukommen. Ich brauche sie fast nicht mehr. (*Er zeigt ihr, wie er auch ohne die rechte Hand sein Gerät handhaben kann.*) Schau, wie ich es mache.

Shen Te   Aber sie darf nicht steif werden! Nimm den Wagen da, verkauf alles und geh mit dem Geld zum Arzt. Ich schäme mich, daß ich bei dir so versagt habe. Und was mußt du denken, daß ich vom Barbier die Baracken angenommen habe!

Wang   Dort können die Obdachlosen jetzt wohnen, du selber, das ist doch wichtiger als meine Hand. Ich gehe jetzt, den Schreiner holen. (*Ab.*)

Shen Te (*ruft ihm nach*)   Versprich mir, daß du mit mir zum Arzt gehen wirst!

Die Shin *ist zurückgekommen und hat ihr immerfort gewinkt.*

Shen Te   Was ist es?

Die Shin   Sind Sie verrückt, auch noch den Wagen mit dem Letzten, was Sie haben, wegzuschenken? Was geht Sie seine Hand an? Wenn es der Barbier erfährt, jagt er Sie noch aus dem einzigen Obdach, das Sie kriegen können. Mir haben Sie die Wäsche noch nicht bezahlt!

Shen Te   Warum sind Sie so böse?

(*To* **Wang**.) He can go live in Mr Shu Fu's cattle sheds, that's where I'm going, probably. I am going to have a child myself. But don't tell anyone, or Yang Sun will hear, and he doesn't need that. Look for Mr Lin To downtown and tell him he should come here.

Wang   Thank you very much, Shen Te. I knew you'd know the way out.

(*To the child.*) I told you so, didn't I? A good person always knows ways out. I'll find your father. (*He starts to leave.*)

Shen Te   Oh, how's your hand, Wang? I wanted to be your witness but my cousin didn't —

Wang   Don't worry about my hand. Already I've learned how to get by without it. Who needs a right hand? (*He shows her he can handle his gear without his right hand.*) See?

Shen Te   Don't let it get stiff! Take the cart, sell everything in it and go with the money to a doctor. I'm ashamed I failed you so badly. I can't imagine what you must think of me for accepting use of the barber's buildings.

Wang   Homes for the homeless, and for you, too, that's more important than my hand. I'll go locate the carpenter. (*He exits.*)

Shen Te (*calling after him*)   Promise me that you'll come with me to the doctor!

Mrs Shin *has returned. She's heard all this, and has been waving her arm at* **Shen Te** *continuously.*

Shen Te   What is it?

Mrs Shin   Have you lost the last of your mind? Giving away the cart and what little you have left? What do you care about his hand? When the barber finds out you're aiding him of all people, he'll take back the buildings and you'll be homeless too. And you haven't paid me for the laundry yet!

Shen Te   Why are you so furious?

Den Mitmenschen zu treten
Ist es nicht anstrengend? Die Stirnader
Schwillt Ihnen an, vor Mühe, gierig zu sein.
Natürlich ausgestreckt
Gibt eine Hand und empfängt mit gleicher Leichtigkeit.
  Nur
Gierig zupackend muß sie sich anstrengen. Ach
Welche Verführung, zu schenken! Wie angenehm
Ist es doch, freundlich zu sein! Ein gutes Wort
Entschlüpft wie ein wohliger Seufzer.

Die Shin *geht zornig weg.*

Shen Te (*zum Kind*)   Setz dich hierher und wart, bis dein
Vater kommt.

Das Kind setzt sich auf den Boden.

Auf den Hof kommt das ältliche Paar, das **Shen Te** *am Tag der
Eröffnung ihres Ladens besuchte.* **Mann** *und* **Frau** *schleppen
große Säcke.*

Die Frau   Bist du allein, Shen Te?

Da **Shen Te** *nickt, ruft sie ihren Neffen herein, der ebenfalls
einen Sack trägt.*

Die Frau   Wo ist dein Vetter?

Shen Te   Er ist weggefahren.

Die Frau   Und kommt er wieder?

Shen Te   Nein. Ich gebe den Laden auf.

Die Frau   Das wissen wir. Deshalb sind wir gekommen.
Wir haben hier ein paar Säcke mit Rohtabak, den uns
jemand geschuldet hat, und möchten dich bitten, sie mit
deinen Habseligkeiten zusammen in dein neues Heim zu
transportieren. Wir haben noch keinen Ort, wohin wir sie
bringen könnten, und fallen auf der Straße zu sehr auf
mit ihnen. Ich sehe nicht, wie du uns diese kleine
Gefälligkeit abschlagen könntest, nachdem wir in deinem
Laden so ins Unglück gebracht worden sind.

Shen Te   Ich will euch die Gefälligkeit gern tun.

To the audience.

Isn't trampling other people
Exhausting work? The vein on your forehead
Bulges from the strain of being greedy.
A hand naturally reaches out, and
It gives and receives with equal ease. Only
Grasping acquisitively is an effort. Oh,
Giving's so seductive! A good word
Slips out like a sigh of relief.

Mrs Shin *goes away, angrily.*

Shen Te (*to the child*)   Sit here and wait till your father
comes.

The child sits on the ground. The couple that stayed with **Shen
Te** *on the opening day of her shop enter the courtyard.* **The
Husband** *and* **The Wife** *carry big bundles.*

The Wife   Are you alone, Shen Te?

Shen Te *nods 'yes'.* **The Wife** *calls her nephew in, who's also
carrying a bundle.*

The Wife   Where's your cousin?

Shen Te   He's gone.

The Wife   Is he expected back?

Shen Te   No. I'm giving up the shop.

The Wife   We heard. That's why we're here. We've got
these bundles of raw tobacco, somebody owed us, and
we'd like you to transport them with your belongings to
your new place. We're still homeless, we've got no place
to put them, and they're attracting too much of the
wrong kind of attention on the street. You really can't
refuse this small request, after the awful things that befell
us in your shop.

Shen Te   I would be glad to do you the favour.

Der Mann   Und wenn du von irgend jemand gefragt werden solltest, wem die Säcke gehören, dann kannst du sagen, sie gehörten dir.

Shen Te   Wer sollte mich denn fragen?

Die Frau (*sie scharf anblickend*)   Die Polizei zum Beispiel. Sie ist voreingenommen gegen uns und will uns ruinieren. Wohin sollen wir die Säcke stellen?

Shen Te   Ich weiß nicht, gerade jetzt möchte ich nicht etwas tun, was mich ins Gefängnis bringen könnte.

Die Frau   Das sieht dir allerdings gleich. Wir sollen auch noch die paar elenden Säcke mit Tabak verlieren, die alles sind, was wir von unserem Hab und Gut gerettet haben!

Shen Te *schweigt störrisch.*

Der Mann   Bedenk, daß dieser Tabak für uns den Grundstock zu einer kleinen Fabrikation abgeben könnte. Da könnten wir hochkommen.

Shen Te   Gut, ich will die Säcke für euch aufheben. Wir stellen sie vorläufig in das Gelaß.

Sie geht mit ihnen hinein. Das Kind hat ihr nachgesehen. Jetzt geht es, sich scheu umschauend, zum Mülleimer und fischt darin herum. Es fängt an, daraus zu essen. **Shen Te** *und die drei kommen zurück.*

Die Frau   Du verstehst wohl, daß wir uns vollständig auf dich verlassen.

Shen Te   Ja. *Sie erblickt das Kind und erstarrt.*

Der Mann   Wir suchen dich übermorgen in den Häusern des Herrn Shu Fu auf.

Shen Te   Geht jetzt schnell, mir ist nicht gut.

Sie schiebt sie weg. Die drei ab.

Shen Te   Es hat Hunger. Es fischt im Kehrichteimer.* (*Sie hebt das Kind auf, und in einer Rede drückt sie ihr Entsetzen aus über das Los armer Kinder, dem Publikum das*

The Husband   And if anyone asks whose bundles they are, just tell them they're yours.

Shen Te   Who'd ask?

The Wife (*looking at her sharply*)   The police, for instance. They've got it in for us, they want us ruined. Where should we put the bundles?

Shen Te   I don't know, I wouldn't want to do anything that could land me in jail.

The Wife   Well isn't that typical of you. So we should lose these few miserable bales of tobacco, all we have left of our worldly possessions?

Shen Te *is stubborn, silent.*

The Husband   This tobacco could be the ground floor for a small factory. It could put us back on our feet.

Shen Te   Very well, I'll keep the bundles for you. We'll put them in the back room temporarily.

She goes in with them. The child watches them leave. Then, looking shyly about, he goes to the garbage container and fishes around in it. He begins to eat out of it. **Shen Te** *and the other three return.*

The Wife   We're putting all our trust in you.

Shen Te   I know. (*She sees the child and freezes.*)

The Husband   We'll come by Mr Shu Fu's buildings tomorrow to see how you're making out.

Shen Te   Go, quickly, I don't feel good.

She picks up the child and expresses her revulsion over the fate of poor children in a speech, showing the audience the little grey mouth. She vows never to let her child be treated so mercilessly.

graue Mäulchen zeigend. Sie beteuert ihre Entschlossenheit, ihr eigenes Kind keinesfalls mit solcher Unbarmherzigkeit zu behandeln.)

O Sohn, o Flieger! In welche Welt
Wirst du kommen? Im Abfalleimer
Wollen sie dich fischen lassen, auch dich? Seht doch
Dies graue Mäulchen!

Sie zeigt das Kind.

Wie
Behandelt ihr euresgleichen? Habt ihr
Keine Barmherzigkeit mit der Frucht
Eures Leibes? Kein Mitleid
Mit euch selber, ihr Unglücklichen? So werde ich
Wenigstens das meine verteidigen und müßte ich
Zum Tiger werden. Ja, von Stund an
Da ich das gesehen habe, will ich mich scheiden
Von allen und nicht ruhen
Bis ich meinen Sohn gerettet habe, wenigstens ihn!
Was ich gelernt in der Gosse, meiner Schule
Durch Faustschlag und Betrug, jetzt
Soll es dir dienen, Sohn, zu dir
Will ich gut sein, und Tiger und wildes Tier
Zu allen andern, wenn's sein muß. Und
Es muß sein.

Sie geht ab, sich in den Vetter zu verwandeln.

Shen Te (*im Abgehen*)   Einmal ist es noch nötig, das letzte Mal, hoffe ich.

*Sie hat die Hose des **Shui Ta** mitgenommen. Die zurückkehrende **Shin** sieht ihr neugierig nach. Herein **Die Schwägerin** und **Der Großvater**.*

Die Schwägerin   Der Laden geschlossen, der Hausrat im Hof! Das ist das Ende!

Die Shin   Die Folgen des Leichtsinns, der Sinnlichkeit und der Eigenliebe! Und wohin geht die Fahrt? Hinab! In die Baracken des Herrn Shu Fu, zu euch!

Shen Te
Oh son, oh pilot! What kind of world
Are you coming to? Will you too
Be an ashcan scavenger? Look
At this grey little mouth! (*She shows the child.*) See
The way you treat your own! Have you
No feelings for the fruit
Your own bodies produce? No sympathy
For yourselves, you miserable people? I at least
Will defend my own, even if I must
Become a tiger. Yes, from the moment
I saw this: I'll cut myself off
From everyone else and spare myself nothing
Till my son is safe! At least my son!
Everything I've learned
In the gutter-school of my life,
Fighting and betraying, now
It'll serve you, my son, to you
I'll be good; a tiger, a wild animal
To everybody else, if that's how it's got to be. And
It must be.

She goes out to change into her cousin. Exiting.

Once more it's necessary, the last time, I hope.

She has taken **Shui Ta**'s *pants with her.* **Mrs Shin**, *returning, looks after her with curiosity. Enter* **The Sister-in-Law** *and* **The Grandfather**.

The Sister-in-Law   The shop's shut tight, her belongings in the yard! This is the end!

Mrs Shin   The consequences of sensuality, narcissism and flightiness! Three stepping stones that lead you where? Down! Off to Mr Shu Fu's barracks you go!

Die Schwägerin   Da wird sie sich aber wundern! Wir sind
gekommen, um uns zu beschweren! Feuchte
Rattenlöcher mit verfaulten Böden! Der Barbier hat sie
nur gegeben, weil ihm seine Seifenvorräte darin
verschimmelt sind. 'Ich habe ein Obdach für euch, was
sagt ihr dazu?' Schande! sagen wir dazu.

Herein **Der Arbeitslose**.

Der Arbeitslose   Ist es wahr, daß Shen Te wegzieht?

Die Schwägerin   Ja. Sie wollte sich wegschleichen, man
sollte es nicht erfahren.

Die Shin   Sie schämt sich, da sie ruiniert ist.

Der Arbeitslose (*aufgeregt*)   Sie muß ihren Vetter rufen!
Ratet ihr alle, daß sie den Vetter ruft! Er allein kann noch
etwas machen.

Die Schwägerin   Das ist wahr! Er ist geizig genug, aber
jedenfalls rettet er ihr den Laden, und sie gibt ja dann.

Der Arbeitslose   Ich dachte nicht an uns, ich dachte an
sie. Aber es ist richtig, auch unseretwegen müßte man
ihn rufen.

Herein **Wang** *mit dem* **Schreiner**. *Er führt zwei Kinder an der
Hand.*

Der Schreiner   Ich kann Ihnen wirklich nicht genug
danken. (*Zu den andern.*) Wir sollen eine Wohnung
kriegen.

Die Shin   Wo?

Der Schreiner   In den Häusern des Herrn Shu Fu! Und
der kleine Feng war es, der die Wendung herbeigeführt
hat! Hier bist du ja! 'Da ist einer, der bittet um Obdach',
soll Fräulein Shen Te gesagt haben, und sogleich
verschaffte sie uns die Wohnung. Bedankt euch bei
eurem Bruder, ihr!

Der Schreiner *und seine Kinder verbeugen sich lustig vor dem
Kind.*

Der Schreiner   Unsern Dank, Obdachbitter!

The Sister-in-Law   She'll be impressed when she gets there! We're here to complain! Damp rats' nests with rotted flooring! The barber only gave them to us because his stock of lye went rancid there. 'I'll give you shelters, now what do you think of me?' Shame! That's what we think.

The Unemployed Man *enters.*

The Unemployed Man   So she's really moving away?

The Sister-in-Law   Yes. She tried to slip out before we got here.

Mrs Shin   She's ashamed.

The Unemployed Man   Tell her to call her cousin! Everyone should urge her to call her cousin! He's the only one who can help her now.

The Sister-in-Law   He's stingy and mean enough, that's true, and I suppose if he saves the shop she'll be able to give out rice again.

The Unemployed Man   I was thinking about her, not about us, but you have a point, she should call him for our sakes too.

Wang *enters with* **The Carpenter**, *who leads two children by the hands.*

The Carpenter   I'll never be able to thank you enough.

(*To the others.*) We're getting an apartment.

Mrs Shin   Where?

The Carpenter   In Mr Shu Fu's buildings. And little Feng's the one who brought about this change. Ah, there he is! 'Here's someone asking for shelter,' Shen Te says, and then she finds us an apartment. Thank your brother, both of you!

The Carpenter *and his children bow to the child.*

The Carpenter   Our thanks, shelter-supplicant!

Hereingetreten ist **Shui Ta**.

Shui Ta   Darf ich fragen, was Sie alle hier wollen?

Der Arbeitslose   Herr Shui Ta!

Wang   Guten Tag, Herr Shui Ta. Ich wußte nicht, daß Sie zurückgekehrt sind. Sie kennen den Schreiner Lin To. Fräulein Shen Te hat ihm einen Unterschlupf in den Häusern des Herrn Shu Fu zugesagt.

Shui Ta   Die Häuser des Herrn Shu Fu sind nicht frei.

Der Schreiner   So können wir dort nicht wohnen?

Shui Ta   Nein. Diese Lokalitäten sind zu anderem bestimmt.

Die Schwägerin   Soll das heißen, daß auch wir heraus müssen?

Shui Ta   Ich fürchte.

Die Schwägerin   Aber wo sollen wir da alle hin?

Shui Ta (*die Achsel zuckend*)   Wie ich Fräulein Shen Te, die verreist ist, verstehe, hat sie nicht die Absicht, die Hand von Ihnen allen abzuziehen. Jedoch soll alles etwas vernünftiger geregelt werden in Zukunft. Die Speisungen ohne Gegendienst werden aufhören. Statt dessen wird jedermann die Gelegenheit gegeben werden, sich auf ehrliche Weise wieder emporzuarbeiten. Fräulein Shen Te hat beschlossen, Ihnen allen Arbeit zu geben. Wer von Ihnen mir jetzt in die Häuser des Herrn Shu Fu folgen will, wird nicht ins Nichts geführt werden.

Die Schwägerin   Soll das heißen, daß wir jetzt alle für Shen Te arbeiten sollen?

Shui Ta   Ja. Sie werden Tabak verarbeiten. Im Gelaß drinnen liegen drei Ballen mit Ware. Holt sie!

Die Schwägerin   Vergessen Sie nicht, daß wir selber Ladenbesitzer waren. Wir ziehen vor, für uns selbst zu arbeiten. Wir haben unseren eigenen Tabak.

Shui Ta *has entered.*

Shui Ta What do you want here?

The Unemployed Man Mr Shui Ta!

Wang Good day, Mr Shui Ta. I didn't know you'd come back. You remember the carpenter Lin To. Miss Shen Te promised him refuge in Mr Shu Fu's buildings.

Shui Ta Mr Shu Fu's buildings aren't available any longer.

The Carpenter You mean we can't live there?

Shui Ta No, they're entirely booked up.

The Sister-in-Law Do we have to leave?

Shui Ta Afraid so.

The Sister-in-Law But where should we go?

Shui Ta (*shrugging his shoulders*) My understanding with Miss Shen Te, who has had to go away, was that she didn't intend to withdraw support entirely. However, in the future the arrangements will be more reciprocal. This feeding without producing in return will stop. Instead, everyone gets an opportunity to work like honourable people. Miss Shen Te has decided to employ you. Those who'll follow me to Mr Shu Fu's buildings won't find themselves enmired in the usual dead end.

The Sister-in-Law So we're working for Shen Te now?

Shui Ta Processing tobacco. There are three bales in the back room. Fetch them!

The Sister-in-Law We used to be shop owners. We work for ourselves. We have our own tobacco.

Shui Ta (*zum* **Arbeitslosen** *und zum* **Schreiner**)   Vielleicht
wollt ihr für Shen Te arbeiten, da ihr keinen eigenen
Tabak habt?

Der Schreiner *und* **Der Arbeitslose** *gehen mißmutig hinein.*
Die Hausbesitzerin *kommt.*

Die Hausbesitzerin   Nun, Herr Shui Ta, wie steht es mit
dem Verkauf. Hier habe ich 300 Silberdollar.

Shui Ta   Frau Mi Tzü, ich hab mich entschlossen, nicht
zu verkaufen, sondern den Mietskontrakt zu
unterzeichnen.

Die Hausbesitzerin   Was? Brauchen Sie plötzlich das
Geld für den Flieger nicht mehr?

Shui Ta   Nein.

Die Hausbesitzerin   Und haben Sie denn die Miete?

Shui Ta (*nimmt vom Wagen mit dem Hausrat den Scheck des
Barbiers und füllt ihn aus*)   Ich habe hier einen Scheck
auf 10,000 Silberdollar, ausgestellt von Herrn Shu Fu, der
sich für meine Kusine interessiert. Überzeugen Sie sich,
Frau Mi Tzü! Ihre 200 Silberdollar für die Miete des
nächsten Halbjahres werden Sie noch vor sechs Uhr
abends in Händen haben. Und nun, Frau Mi Tzü,
erlauben Sie mir, daß ich mit meiner Arbeit fortfahre. Ich
bin heute sehr beschäftigt und muß um Entschuldigung
bitten.

Die Hausbesitzerin   Ach, Herr Shu Fu tritt in die
Fußtapfen des Fliegers! 10,000 Silberdollar! Immerhin,
ich bin erstaunt über die Wankelmütigkeit und
Oberflächlichkeit der jungen Mädchen von heutzutage,
Herr Shui Ta. (*Ab.*)

Der Schreiner *und* **Der Arbeitslose** *bringen die Säcke.*

Der Schreiner   Ich weiß nicht, warum ich Ihnen Ihre
Säkke schleppen muß.

Shui Ta   Es genügt, daß ich es weiß. Ihr Sohn hier zeigt
einen gesunden Appetit. Er will essen, Herr Lin To.

Shui Ta (*to* **The Unemployed Man** *and* **The Carpenter**)
Perhaps, since you don't have your own tobacco, you
would be interested in working for Shen Te?

The Carpenter *and* **The Unemployed Man** *go in sullenly.*
The Landlady *enters.*

The Landlady   Ah, Mr Shui Ta. What about our deal? I
have 300 silver dollars here.

Shui Ta   Mrs Mi Tzu, I've decided not to sell. I'll sign the
rental agreement.

The Landlady   Really? Don't you need the money for
that pilot?

Shui Ta   No longer.

The Landlady   And you have the rent?

Shui Ta (*taking the barber's cheque from the cart and filling it
out*)   This is a cheque for 10,000 silver dollars, signed by
Mr Shu Fu, who's interested in my cousin. I will get you
your 200 silver dollars for half the year's rent by six
tonight. And now, Mrs Mi Tzu, allow me to resume my
work. I'm very busy today and so I beg your pardon.

The Landlady   Aha. The pilot slides over and Mr Shu Fu
slips in! 10,000 silver dollars!

I'm saddened and chagrined by the fickleness and
superficiality of young girls today, Mr Shui Ta! (*She exits.*)

The Carpenter *and* **The Unemployed Man** *bring out the
bundles.*

The Carpenter   Why should I carry your bundles?

Shui Ta   Because your little son has a healthy appetite.
He likes to eat, Mr Lin To.

Die Schwägerin (*sieht die Säcke*)   Ist mein Schwager hier gewesen?

Die Shin   Ja.

Die Schwägerin   Eben. Ich kenne doch die Säcke. Das ist unser Tabak!

Shui Ta   Besser, Sie sagen das nicht so laut. Das ist mein Tabak, was Sie daraus ersehen können, daß er in meinem Gelaß stand. Wenn Sie einen Zweifel haben, können wir aber zur Polizei gehen und Ihren Zweifel beseitigen. Wollen Sie das?

Die Schwägerin (*böse*)   Nein.

Shui Ta   Es scheint, daß Sie doch keinen eigenen Tabak besitzen. Vielleicht ergreifen Sie unter diesen Umständen die rettende Hand, die Fräulein Shen Te Ihnen reicht? Haben Sie die Güte, mir jetzt den Weg zu den Häusern des Herrn Shu Fu zu zeigen.

Das jüngste Kind des Schreiners an die Hand nehmend, geht **Shui Ta** *ab, gefolgt von dem* **Schreiner***, seinen anderen Kindern,* **Der Schwägerin***, dem* **Großvater***, dem* **Arbeitslosen***.* **Schwägerin***,* **Schreiner** *und* **Arbeitsloser** *schleppen die Säcke.*

Wang   Er ist ein böser Mensch, aber Shen Te ist gut.

Die Shin   Ich weiß nicht. Von der Wäscheleine fehlt eine Hose und der Vetter trägt sie. Das muß etwas bedeuten. Ich möchte wissen, was.

Herein die beiden Alten.

Die Alte   Ist Fräulein Shen Te nicht hier?

Die Shin (*abwesend*)   Verreist.

Die Alte   Das ist merkwürdig. Sie wollte uns etwas bringen.

Wang (*schmerzlich seine Hand betrachtend*)   Sie wollte auch mir helfen. Meine Hand wird steif. Sicher kommt sie bald zurück. Der Vetter ist ja immer nur ganz kurz da.

Die Shin   Ja, nicht wahr?

The Sister-in-Law (*looking at the bundles*)   Was my brother-in-law here?

Mrs Shin   Yes.

The Sister-in-Law   I thought as much. I know these bundles! This is our tobacco!

Shui Ta   I think perhaps you should not say that so loudly. That the tobacco's mine may be deduced from the fact that it was in my back room. If you still have doubts we can go to the police. Shall I call them?

The Sister-in-Law (*angry*)   No.

Shui Ta   You own no tobacco, as it turns out. Perhaps under the circumstances you wish to grasp the rescuing hand which Miss Shen Te extends to you? Be so good as to show me the path to Mr Shu Fu's buildings.

Taking the youngest child of the carpenter by the hand, **Shui Ta** *exits, followed by* **The Carpenter** *and his other children,* **The Sister-in-Law**, **The Grandfather** *and* **The Unemployed Man**. **The Sister-in-Law**, **The Carpenter** *and* **The Unemployed Man** *carry the bundles.*

Wang   He's a bad man, but Shen Te's good.

Mrs Shin   A pair of pants was taken from the laundry, and now the cousin is wearing them. That must mean something. I'd like to know what it means.

The old couple enter.

The Old Woman   Isn't Miss Shen Te here?

Mrs Shin (*coldly*)   Gone.

The Old Woman   That's strange. She wanted to bring us something.

Wang (*looking, in pain, at his hand*)   She wanted to help me, too. My hand's growing stiff. I'm sure she'll come back soon. The cousin never stays long.

Mrs Shin   That's a fact, isn't it?

ZWISCHENSPIEL
WANGS NACHTLAGER

*Musik. Im Traum teilt der Wasserverkäufer den Göttern seine
Befürchtungen mit. Die Götter sind immer noch auf ihrer langen
Wanderung begriffen. Sie scheinen müde. Für eine kleine Weile
innehaltend, wenden sie die Köpfe über die Schultern nach dem
Wasserverkäufer zurück.*

Wang Bevor mich euer Erscheinen erweckte,
Erleuchtete, träumte ich und sah meine liebe Schwester
Shen Te in großer Bedrängnis im Schilf des Flusses, an
der Stelle, wo die Selbstmörder gefunden werden. Sie
schwankte merkwürdig daher und hielt den Nacken
gebeugt, als schleppe sie an etwas Weichem, aber
Schwerem, das sie hinunterdrückte in den Schlamm. Auf
meinen Anruf rief sie mir zu, sie müsse den Ballen der
Vorschriften ans andere Ufer bringen, daß er nicht naß
würde, da sonst die Schriftzeichen verwischten.
Ausdrücklich: ich sah nichts auf ihren Schultern. Aber
ich erinnerte mich erschrocken, daß ihr Götter ihr über
die großen Tugenden gesprochen habt, zum Dank dafür,
daß sie euch bei sich aufnahm, als ihr um ein Nachtlager
verlegen wart, o Schande! Ich bin sicher, ihr versteht
meine Sorge um sie.

Der Dritte Gott Was schlägst du vor?

Wang Eine kleine Herabminderung der Vorschriften,
Erleuchtete. Eine kleine Erleichterung des Ballens der
Vorschriften, Gütige, in Anbetracht der schlechten
Zeiten.

Der Dritte Gott Als da wäre, Wang, als da wäre?

Wang Als da zum Beispiel wäre, daß nur Wohlwollen
verlangt würde anstatt Liebe oder …

Der Dritte Gott Aber das ist doch noch schwerer, du
Unglücklicher!

Wang Oder Billigkeit anstatt Gerechtigkeit.

Der Dritte Gott Aber das bedeutet mehr Arbeit!

INTERLUDE
WANG'S NIGHT LODGING

Music. **Wang** *the waterseller shares his fears with* **the Gods** *in a dream.* **The Gods** *are still on their long journey. They seem tired. Stopping in their tracks, they turn their heads over their shoulders, looking back at* **Wang**.

Wang   Before you appeared and woke me up, Awakened Ones, I was having a nightmare concerning my dear sister Shen Te who was in great distress amongst the bulrushes by the river, at the spot where suicides are usually found. She staggered and she was stooped as if she carried something soft and heavy which made her sink in the mud. Hearing me call her name, she told me that she had to bring the commandments in a bundle to the other bank without letting the water blur the pages. In fact: She carried nothing. But like a sharp blow I remembered then how you Gods lectured her about the great virtues which were the thanks she got for taking you in when no one would, Oh Shame! I knew you'd share my fears for her.

The Third God   What do you propose?

Wang   A lightening of the burden of the commandments, Awakened Ones, in consideration of the badness of the times.

The Third God   For instance, Wang, for instance?

Wang   For instance, that only good will would be demanded, instead of love, or —

The Third God   But good will's harder than love, unlucky man!

Wang   Or simple fairness instead of justice.

The Third God   But simple fairness is even harder work!

Wang   Dann bloße Schicklichkeit anstatt Ehre!

Der Dritte Gott   Aber das ist doch mehr, du Zweifelnder!

Sie wandern müde weiter.

Wang Ordinary decency instead of honour!

The Third God But that's much much more difficult, you doubter!

They continue their progress, tired.

8
Shui Tas Tabakfabrik

*In den Baracken des Herrn **Shu Fu** hat **Shui Ta** eine kleine Tabakfabrik eingerichtet. Hinter Gittern hocken, entsetzlich zusammengepfercht, einige Familien, besonders Frauen und Kinder, darunter **Die Schwägerin**, **Der Großvater**, **Der Schreiner** und seine Kinder.*

*Davor tritt **Frau Yang** auf, gefolgt von ihrem Sohn **Sun**.*

Frau Yang (*zum Publikum*)   Ich muß Ihnen berichten, wie mein Sohn Sun durch die Weisheit und Strenge des allgemein geachteten Herrn Shui Ta aus einem verkommenen Menschen in einen nützlichen verwandelt wurde. Wie das ganze Viertel erfuhr, eröffnete Herr Shui Ta in der Nähe des Viehhofs eine kleine, aber schnell aufblühende Tabakfabrik. Vor drei Monaten sah ich mich veranlaßt, ihn mit meinem Sohn dort aufzusuchen. Er empfing mich nach kurzer Wartezeit.

*Aus der Fabrik tritt **Shui Ta** auf **Frau Yang** zu.*

Shui Ta   Womit kann ich Ihnen dienen, Frau Yang?

Frau Yang   Herr Shui Ta, ich möchte ein Wort für meinen Sohn bei Ihnen einlegen. Die Polizei war heute morgen bei uns, und man hat uns gesagt, daß Sie im Namen von Fräulein Shen Te Anklage wegen Bruch des Heiratsversprechens und Erschleichung von 200 Silberdollar erhoben haben.

Shui Ta   Ganz richtig, Frau Yang.

Frau Yang   Herr Shui Ta, um der Götter willen, können Sie nicht noch einmal Gnade vor Recht ergehen lassen? Das Geld ist weg. In zwei Tagen hat er es durchgebracht, als der Plan mit der Fliegerstelle scheiterte. Ich weiß, er ist ein Lump. Er hat auch meine Möbel schon verkauft gehabt und wollte ohne seine alte Mama nach Peking. *Sie weint.* Fräulein Shen Te hielt einmal große Stücke auf ihn.

8
Shui Ta's Tobacco Factory

In **Shu Fu**'s *buildings* **Shui Ta** *has set up a small tobacco factory. A number of families squat behind bars, severely crowded together, women and children mostly, among them* **The Sister-in-Law**, **The Grandfather**, **The Carpenter** *and his children.* **Mrs Yang** *enters in front of the bars, followed by* **Sun**.

Mrs Yang (*to the audience*)   I must make a report to you about how, through the wisdom and severe instruction of the estimable and popular Mr Shui Ta, my son, Sun, has been changed from a ruined man to a useful one. As everyone in the neighbourhood soon heard, Mr Shui Ta opened a small but thriving tobacco factory in the sheds behind the cattleyards. Three months ago I found myself faced with the necessity of seeking him out. Sun, my son, accompanied me. He received us after a short wait.

Shui Ta *comes out of the factory and crosses to* **Mrs Yang**.

Shui Ta   Can I help you, Mrs Yang?

Mrs Yang   Mr Shui Ta I'm here on behalf of my son. The police came to our house this morning, and they told us you've filed suit in Miss Shen Te's name for breach of promise over the broken engagement, and for defrauding her of 200 silver dollars.

Shui Ta   Correct in every particular, Mrs Yang.

Mrs Yang   Mr Shui Ta, for the love of God, couldn't you temper justice with mercy? The money's all gone. When the plans for the pilot's job fell through he squandered it in two days. I know he's a louse. He sold my furniture to book passage for Peking, though he never intended to take his old mother.

(*She cries.*) Miss Shen Te once had a high opinion of him.

Shui Ta   Was haben Sie mir zu sagen, Herr Yang Sun?

Sun (*finster*)   Ich habe das Geld nicht mehr.

Shui Ta   Frau Yang, der Schwäche wegen, die meine
Kusine aus irgendwelchen, mir unbegreiflichen Gründen
für Ihren verkommenen Sohn hatte, bin ich bereit, es
noch einmal mit ihm zu versuchen. Sie hat mir gesagt,
daß sie sich durch ehrliche Arbeit eine Besserung
erwartet. Er kann eine Stelle in meiner Fabrik haben.
Nach und nach werden ihm die 200 Silberdollar vom
Lohn abgezogen werden.

Sun   Also Kittchen oder Fabrik?

Shui Ta   Sie haben die Wahl.

Sun   Und mit Shen Te kann ich wohl nicht mehr
sprechen?

Shui Ta   Nein.

Sun   Wo ist mein Arbeitsplatz?

Frau Yang   Tausend Dank, Herr Shui Ta! Sie sind
unendlich gütig, und die Götter werden es Ihnen
vergelten. (*Zu* **Sun**.) Du bist vom rechten Wege
abgewichen. Versuch nun, durch ehrliche Arbeit wieder
so weit zu kommen, daß du deiner Mutter in die Augen
schauen kannst.

Sun *folgt* **Shui Ta** *in die Fabrik.* **Frau Yang** *kehrt an die Rampe
zurück.*

Frau Yang   Die ersten Wochen waren hart für Sun. Die
Arbeit sagte ihm nicht zu. Er hatte wenig Gelegenheit,
sich auszuzeichnen. Erst in der dritten Woche kam ihm
ein kleiner Vorfall zu Hilfe. Er und der frühere Schreiner
Lin To mußten Tabakballen schleppen.

Sun *und* **Der Frühere Schreiner** *Lin To schleppen je zwei
Tabakballen.*

Der Frühere Schreiner (*hält ächzend inne und läßt sich auf
einem Ballen nieder*)   Ich kann kaum mehr. Ich bin nicht
mehr jung genug für diese Arbeit.

Shui Ta Anything you'd like to tell me, Mr Yang Sun?

Sun (*sullen*) I don't have the money any more.

Shui Ta Mrs Yang, because of my cousin's incomprehensible weakness for your corrupt and degraded son, I'm prepared to try with him once more. She told me he might improve after some honourable work. He can have a job in my factory. His wages will be garnisheed till the 200 silver dollars are paid back.

Sun In other words, the factory or jail.

Shui Ta The choice is yours.

Sun And I suppose I can't speak to Shen Te?

Shui Ta No.

Sun When do I start?

Mrs Yang A thousand thanks, Mr Shui Ta! You are infinitely good, the Gods will reward you for it. (*To* **Sun**.) You have swerved from the straight and narrow. Try to redeem yourself sufficiently to be able to look your mother in her eyes again.

Sun *follows* **Shui Ta** *into the factory.* **Mrs Yang** *turns back down the ramp.*

Mrs Yang (*to the audience*) The first weeks were hard for Sun. He didn't like the work. There was no chance to show his special talents. Then in the third week a minor incident rescued him. He and the former carpenter Lin To were carrying bundles of tobacco.

Sun *and Lin To* **The Carpenter**, *who is now* **The Former Carpenter**, *each carry two bundles of tobacco.* **The Former Carpenter** *stops with a groan and sits on one of the bundles.*

The Former Carpenter I can barely stand. I'm too old for this kind of work.

Sun (*setzt sich ebenfalls*)   Warum schmeißt du ihnen die Ballen nicht einfach hin?

Der Frühere Schreiner   Und wovon sollen wir leben? Ich muß doch sogar, um das Notwendigste zu haben, die Kinder einspannen. Wenn das Fräulein Shen Te sähe! Sie war gut.

Sun   Sie war nicht die Schlechteste. Wenn die Verhältnisse nicht so elend gewesen wären, hätten wir es ganz gut miteinander getroffen. Ich möchte wissen, wo sie ist. Besser, wir machen weiter. Um diese Zeit pflegt er zu kommen.

Sie stehen auf.

Sun (*sieht* **Shui Ta** *kommen*)   Gib den einen Sack her, du Krüppel! **Sun** *nimmt auch noch den einen Ballen Lin Tos auf.*

Der Frühere Schreiner   Vielen Dank! Ja, wenn sie da wäre, würdest du gleich einen Stein im Brett haben, wenn sie sähe, daß du einem alten Mann so zur Hand gehst. Ach ja!

Herein **Shui Ta**.

Frau Yang   Und mit einem Blick sieht natürlich Herr Shui Ta, was ein guter Arbeiter ist, der keine Arbeit scheut. Und er greift ein.

Shui Ta   Halt, ihr! Was ist da los? Warum trägst du nur einen einzigen Sack?

Der Frühere Schreiner   Ich bin ein wenig müde heute, Herr Shui Ta, und Yang Sun war so freundlich ...

Shui Ta   Du kehrst um und nimmst drei Ballen, Freund. Was Yang Sun kann, kannst du auch. Yang Sun hat guten Willen und du hast keinen.

Frau Yang (*während* **Der Frühere Schreiner** *zwei weitere Ballen holt*)   Kein Wort natürlich zu Sun, aber Herr Shui Ta war im Bilde. Und am nächsten Samstag bei der Lohnauszahlung ...

Sun   So quit.

The Former Carpenter   And live on what? I have to put the kids in the harness just to scrape by. I wish Miss Shen Te could see this! She was good.

Sun   There are worse. Under less miserable circumstances we'd really have been alright. I'd like to know where she is. We'd better get back to it. This is when he usually makes the rounds.

They stand up. **Sun** *sees* **Shui Ta** *coming.*

Sun   Give me a bundle, cripple!

Sun *takes one of Lin To's bundles as well as his own.*

The Former Carpenter   Thank you very much! If she was here, you'd score big points with her for lending an old man your hand. Yessir!

Shui Ta *enters.*

Mrs Yang (*to the audience*)   And right off Mr Shui Ta recognises a good worker who goes the extra mile. And he acts.

Shui Ta   Stop, both of you! What's going on here? Why are you carrying only one bundle?

The Former Carpenter   I'm a little worn out today, Mr Shui Ta, and Yang Sun was kind enough to —

Shui Ta   Kindly go back and get three bundles, friend. If Yang Sun can do it, so can you. Yang Sun's simply got a positive attitude, and you don't.

The Former Carpenter *goes to get two more bundles.*

Mrs Yang (*to the audience*)   Naturally nothing said to Sun, but Mr Shui Ta took note. And on next Saturday, while wages were being paid ...

Ein Tisch wird aufgestellt und **Shui Ta** *kommt mit einem Säckchen Geld. Neben dem* **Aufseher** *– dem früheren* **Arbeitslosen** *– stehend, zahlt er den Lohn aus.* **Sun** *tritt vor den Tisch.*

Der Aufseher   Yang Sun – sechs Silberdollar.

Sun   Entschuldigen Sie, es können nur funf sein. Nur funf Silberdollar. (*Er nimmt die Liste, die* **Der Aufseher** *hält.*) Sehen Sie bitte, hier stehen fälschlicherweise sechs Arbeitstage, ich war aber einen Tag abwesend, eines Gerichtstermins wegen. (*Heuchlerisch.*) Ich will nichts bekommen, was ich nicht verdiene, und wenn der Lohn noch so lumpig ist!

Der Aufseher   Also funf Silberdollar! (*Zu* **Shui Ta**.) Ein seltener Fall, Herr Shui Ta!

Shui Ta   Wie können hier sechs Tage stehen, wenn es nur fünf waren?

Der Aufseher   Ich muß mich tatsächlich geirrt haben, Herr Shui Ta. (*Zu* **Sun**, *kalt.*) Es wird nicht mehr vorkommen.

Shui Ta (*winkt* **Sun** *zur Seite*)   Ich habe neulich beobachtet, daß Sie ein kräftiger Mensch sind und Ihre Kraft auch der Firma nicht vorenthalten. Heute sehe ich, daß Sie sogar ein ehrlicher Mensch sind. Passiert das öfter, daß der Aufseher sich zuungunsten der Firma irrt?

Sun   Er hat Bekannte unter den Arbeitern und wird als einer der ihren angesehen.

Shui Ta   Ich verstehe. Ein Dienst ist des andern wert. Wollen Sie eine Gratifikation?

Sun   Nein. Aber vielleicht darf ich darauf hinweisen, daß ich auch ein intelligenter Mensch bin. Ich habe eine gewisse Bildung genossen, wissen Sie. Der Aufseher meint es sehr gut mit der Belegschaft, aber er kann, ungebildet wie er ist, nicht verstehen, was die Firma benötigt. Geben Sie mir eine Probezeit von einer Woche, Herr Shui Ta, und ich glaube, Ihnen beweisen zu können, daß meine Intelligenz für die Firma mehr wert ist als meine pure Muskelkraft.

A table is set up, and **Shui Ta** *enters with a small sack of money. Standing next to* **The Foreman** – *the former* **Unemployed Man** – *he pays out the wages.* **Sun** *steps up to the table.*

The Unemployed Man, *who is now* **The Foreman**   Yang Sun – six silver dollars.

Sun   Excuse me, it's only supposed to be five silver dollars.

He takes the paylist from **The Foreman**.

Sun   Look, please, you incorrectly wrote six days worked, but I missed a day because of a court date. (*Piously.*) I don't want anything I didn't earn, even if the wages are lousy!

The Foreman   Alright, alright, five silver dollars! (*To* **Shui Ta**.) Weird, huh, Mr Shui Ta?

Shui Ta   How come it says six days if he worked five?

The Foreman   I must've made a mistake, Mr Shui Ta. (*To* **Sun**, *coldly.*) It won't happen again.

Shui Ta *beckons* **Sun** *to the side.*

Shui Ta   I've recently observed you're a strong person and when it comes to the firm you don't spare your strength. Today I see you're also honest. Does the foreman frequently make mistakes to the firm's disadvantage?

Sun   The workers are mostly his friends, he's really one of them.

Shui Ta   I understand. One hand washes the other. Would you like a bonus?

Sun   No. But perhaps I might point out that I'm an intelligent man. I've got education, not a lot but a degree. Of education, I have a degree of education, I don't have a degree.* The foreman's well-meaning with the workers but completely uneducated, he can't really give the firm what it needs. Try me for a week, Mr Shui Ta, and I think I can prove to you that my brains are worth more to the firm than my sheer muscle power.

Frau Yang Das waren kühne Worte, aber an diesem Abend sagte ich zu meinem Sun: 'Du bist ein Flieger. Zeig, daß du auch, wo du jetzt bist, in die Höhe kommen kannst! Flieg, mein Falke!' Und tatsächlich, was bringen doch Bildung und Intelligenz für große Dinge hervor! Wie will einer ohne sie zu den besseren Leuten gehören? Wahre Wunderwerke verrichtete mein Sohn in der Fabrik des Herrn Shui Ta!

Sun *steht breitbeinig hinter den Arbeitenden. Sie reichen sich über die Köpfe einen Korb Rohtabak zu.*

Sun Das ist keine ehrliche Arbeit, ihr! Dieser Korb muß fixer wandern! (*Zu einem Kind.*) Du kannst dich doch auf den Boden setzen, da nimmst du keinen Platz weg! Und du kannst noch ganz gut auch das Pressen übernehmen, ja, du dort! Ihr faulen Hunde, wofür bezahlen wir euch Lohn? Fixer mit dem Korb! Zum Teufel! Setzt den Großpapa auf die Seite und laßt ihn mit den Kindern nur zupfen! Jetzt hat es sich ausgefaulenzt hier! Im Takt das Ganze! (*Er klatscht mit den Händen den Takt, und der Korb wandert schneller.*)

Frau Yang Und keine Anfeindung, keine Schmähung von seiten ungebildeter Menschen, denn das blieb nicht aus, hielten meinen Sohn von der Erfüllung seiner Pflicht zurück.

Einer der Arbeiter stimmt das Lied vom Achten Elefanten *an. Die andern fallen in den Refrain ein.*

1
Sieben Elefanten hatte Herr Dschin
Und da war dann noch der achte.
Sieben waren wild und der achte war zahm
Und der achte war's, der sie bewachte.
  Trabt schneller!
  Herr Dschin hat einen Wald
  Der muß vor Nacht gerodet sein
  Und Nacht ist jetzt schon bald!

Mrs Yang (*to the audience*)   Bold words, but that evening I
told my son, 'You are a pilot. Prove that you can attain
the heights even from the depths. Fly, my falcon!' And
isn't it great what education and intelligence can do?
How can you join a better class of people without them?
My son became a wonder-worker in Mr Shui Ta's factory!

*Sun stands, legs akimbo, behind the workers. They're in a line,
passing a basket of raw tobacco over their heads.*

Sun   Sloppy work, over there! Move that basket faster!
(*To a child.*) You take up too much space, sit on the floor
there. And you get on those presses, yeah you! What do
we pay you slobs for? Faster with the goddamn basket! No
YOU go to hell! Yeah I heard that. Move grandpa over to
the side, let him pluck leaves with the kids! Turn my back
for a minute the whole place breaks down! Move to the
beat!

*He claps a rhythm with his hands, and the baskets move more
quickly.*

Mrs Yang (*to the audience*)   And no amount of envy or
abuse on the part of ignoramuses – and they didn't spare
the abuse – could deter my son from doing the best job
possible.

One of the workers begins The Song of Eight Elephants. *The
others join in the refrain.*

Workers

1
Seven elephants had Mr Dschin.
And the eighth was Mr Dschin's too.
The Seven 'Shame! Number Eight's gone tame!'
Number Eight told the rest what to do.
    Trot faster!
    In the forest of Mr Dschin
    We clear the way from break of day
    Until night closes in.

2
Sieben Elefanten roden den Wald
Und Herr Dschin ritt hoch auf dem achten.
All den Tag Nummer acht stand faul auf der Wacht
Und sah zu, was sie hinter sich brachten.
  Grabt schneller!
  Herr Dschin hat einen Wald
  Der muß vor Nacht gerodet sein
  Und Nacht ist jetzt schon bald!

3
Sieben Elefanten wollten nicht mehr
Hatten satt das Bäumeabschlachten
Herr Dschin war nervös, auf die sieben war er bös
Und gab ein Schaff Reis dem achten.
  Was soll das?
  Herr Dschin hat einen Wald
  Der muß vor Nacht gerodet sein
  Und Nacht ist jetzt schon bald!

4
Sieben Elefanten hatten keinen Zahn
Seinen Zahn hatte nur noch der achte.
Und Nummer acht war vorhanden, schlug die sieben
zuschanden
Und Herr Dschin stand dahinten und lachte.
  Grabt weiter!
  Herr Dschin hat einen Wald
  Der muß vor Nacht gerodet sein
  Und Nacht ist jetzt schon bald!

Shui Ta *ist gemächlich schlendernd und eine Zigarre rauchend nach vorn gekommen. Yang* **Sun** *hat den Refrain der dritten Strophe lachend mitgesungen und in der letzten Strophe durch Händeklatschen das Tempo beschleunigt.*

Frau Yang   Wir können Herrn Shui Ta wirklich nicht genug danken. Beinahe ohne jedes Zutun, aber mit Strenge und Weisheit hat er alles Gute herausgeholt, was in Sun steckte! Er hat nicht allerhand phantastische Versprechungen gemacht wie seine so sehr gepriesene Kusine, sondern ihn zu ehrlicher Arbeit gezwungen.

2
Seven elephants uprooted trees,
While Dschin rode on number eight's back.
And number eight sneered as the other ones cleared,
'Do it faster,' he'd bellow, 'No slack!'
    Dig faster!
    In the forest of Mr Dschin
    We clear the way from break of day
    Until night closes in.

Shui Ta *saunters forward, smoking a cigar.* **Sun** *sings the third verse of the song, laughing, and in the last verse he speeds up the tempo of his clapping.*

Workers and Sun

3
Seven elephants said 'We refuse!
No work unless we're fed!'
Dschin lost his cool, served 'em watery gruel;
Number eight ate butter and bread.
    I mean, what is that?
    In the forest of Mr Dschin
    We clear the way from break of day
    Until night closes in.

4
Mr Dschin removed the tusks
Of each of number eight's brothers.
But the tusks of number eight could lacerate –
Number eight slaughtered all the others.
    Get new elephants!
    In the forest of Mr Dschin
    We clear the way from break of day
    Till night-time closes in.

Mrs Yang (*to the audience*)   Our indebtedness to Mr Shui Ta is inexpressible. He almost didn't do anything, but his strict wisdom has brought out all the good that was hidden in Sun. He didn't set him up with all sorts of fantastic promises the way his egregiously overpraised cousin had done, but instead forced him into honourable

Heute ist Sun ein ganz anderer Mensch als vor drei
Monaten. Das werden Sie wohl zugeben! 'Der Edle ist wie
eine Glokke, schlägt man sie, so tönt sie, schlägt man sie
nicht, so tönt sie nicht', wie die Alten sagten.

toil. Today Sun is a completely different person than he was three months ago. You can see it yourselves! As the ancients said: 'Goodness is like a bell: if you want it to ring, you have to hit it.'

9
Shen Tes Tabakladen

Der Laden ist zu einem Kontor mit Klubsesseln und schönen
Teppichen geworden. Es regnet. **Shui Ta**, *nunmehr dick,*
verabschiedet das Teppichhändlerpaar. **Die Shin** *schaut*
amüsiert zu. Sie ist auffallend neu gekleidet.

Shui Ta Es tut mir leid, daß ich nicht sagen kann, wann
sie zurückkehrt.

Die Alte Wir haben heute einen Brief mit den 200
Silberdollar bekommen, die wir ihr einmal geliehen
haben. Es war kein Absender genannt. Aber der Brief
muß doch wohl von Shen Te kommen. Wir möchten ihr
gern schreiben, wie ist ihre Adresse?

Shui Ta Auch das weiß ich leider nicht.

Der Alte Gehen wir.

Die Alte Irgendwann muß sie ja wohl zurückkehren.

Shui Ta *verbeugt sich. Die beiden Alten gehen unsicher und*
unruhig ab.

Die Shin Sie haben ihr Geld zu spät zurückgekriegt.
Jetzt haben sie ihren Laden verloren, weil sie ihre
Steuern nicht bezahlen konnten.

Shui Ta Warum sind sie nicht zu mir gekommen?

Die Shin Zu Ihnen kommt man nicht gern. Zuerst
warteten sie wohl, daß Shen Te zurückkäme, da sie nichts
Schriftliches hatten. In den kritischen Tagen fiel der Alte
in ein Fieber, und die Frau saß Tag und Nacht bei ihm.

Shui Ta (*muß sich setzen, da es ihm schlecht wird*) Mir
schwindelt wieder!

Die Shin (*bemüht sich um ihn*) Sie sind im siebenten
Monat! Die Aufregungen sind nichts für Sie. Seien Sie
froh, daß Sie mich haben. Ohne jede menschliche Hilfe
kann niemand auskommen. Nun, ich werde in Ihrer
schweren Stunde an Ihrer Seite stehen. (*Sie lacht.*)

9

Shui Ta's Tobacco Shop

The shop has become an office with leather armchairs and nice carpets. It's raining. **Shui Ta**, *now fat, is taking his leave of the rug merchant and his wife.* **Mrs Shin** *looks on, amused. She has conspicuously new clothes.*

Shui Ta   I'm sorry, but I don't know when she'll return.

The Old Woman   An envelope arrived today with the 200 silver dollars we once lent her. There was no note inside and no return address. But it must have come from Shen Te. We would very much like to thank her, but where would we send the letter?

Shui Ta   I'm sorry, but I don't know that either.

The Old Man   Let's go.

The Old Woman   She has to return eventually.

Shui Ta *bows. The old couple leave, uncertain and troubled.*

Mrs Shin   The money was returned but too late for them. They couldn't pay their taxes in time, and they lost the rug shop.

Shui Ta   Why didn't they come and tell me?

Mrs Shin   People don't like to come to you. They didn't have anything in writing, so they waited for Shen Te to return. Then just at tax-time the old man had a fever, and the old woman sat with him day and night; they fell into arrears.

Shui Ta (*sitting down because he feels sick*)   I feel nauseous again!

Mrs Shin (*attending him*)   You're in your seventh month! It's not good to get agitated. Be glad I'm here. This is something nobody gets through without help. I'll be by your side when your hour of need arrives. (*She laughs.*)

Shui Ta (*schwach*)   Kann ich darauf zählen, Frau Shin?

Die Shin   Und ob! Es kostet freilich eine Kleinigkeit. Machen Sie den Kragen auf, da wird Ihnen leichter.

Shui Ta (*jämmerlich*)   Es ist alles nur für das Kind, Frau Shin.

Die Shin   Alles für das Kind.

Shui Ta   Ich werde nur zu schnell dick. Das muß auffallen.

Die Shin   Man schiebt es auf den Wohlstand.

Shui Ta   Und was soll mit dem Kleinen werden?

Die Shin   Das fragen Sie jeden Tag dreimal. Es wird in Pflege kommen. In die beste, die für Geld zu haben ist.

Shui Ta Ja. (*Angstvoll.*)   Und es darf niemals Shui Ta sehen.

Die Shin   Niemals. Immer nur Shen Te.

Shui Ta   Aber die Gerüchte im Viertel! Der Wasserverkäufer mit seinen Redereien! Man belauert den Laden!

Die Shin   Solang der Barbier nichts weiß, ist nichts verloren. Trinken Sie einen Schluck Wasser.

Herein **Sun** *in dem flotten Anzug und mit der Mappe eines Geschäftsmannes. Er sieht erstaunt* **Shui Ta** *in den Armen der* **Shin**.

Sun   Ich störe wohl?

Shui Ta (*steht mühsam auf und geht schwankend zur Tür*) Auf morgen, Frau Shin!

Die Shin, *ihre Handschuhe anziehend, lächelnd ab.*

Sun   Handschuhe! Woher, wieso, wofür? Schröpft die Sie etwa? (*Da* **Shui Ta** *nicht antwortet.*) Sollten auch Sie zarteren Gefühlen zugänglich sein? Komisch. (*Er nimmt ein Blatt aus seiner Mappe.*) Jedenfalls sind Sie nicht auf der Höhe in der letzten Zeit, nicht auf Ihrer alten Höhe.

Shui Ta (*weak*)   Can I count on that, Mrs Shin?

Mrs Shin   And how! For a little fee of course. Open your collar button, you'll breathe easier.

Shui Ta (*pitiful*)   I'm doing this for the child, Mrs Shin.

Mrs Shin   For the child, anything.

Shui Ta   But I'm getting huge too quickly. People must be wondering.

Mrs Shin   Rich people get fat fast.

Shui Ta   And what about when the baby comes?

Mrs Shin   You ask that three times a day. It'll stay with a wet nurse. The best money can buy.

Shui Ta   OK. (*Fearful.*) And it'll never be allowed to see Shui Ta.

Mrs Shin   Only Shen Te.

Shui Ta   But the whole neighbourhood suspects something's amiss! The waterseller's the worst! People are spying on the shop!

Mrs Shin   As long as the barber doesn't know, everything will be fine. Drink some water.

Sun *enters in a stylish suit and carrying a briefcase, looking like a businessman. He's astonished to see* **Shui Ta** *in* **Mrs Shin**'s *arms.*

Sun   Am I disturbing you?

Shui Ta *stands, unsteadily, and walks to the door.*

Shui Ta   Until tomorrow, Mrs Shin!

Mrs Shin *pulls on her gloves and exits, smiling.*

Sun   Gloves! How'd she get her hands in gloves? She blackmailing you or something?

No answer from **Shui Ta**.

Launen. Unentschlossenheit. Sind Sie krank? Das Geschäft leidet darunter. Da ist wieder ein Schrieb von der Polizei. Sie wollen die Fabrik schließen. Sie sagen, sie können allerhöchstens doppelt so viele Menschen pro Raum zulassen, als gesetzlich erlaubt ist. Sie müssen da endlich etwas tun, Herr Shui Ta!

Shui Ta *sieht ihn einen Augenblick geistesabwesend an. Dann geht er ins Gelaß und kehrt mit einer Tüte zurück. Aus ihr zieht er einen neuen Melonenhut und wirft ihn auf den Schreibtisch.*

Shui Ta Die Firma wünscht ihre Vertreter anständig gekleidet.

Sun Haben Sie den etwa für mich gekauft?

Shui Ta (*gleichgültig*) Probieren Sie ihn, ob er Ihnen paßt.

Sun *blickt erstaunt und setzt ihn auf.* **Shui Ta** *rückt die Melone prüfend zurecht.*

Sun Ihr Diener, aber weichen Sie mir nicht wieder aus. Sie müssen heute mit dem Barbier das neue Projekt besprechen.

Shui Ta Der Barbier stellt unerfüllbare Bedingungen.

Sun Wenn Sie mir nur endlich sagen wollten, was für Bedingungen.

Shui Ta (*ausweichend*) Die Baracken sind gut genug.

Sun Ja, gut genug für das Gesindel, das darin arbeitet, aber nicht gut genug für den Tabak. Er wird feucht. Ich werde noch vor der Sitzung mit der Mi Tzü über ihre Lokalitäten reden. Wenn wir die haben, können wir unsere Bittfürmichs, Wracks und Stümpfe an die Luft setzen. Sie sind nicht gut genug. Ich tätschele der Mi Tzü bei einer Tasse Tee die dicken Knie, und die Lokalitäten kosten uns die Hälfte.

Shui Ta (*scharf*) Das wird nicht geschehen. Ich wünsche, daß Sie sich im Interesse des Ansehens der Firma stets persönlich zurückhaltend und kühl geschäftsmäßig benehmen.

Sun Don't tell me you have a soft spot? I'd never have guessed. (*He takes a paper from his briefcase.*) Maybe you do, you've been a little soft lately, not up to snuff. Moody, indecisive. Are you sick? It's bad for the firm. Another warning from the police. They're threatening to shut us down. They've let you have twice the number of workers permissible by law in the workrooms, but no more than that, yet you keep packing them in! It's getting out of hand, Mr Shui Ta!

Shui Ta *looks at him absentmindedly for a moment. Then he goes onto the backroom and returns with a box. He pulls a new bowler out of it and throws it on the desk.*

Shui Ta The firm wishes to see her representative respectably dressed.

Sun Did you buy this for me?

Shui Ta (*indifferently*) Try it on, see if it fits.

Sun *looks astonished and puts it on.* **Shui Ta** *adjusts the bowler so it's sitting correctly.*

Sun Your devoted servant, now let's get back to business. You have to speak to the barber about the new project today.

Shui Ta The barber's conditions are unacceptable.

Sun But you won't tell me what his conditions are.

Shui Ta (*evasively*) The barracks are good enough.

Sun Good enough for the zombies you hire, but not good enough for the tobacco. It's getting damp. When Mi Tzu gets here I'll ask about leasing warehouse space from her. With a better physical plant we could get better workers, fire the beggars, wrecks and stumps we're paying now. They can't do anything right. I'll rub Mi Tzu's fat knees under the tea table, she'll only charge us half.

Shui Ta (*sharply*) You'll do no such thing. I wish you could learn to conduct yourself with restraint and an appro-priately professional demeanour. For the firm's sake.

Sun   Warum sind Sie so gereizt? Sind es die unangenehmen Gerüchte im Viertel?

Shui Ta   Ich kümmere mich nicht um Gerüchte.

Sun   Dann muß es wieder der Regen sein. Regen macht Sie immer so reizbar und melancholisch. Ich möchte wissen, warum.

Wangs stimme (*von draußen*)
   Ich hab Wasser zu verkaufen
   Und nun steh ich hier im Regen
   Und ich bin weither gelaufen
   Meines bißchen Wassers wegen.
   Und jetzt schrei ich mein: Kauft Wasser!
   Und niemand kauft es
   Verschmachtend und gierig
   Und zahlt es und sauft es.

Sun   Da ist dieser verdammte Wasserverkäufer. Gleich wird er wieder mit seinem Gehetze anfangen.

Wangs stimme (*von draußen*)   Gibt es denn keinen guten Menschen mehr in der Stadt? Nicht einmal hier am Platz, wo die gute Shen Te lebte? Wo ist sie, die mir auch bei Regen ein Becherchen abkaufte, vor vielen Monaten, in der Freude ihres Herzens? Wo ist sie jetzt? Hat sie keiner gesehen? Hat keiner von ihr gehört? In dieses Haus ist sie eines Abends gegangen und kam nie mehr heraus!

Sun   Soll ich ihm nicht endlich das Maul stopfen? Was geht es ihn an, wo sie ist! Ich glaube übrigens, Sie sagen es nur deshalb nicht, damit ich es nicht erfahre.

Wang (*herein*)   Herr Shui Ta, ich frage Sie wieder, wann Shen Te zurückkehren wird. Sechs Monate sind jetzt vergangen, daß sie sich auf Reisen begeben hat. (*Da* **Shui Ta** *schweigt.*) Vieles ist inzwischen hier geschehen, was in ihrer Anwesenheit nie geschehen wäre. (*Da* **Shui Ta** *immer noch schweigt.*) Herr Shui Ta, im Viertel sind Gerüchte verbreitet, daß Shen Te etwas zugestoßen sein muß. Wir, ihre Freunde, sind sehr beunruhigt. Haben Sie

Sun What's eating you? You been hearing the rumours?

Shui Ta I don't listen to rumours.

Sun I'll bet it's the rain, then. Every time it rains you get crabby and blue. I'd like to know why that is.

Wang's Voice (*singing, outside*)
I've got water here for sale,
But I'm standing in the rain,
Walked for miles with this pail,
And my labours were in vain.
And now I'm shouting: Buy Water!
Nobody will buy.
No one's fishing out their money,
No one's greedy gullet's dry.

Sun The goddam waterseller. As soon as he's finished singing he'll start raising a ruckus again.

Wang's Voice (*from outside*) Are there no more good people in this city? On this square, where once the good Shen Te lived? She bought a cup of water from me in the rain once, many months ago, in the joy of her heart! And where is she? Where is she now? Hasn't anyone heard from her? One evening she went into her shop and she's never come out again!

Sun Shouldn't I shut him up for good? Why does he care where she is? You're not telling where she is because you don't want me to know.

Wang (*entering*) Mr Shui Ta, I ask you again, when will Shen Te return? Seven months have passed since she embarked on her journey.

Shui Ta *is silent.*

A lot has happened in the meanwhile that would never've happened if she'd been here.

Shui Ta *is silent.*

Mr Shui Ta, people in the neighbourhood speculate that some accident's befallen Shen Te. We're her friends,

doch die Freundlichkeit, uns jetzt Bescheid über ihre Adresse zu geben!

Shui Ta   Leider habe ich im Augenblick keine Zeit, Herr Wang. Kommen Sie in der nächsten Woche wieder.

Wang (*aufgeregt*)   Es ist auch aufgefallen, daß der Reis, den die Bedürftigen hier immer erhielten, seit einiger Zeit morgens wieder vor der Tür steht.

Shui Ta   Was schließt man daraus?

Wang   Daß Shen Te überhaupt nicht verreist ist.

Shui Ta   Sondern? (*Da* **Wang** *schweigt.*) Dann werde ich Ihnen meine Antwort erteilen. Sie ist endgültig. Wenn Sie Shen Tes Freund sind, Herr Wang, dann fragen Sie möglichst wenig nach ihrem Verbleiben. Das ist mein Rat.

Wang   Ein schöner Rat! Herr Shui Ta, Shen Te teilte mir vor ihrem Verschwinden mit, daß sie schwanger sei!

Sun   Was?

Shui Ta (*schnell*)   Lüge!

Wang (*mit großem Ernst zu* **Shui Ta**)   Herr Shui Ta, Sie müssen nicht glauben, daß Shen Tes Freunde je aufhören werden, nach ihr zu fragen. Ein guter Mensch wird nicht leicht vergessen. Es gibt nicht viele. (*Ab.*)

Shui Ta *sieht ihm erstarrt nach. Dann geht er schnell in das Gelaß.*

Sun (*zum Publikum*)   Shen Te schwanger! Ich bin außer mir! Ich bin hereingelegt worden! Sie muß es sofort ihrem Vetter gesagt haben, und dieser Schuft hat sie selbstverständlich gleich weggeschafft. 'Pack deinen Koffer und verschwind, bevor der Vater des Kindes davon Wind bekommt!' Es ist ganz und gar unnatürlich. Unmenschlich ist es. Ich habe einen Sohn. Ein Yang erscheint auf der Bildfläche! Und was geschieht? Das Mädchen verschwindet, und man läßt mich hier schuften! (*Er gerät in Wut.*) Mit einem Hut speist man

we're extremely disturbed. Please for once show friendliness, tell us her address.

Shui Ta   I'm sorry, I'm too busy now, Mr Wang. Next week perhaps.

Wang (*excitedly*)   It's also been observed that the rice which the needy used to get at her door every morning has, each morning of late, been set outside again.

Shui Ta   From which you conclude what, exactly?

Wang   That Shen Te hasn't gone away at all.

Shui Ta   But instead?

Wang *is silent.*

Shui Ta   This is my final answer to you. If you really are Miss Shen Te's friend, Mr Wang, you will give up asking about her whereabouts. That's my best advice.

Wang   Some advice! Mr Shui Ta, before she disappeared Shen Te told me she was pregnant.

Sun   What?

Shui Ta (*quickly*)   Liar!

Wang (*with great seriousness to* **Shui Ta**)   Mr Shui Ta, you must not believe that Shen Te's friends will ever stop asking about her. A good person is not easily forgotten. There aren't many. (*Exits.*)

Shui Ta *looks at him, frozen. Then he goes quickly to the back room.*

Sun (*to the audience, like a changed man*)   She's pregnant! Oh God I can't stand this! I've been robbed! She must have told her cousin, and the sonofabitch got rid of her. 'Pack up and vanish before the little bastard's father hears about it!' It's unnatural. It's inhuman. I have a son. A new Yang enters the stage!* And what happens? She leaves me behind to slave in the mines! (*He flies into a rage.*) I get a hat! (*He tramples the hat underfoot.*) Housewrecker! Burglar! Kidnapper! And no one to protect the girl!

mich ab! (*Er zertrampelt ihn mit den Füßen.*) Verbrecher!
Räuber! Kindesentführer! Und das Mädchen ist praktisch
ohne Beschützer! (*Man hört aus dem Gelaß ein Schluchzen.
Er steht still.*) War das nicht ein Schluchzen? Wer ist das?
Es hat aufgehört. Was ist das für ein Schluchzen im
Gelaß? Dieser ausgekochte Hund Shui Ta schluchzt doch
nicht. Wer schluchzt also? Und was bedeutet es, daß der
Reis immer noch morgens vor der Tür stehen soll? Ist das
Mädchen doch da? Versteckt er sie nur? Wer sonst soll da
drin schluchzen? Das wäre ja ein gefundenes Fressen! Ich
muß sie unbedingt auftreiben, wenn sie schwanger ist!

Shui Ta *kehrt aus dem Gelaß zurück. Er geht an die Tür und
blickt hinaus in den Regen.*

Sun   Also wo ist sie?

Shui Ta (*hebt die Hand und lauscht*)   Einen Augenblick!
Es ist neun Uhr. Aber man hört nichts heute. Der Regen
ist zu stark.

Sun (*ironisch*)   Was wollen Sie denn hören?

Shui Ta   Das Postflugzeug.

Sun   Machen Sie keine Witze.

Shui Ta   Ich habe mir einmal sagen lassen, Sie wollten
fliegen? Haben Sie dieses Interesse verloren?

Sun   Ich beklage mich nicht über meine jetzige
Stellung, wenn Sie das meinen. Ich habe keine Vorliebe
für Nachtdienst, wissen Sie. Postfliegen ist Nachtdienst.
Die Firma ist mir sozusagen ans Herz gewachsen. Es ist
immerhin die Firma meiner einstigen Zukünftigen, wenn
sie auch verreist ist. Sie ist doch verreist?

Shui Ta   Warum fragen Sie das?

Sun   Vielleicht, weil mich ihre Angelegenheiten immer
noch nicht kalt lassen.

Shui Ta   Das könnte meine Kusine interessieren.

Sun   Ihre Angelegenheiten beschäftigen mich jedenfalls
genug, daß ich nicht meine Augen zudrückte, wenn sie
zum Beispiel ihrer Bewegungsfreiheit beraubt würde.

A sob is heard from the back room. He stands still.

Someone's crying. Who was that? It's stopped. Why was
someone crying back there? It's not that heartless prick
Shui Ta, he never cried in his life. And what, by the way,
should be concluded from the rice again in the
mornings? Is she back there? Is he helping her hide? Or
is he hiding her? Rice is nice but I'd rather find her in
the morning. If she's knocked up back there I've got to
flush her out!

Shui Ta *comes out of the back room. He goes to the door and
looks out into the rain.*

So where is she?

Shui Ta (*holds up his hand and listens*)   Just a moment. It's
nine o'clock. But you can't hear it today. It's raining too
hard.

Sun (*sarcastically*)   You're listening for something.

Shui Ta   The mail plane.

Sun   That's not funny.

Shui Ta   I remember you wanted to fly. Lose interest?

Sun   If you're asking am I satisfied with my position, the
answer's yes, I am, at present. I don't care much for night
work. Airmail pilots do night work. The firm's got a firm
place in my heart now. After all, it's the firm of my former
fiancée, even if in absentia. If in fact she is in absentia.

Shui Ta   What's it to you?

Sun   I retain an interest in her welfare.

Shui Ta   That might interest my cousin.

Sun   I'm interested at least to the extent that I wouldn't
just close my eyes if, for example, I learned she was being
forcibly deprived of her freedom.

Shui Ta   Durch wen?

Sun   Durch Sie!

Pause.

Shui Ta   Was würden Sie in einem solchen Falle tun?

Sun   Ich würde vielleicht zunächst meine Stellung in der Firma neu diskutieren.

Shui Ta   Ach so. Und wenn die Firma, das heißt ich, Ihnen eine entsprechende Stellung einräumte, könnte sie damit rechnen, daß Sie jede weitere Nachforschung nach Ihrer früheren Zukünftigen aufgäben?

Sun   Vielleicht.

Shui Ta   Und wie denken Sie sich Ihre neue Stellung in der Firma?

Sun   Dominierend. Ich denke zum Beispiel an Ihren Hinauswurf.

Shui Ta   Und wenn die Firma statt mich Sie hinauswürfe?

Sun   Dann würde ich wahrscheinlich zurückkehren, aber nicht allein.

Shui Ta   Sondern?

Sun   Mit der Polizei.

Shui Ta   Mit der Polizei. Angenommen, die Polizei fände niemand hier?

Sun   So würde sie vermutlich in diesem Gelaß nachschauen! Herr Shui Ta, meine Sehnsucht nach der Dame meines Herzens wird unstillbar. Ich fühle, daß ich etwas tun muß, sie wieder in meine Arme schließen zu können. (*Ruhig.*) Sie ist schwanger und braucht einen Menschen um sich.* Ich muß mich mit dem Wasserverkäufer darüber besprechen. (*Er geht.*)

Shui Ta   By whom?

Sun   By you!

Pause.

Shui Ta   What would you do, if you learned such a thing?

Sun   I might want to talk about my position in the firm.

Shui Ta   Aha. So if the firm were to offer you an elevated position, it could count on your willingness to abandon any further inquiries into your former fiancée's freedom?

Sun   It's possible.

Shui Ta   And how elevated, do you think?

Sun   To the top. After which, I think, I'd kick you out.

Shui Ta   And what if you get kicked out before I do?

Sun   I'll come right back. With company.

Shui Ta   Who?

Sun   The police.

Shui Ta   The police. And when they found nothing amiss?

Sun   They'd look in the back room! Mr Shui Ta, my desire for the woman of my dreams can't be stilled. I feel that I must do something, if I'm ever going to hold her in my arms again. I think I should talk to the waterseller. (*He exits.*)

Shui Ta *sieht ihm unbeweglich nach. Dann geht er schnell in das Gelaß zurück. Er bringt allerlei Gebrauchsgegenstände* **Shen Tes**, *Wäsche, Kleider, Toiletteartikel. Lange betrachtet er den Shawl, den* **Shen Te** *von dem Teppichhändlerpaar kaufte. Dann packt er alles zu einem Bündel zusammen und versteckt es unter dem Tisch, da er Geräusche hört. Herein* **Die Hausbesitzerin** *und* **Herr Shu Fu**. *Sie begrüßen* **Shui Ta** *und entledigen sich ihrer Schirme und Galoschen.*

Die Hausbesitzerin   Es wird Herbst, Herr Shu Ta.

Herr Shu Fu   Eine melancholische Jahreszeit!

Die Hausbesitzerin   Und wo ist Ihr charmanter Prokurist? Ein schrecklicher Damenkiller! Aber Sie kennen ihn wohl nicht von dieser Seite. Immerhin, er versteht es, diesen seinen Charme auch mit seinen geschäftlichen Pflichten zu vereinen, so daß Sie nur den Vorteil davon haben dürften.

Shui Ta (*verbeugt sich*)   Nehmen Sie bitte Platz!

Man setzt sich und beginnt zu rauchen.

Shui Ta   Meine Freunde, ein unvorhergesehener Vorfall, der gewisse Folgen haben kann, zwingt mich, die Verhandlungen, die ich letzthin über die Zukunft meines Unternehmens führte, sehr zu beschleunigen. Herr Shu Fu, meine Fabrik ist in Schwierigkeiten.

Herr Shu Fu   Das ist sie immer.

Shui Ta   Aber nun droht die Polizei offen, sie zu schließen, wenn ich nicht auf Verhandlungen über ein neues Objekt hinweisen kann. Herr Shu Fu, es handelt sich um den einzigen Besitz meiner Kusine, für die Sie immer ein so großes Interesse gezeigt haben.

Herr Shu Fu   Herr Shui Ta, ich fühle eine tiefe Unlust, Ihre sich ständig vergrößernden Projekte zu besprechen. Ich rede von einem kleinen Abendessen mit Ihrer Kusine, Sie deuten finanzielle Schwierigkeiten an. Ich stelle Ihrer Kusine Häuser für Obdachlose zur Verfügung, Sie etablieren darin eine Fabrik. Ich überreiche ihr einen Scheck, Sie präsentieren ihn. Ihre

Shui Ta *looks after him, motionless. Then he goes quickly into the back room. He brings out* **Shen Te** '*s things: linens, clothes, toiletries. He looks for a long time at the shawl* **Shen Te** *had bought from the rug merchant. Then, hearing a noise, he makes a bundle of everything and hides it.* **The Landlady** *and* **Shu Fu** *enter. They greet* **Shui Ta**, *fold their umbrellas and take off their galoshes.*

The Landlady   Autumn's coming, Mr Shui Ta.

Shu Fu   A melancholy time of year!

The Landlady   And where's your charming field representative? He's a terrible flirt! Of course you don't know that about him, he doesn't flirt with you. But he's a real professional, charisma and business acumen perfectly blended and I'm sure your profits are showing it.

Shui Ta (*bowing*)   Please be seated!

They sit and begin to smoke.

Shui Ta   My friends, an unforeseen circumstance which could have repercussions forces me to greatly accelerate our negotiations over the future of my business. Mr Shu Fu, the factory's in a crisis.

Shu Fu   As always.

Shui Ta   But the police are publicly threatening to close it now, unless I can demonstrate progress in the negotiations over a new location. These holdings are my cousin's, Mr Shu Fu, for whom you have always shown great concern.

Shu Fu   Mr Shui Ta, I'm extremely loathe to discuss further with you your endlessly expanding enterprises. I invite your cousin to an intimate dinner, you come back with financial woes. I give your cousin my buildings as homeless shelters, you turn them into a tobacco factory. I give her a cheque, you cash the cheque. And then your cousin vanishes. And then you ask for 100,000 silver

Kusine verschwindet, Sie wünschen 100,000 Silberdollar mit der Bemerkung, meine Häuser seien zu klein. Herr, wo ist Ihre Kusine?

Shui Ta   Herr Shu Fu, beruhigen Sie sich. Ich kann Ihnen heute die Mitteilung machen, daß sie sehr bald zurückkehren wird.

Herr Shu Fu   Bald? Wann? 'Bald' höre ich von Ihnen seit Wochen.

Shui Ta   Ich habe von Ihnen nicht neue Unterschriften verlangt. Ich habe Sie lediglich gefragt, ob Sie meinem Projekt nähertreten würden, wenn meine Kusine zurückkäme.

Herr Shu Fu   Ich habe Ihnen tausendmal gesagt, daß ich mit Ihnen nichts mehr, mit Ihrer Kusine dagegen alles zu besprechen bereit bin. Sie scheinen aber einer solchen Besprechung Hindernisse in den Weg legen zu wollen.

Shui Ta   Nicht mehr.

Herr Shu Fu   Wann also wird sie stattfinden?

Shui Ta (*unsicher*)   In drei Monaten.

Herr Shu Fu (*ärgerlich*)   Dann werde ich in drei Monaten meine Unterschrift geben.

Shui Ta   Aber es muß alles vorbereitet werden.

Herr Shu Fu   Sie können alles vorbereiten, Shui Ta, wenn Sie überzeugt sind, daß Ihre Kusine dieses Mal tatsächlich kommt.

Shui Ta   Frau Mi Tzü, sind Sie Ihrerseits bereit, der Polizei zu bestätigen, daß ich Ihre Fabrikräume haben kann?

Die Hausbesitzerin   Gewiß, wenn Sie mir Ihren Prokuristen überlassen. Sie wissen seit Wochen, daß das meine Bedingung ist. (*Zu Herrn* **Shu Fu**.) Der junge Mann ist geschäftlich so tüchtig, und ich brauche einen Verwalter.

dollars and along the way inform me that my buildings are too small and too damp. Sir, where is your cousin?

Shui Ta   Calm down, Mr Shu Fu. Today I can tell you she will be returning very soon.

Shu Fu   Soon? When is soon? You've been saying 'soon' for seven months.

Shui Ta   I'm not asking you to sign the loan now, just whether you might be more interested in my project if my cousin came back.

Shu Fu   And again, for the thousandth time, I will not talk to you about anything. With your cousin, everything. But you seem intent on being an impediment to our conjoining.

Shui Ta   No longer.

Shu Fu   Then when can I conjoin with her?

Shui Ta (*uncertainly*)   Three months.

Shu Fu (*angry*)   Then in three months I'll sign the loan.

Shui Ta   But there are preparations.

Shu Fu   Make them yourself, Shui Ta, if you're sure your cousin will be back by then.

Shui Ta   Mrs Mi Tzu, will you testify to the police that I'll be leasing your warehouses?

The Landlady   I certainly will, provided you let me have your field representative. I told you weeks ago that was my one stipulation. (*To* **Shu Fu**.) This young man is so marvellously thorough, and I need a thorough man to organise my affairs.

Shui Ta Sie müssen doch verstehen, daß ich gerade jetzt Herrn Yang Sun nicht entbehren kann, bei all den Schwierigkeiten und bei meiner in letzter Zeit so schwankenden Gesundheit! Ich war ja von Anfang an bereit, ihn Ihnen abzutreten, aber ...

Die Hausbesitzerin Ja, aber!

Pause.

Shui Ta Schön, er wird morgen in Ihrem Kontor vorsprechen.

Herr Shu Fu Ich begrüße es, daß Sie sich diesen Entschluß abringen konnten, Shui Ta. Sollte Fräulein Shen Te wirklich zurückkehren, wäre die Anwesenheit des jungen Mannes hier höchst ungeziemend. Er hat, wie wir wissen, seinerzeit einen ganz unheilvollen Einfluß auf sie ausgeübt.

Shui Ta (*sich verbeugend*) Zweifellos. Entschuldigen Sie in den beiden Fragen, meine Kusine Shen Te und Herrn Yang Sun betreffend, mein langes Zögern, so unwürdig eines Geschäftsmannes. Diese Menschen standen einander einmal nahe.

Die Hausbesitzerin Sie sind entschuldigt.

Shui Ta (*nach der Tür schauend*) Meine Freunde, lassen Sie uns nunmehr zu einem Abschluß kommen. In diesem einstmals kleinen und schäbigen Laden, wo die armen Leute des Viertels den Tabak der guten Shen Te kauften, beschließen wir, ihre Freunde, nun die Etablierung von zwölf schönen Läden, in denen in Zukunft der gute Tabak der Shen Te verkauft werden soll. Wie man mir sagt, nennt das Volk mich heute den Tabakkönig von Sezuan. In Wirklichkeit habe ich dieses Unternehmen aber einzig und allein im Interesse meiner Kusine geführt. Ihr und ihren Kindern und Kindeskindern wird es gehören.

Von draußen kommen die Geräusche einer Volksmenge. Herein **Sun**, **Wang** *und* **Der Polizist**.

Shui Ta I must crave your understanding, at the moment it's impossible to spare Mr Yang Sun, with the business in crisis and my health recently! I've always been ready to give him to you, but ...

The Landlady Yes? But?

Pause.

Shui Ta He'll report to your office tomorrow.

Shu Fu I applaud your determination to wrest this decision from yourself, Shui Ta. If Miss Shen Te ever does come back you couldn't keep that young man around, that'd be entirely inappropriate. As everyone knows, he in his time wielded an extremely unhealthy influence over her.

Shui Ta (*bowing*) Without question. Please forgive my stupid hesitations, so unworthy of a businessman, in settling the fates of my cousin Shen Te and Mr Yang Sun. Once these two people meant a lot to each other.

The Landlady You're forgiven.

Shui Ta (*looking towards the door*) Let us conclude, my friends. In this formerly shabby shop, from which once the poor of the outskirts bought the tobacco of the good Shen Te, we her friends are bringing forth twelve beautiful boutiques, from which future customers will be buying Shen Te's Good Tobacco. I'm told the neighbourhood's calling me The Tobacco King of Szechwan. But in point of fact everything I've done was done for my cousin. The business is hers, and her children, and her grandchildren.

The sound of a mob outside. **Sun, Wang** *and* **The Policeman** *enter.*

Der Polizist   Herr Shui Ta, zu meinem Bedauern zwingt mich die aufgeregte Stimmung des Viertels, einer Anzeige aus Ihrer eigenen Firma nachzugehen, nach der Sie Ihre Kusine, Fräulein Shen Te, ihrer Freiheit berauben sollen.

Shui Ta   Das ist nicht wahr.

Der Polizist   Herr Yang Sun hier bezeugt, daß er aus dem Gelaß hinter Ihrem Kontor ein Schluchzen gehört hat, das nur von einer Frauensperson herstammen konnte.

Die Hausbesitzerin   Das ist lächerlich. Ich und Herr Shu Fu, zwei angesehene Bürger dieser Stadt, deren Aussagen die Polizei kaum in Zweifel ziehen kann, bezeugen, daß hier nicht geschluchzt wurde. Wir rauchen in Ruhe unsere Zigarren.

Der Polizist   Ich habe leider den Auftrag, das fragliche Gelaß zu inspizieren.

Shui Ta *öffnet die Tür.* **Der Polizist** *tritt mit einer Verbeugung auf die Schwelle. Er schaut hinein, dann wendet er sich um und lächelt.*

Der Polizist   Hier ist tatsächlich kein Mensch.

Sun (*der neben ihn getreten war*)   Aber es war ein Schluchzen! (*Sein Blick fällt auf den Tisch, unter den* **Shui Ta** *das Bündel gestopft hat. Er läuft darauf zu.*) Das war vorhin noch nicht da! (*Es öffnend, zeigt er* **Shen Tes** *Kleider usw.*)

Wang   Das sind Shen Tes Sachen! (*Er läuft zur Tür und ruft hinaus.*) Man hat ihre Kleider hier entdeckt.

Der Polizist (*die Sachen an sich nehmend*)   Sie erklären, daß Ihre Kusine verreist ist. Ein Bündel mit ihr gehörenden Sachen wird unter Ihrem Tisch versteckt gefunden. Wo ist das Mädchen erreichbar, Herr Shui Ta?

Shui Ta   Ich kenne ihre Adresse nicht.

Der Polizist   Das ist sehr bedauerlich.

The Policeman Mr Shui Ta, to my deep regret the agitated voice of the neighbourhood compels me to investigate a denunciation from within your own firm, according to which you are said to have forcibly imprisoned your cousin Shen Te.

Shui Ta That's not true.

The Policeman Mr Yang Sun here claims he heard a woman sobbing in the room behind your office.

The Landlady Ridiculous. Mr Shu Fu and I, two of the city's respected citizens whose testimony the police are accustomed to credit, are hereby witnessing that no one's been sobbing here. We've been peaceably smoking our cigars.

The Policeman Unfortunately I have a search warrant for the room in question.

Shui Ta *opens the door.* **The Policeman** *bows, steps onto the threshold. He looks in, then turns around and smiles.*

The Policeman It's empty.

Yang Sun *looks in.*

Sun Someone was crying!

His gaze falls on the table under which **Shui Ta** *has stuffed the bundle. He goes to it.*

This wasn't there earlier.

Opening it, he shows **Shen Te** *'s clothes etc.*

Wang Those are Shen Te's things!

(*He goes to the door and calls out.*) They found her clothes here!

The Policeman (*gathering up the bundle*) You said your cousin had gone away. A bundle full of things belonging to her is found under your table? Where can we reach the girl, Mr Shui Ta?

Shui Ta I no longer know where she lives.

The Policeman That is very unfortunate.

Rufe Aus Der Volksmenge   Shen Tes Sachen sind
gefunden worden! Der Tabakkönig hat das Mädchen
ermordet und verschwinden lassen!

Der Polizist   Herr Shui Ta, ich muß Sie bitten, mir auf
die Wache zu folgen.

Shui Ta (*sich vor der* **Hausbesitzerin** *und* **Herrn Shu Fu**
verbeugend)   Ich bitte Sie um Entschuldigung für den
Skandal, meine Herrschaften. Aber es gibt noch Richter
in Sezuan. Ich bin überzeugt, daß sich alles in Kürze
aufklären wird. (*Er geht vor dem* **Polizisten** *hinaus.*)

Wang   Ein furchtbares Verbrechen ist geschehen!

Sun (*bestürzt*)   Aber dort war ein Schluchzen!

ZWISCHENSPIEL
WANGS NACHTLAGER

*Musik. Zum letztenmal erscheinen dem Wasserverkäufer im
Traum die Götter. Sie haben sich sehr verändert. Unverkennbar
sind die Anzeichen langer Wanderung, tiefer Erschöpfung und
mannigfaltiger böser Erlebnisse. Einem ist der Hut vom Kopf
geschlagen, einer hat ein Bein in einer Fuchsfalle gelassen, und
alle drei gehen barfuß.*

Wang   Endlich erscheint ihr! Furchtbare Dinge gehen
vor in Shen Tes Tabakladen, Erleuchtete! Shen Te ist
wieder verreist, schon seit Monaten! Der Vetter hat alles
an sich gerissen! Er ist heute verhaftet worden. Er soll sie
ermordet haben, heißt es, um sich ihren Laden
anzueignen. Aber das glaube ich nicht, denn ich habe
einen Traum gehabt, in dem sie mir erschien und
erzählte, daß ihr Vetter sie gefangen hält. Oh,
Erleuchtete, ihr müßt sogleich zurückkommen und sie
finden.

Der Erste Gott   Das ist entsetzlich. Unsere ganze Suche
ist gescheitert. Wenige Gute fanden wir, und wenn wir
welche fanden, lebten sie nicht menschenwürdig. Wir
hatten schon beschlossen, uns an Shen Te zu halten.

Shouts from the Crowd   Shen Te's belongings have been found! The Tobacco King has murdered Shen Te and made her body disappear!

The Policeman   Mr Shui Ta, I must ask you to accompany me to the station.

Shui Ta (*bowing to* **The Landlady** *and* **Shu Fu**)   Please excuse this scandal, my partners and colleagues. But there are still judges in Szechwan. I'm confident that this will be cleared up in no time.

He exits in front of **The Policeman**.

Wang   A horrible crime has been committed.

Sun (*troubled*)   But I know I heard somebody crying in there!

INTERLUDE
WANG'S NIGHT LODGING

Music. For the last time **the Gods** *appear to* **Wang** *in a dream. They are very changed. The signs are unmistakable of a long journey, deep fatigue and many bad experiences. One has had his hat knocked off, one has caught his leg in a foxtrap, and all three are barefoot.*

Wang   Finally you appear! Terrible doings in Shen Te's tobacco shop, Awakened Ones! Shen Te's been missing for months! The cousin's taken over! He was arrested today. He's alleged to have murdered her, they say he did it to get hold of her shop. But I believe otherwise, because in a dream Shen Te appeared to me and said that her cousin was keeping her prisoner. Oh please, Awakened Ones, you must return and find her.

The First God   That's horrifying. Our whole search has been a failure. We travelled so far and found so little and what little we found was dismal. Shen Te was our last hope.

Der Zweite Gott   Wenn sie immer noch gut sein sollte!

Wang   Das ist sie sicherlich, aber sie ist verschwunden!

Der Erste Gott   Dann ist alles verloren.

Der Zweite Gott   Haltung.

Der Erste Gott   Wozu da noch Haltung? Wir müssen abdanken, wenn sie nicht gefunden wird! Was für eine Welt haben wir vorgefunden, Elend, Niedrigkeit und Abfall überall! Selbst die Landschaft ist von uns abgefallen. Die schönen Bäume sind enthauptet von Drähten, und jenseits der Gebirge sehen wir dicke Rauchwolken und hören Donner von Kanonen, und nirgends ein guter Mensch, der durchkommt!

Der Dritte Gott   Ach, Wasserverkäufer, unsere Gebote scheinen tödlich zu sein! Ich fürchte, es muß alles gestrichen werden, was wir an sittlichen Vorschriften aufgestellt haben. Die Leute haben genug zu tun, nur das nackte Leben zu retten. Gute Vorsätze bringen sie an den Rand des Abgrunds, gute Taten stürzen sie hinab. (*Zu den beiden andern Göttern.*) Die Welt ist unbewohnbar, ihr müßt es einsehen!

Der Erste Gott (*heftig*)   Nein, die Menschen sind nichts wert!

Der Dritte Gott   Weil die Welt zu kalt ist!

Der Zweite Gott   Weil die Menschen zu schwach sind!

Der Erste Gott   Würde, ihr Lieben, Würde! Brüder, wir dürfen nicht verzweifeln. Einen haben wir doch gefunden, der gut war und nicht schlecht geworden ist, und er ist nur verschwunden. Eilen wir, ihn zu finden. Einer genügt. Haben wir nicht gesagt, daß alles noch gut werden kann, wenn nur einer sich findet, der diese Welt aushält, nur einer!

Sie entschwinden schnell.

The Second God   If she'd remained good!

Wang   She did, she did but she's disappeared!

The First God   Then all's lost, lost, lost, lost!

The Second God   Composure!

The First God   What good will composure do now? We'll resign in disgrace if she can't be found! What kind of world have we stumbled onto? Deprivation, degradation, dissolution! Even the landscape has grown apostate. The beautiful trees are beheaded by electric wires, and over the mountains we have seen thick clouds of smoke and heard the thunder of cannon, and no good people will survive that!

The Third God   Oh waterseller, apparently our commandments are fatal! I am afraid all our ethical precepts must be stricken from the books. People are stretched to extremes just saving their own skins. Good intentions lead them to the brink of the abyss, and good deeds push them in. (*To the other Gods.*) The world is unliveable, surely you see that!

The First God (*vehemently*)   No, the people are simply worthless!

The Third God   Because the world is too cold!

The Second God   Because people are weak!

The First God   Dignity, dear ones, dignity! Brothers let us not despair. We've found one who was good, who didn't become bad, she merely disappeared. Let's hasten to find her. One is enough. Has it not been decreed that this world is redeemed if one person can be found who can transcend this world's hideousness? Just one?

They quickly disappear.

10
Gerichtslokal

In Gruppen: **Herr Shu Fu** *und* **Die Hausbesitzerin**. **Sun** *und seine Mutter.* **Wang, Der Schreiner**, **Der Großvater, Die Junge Prostituierte**, *die beiden Alten.* **Die Shin. Der Polizist. Die Schwägerin.**

Der Alte   Er ist zu mächtig.

Wang   Er will zwölf neue Läden aufmachen.

Der Schreiner   Wie soll der Richter ein gerechtes Urteil sprechen, wenn die Freunde des Angeklagten, der Barbier Shu Fu und die Hausbesitzerin Mi Tzü, seine Freunde sind?

Die Schwägerin   Man hat gesehen, wie gestern abend die Shin im Auftrag des Herrn Shui Ta eine fette Gans in die Küche des Richters brachte. Das Fett troff durch den Korb.

Die Alte (*zu* **Wang**)   Unsere arme Shen Te wird nie wieder entdeckt werden.

Wang   Ja, nur die Götter können die Wahrheit ausfindig machen.

Der Polizist   Ruhe! Der Gerichtshof erscheint.

Eintreten in Gerichtsroben die drei Götter. Während sie an der Rampe entlang zu ihren Sitzen gehen, hört man sie flüstern.

Der Dritte Gott   Es wird aufkommen. Die Zertifikate sind sehr schlecht gefälscht.

Der Zweite Gott   Und man wird sich Gedanken machen über die plötzliche Magenverstimmung des Richters.

Der Erste Gott   Nein, sie ist natürlich, da er eine halbe Gans aufgegessen hat.

Die Shin   Es sind neue Richter!

10
Courtroom

In groups: **Mr Shu Fu** *and* **The Landlady**. **Sun** *and his mother.*
Wang, **The Former Carpenter**, **The Unemployed Man**,
The Sister-in-Law, **The Grandfather**, **The Young Prostitute**
(**The Niece**), *the old couple.* **Mrs Shin**. **The Policeman**.

The Old Man   He's much too powerful.

Wang   He's opening twelve new shops.

The Former Carpenter   How's the judge going to be
impartial when the defendant's friends, the barber Shu
Fu and the landlady Mi Tzu, are the judge's friends too?

The Sister-in-Law   Mrs Shin was seen yesterday evening
bringing an enormous goose to the judge's kitchen door.
The goosefat dripped right through the basket.

The Old Woman (*to* **Wang**)   Our poor Shen Te will never
be found again.

Wang   Only the Gods can uncover the truth here.

The Policeman   Quiet! Court is in session!

The three Gods *enter wearing judges' robes. As they go along
the ramp to their seats, we hear them whispering.*

The Third God   We're going to get caught. The
signatures were very poorly forged.

The Second God   Won't they be suspicious of the
judge's sudden indigestive incapacitation?

The First God   What's suspicious about indigestion? The
man ate half an enormous goose!

Mrs Shin   They've gotten fresh judges!

Wang   Und sehr gute!

Der dritte Gott, *der als letzter geht, hört ihn, wendet sich um und lächelt ihm zu. Die Götter setzen sich.* **Der Erste Gott** *schlägt mit dem Hammer auf den Tisch.* **Der Polizist** *holt* **Shui Ta** *herein, der mit Pfeifen empfangen wird, aber in herrischer Haltung einhergeht.*

Der Polizist   Machen Sie sich auf eine Überraschung gefaßt. Es ist nicht der Richter Fu Yi Tscheng. Aber die neuen Richter sehen auch sehr mild aus.

Shui Ta *erblickt die Götter und wird ohnmächtig.*

Die Junge Prostituierte   Was ist da? Der Tabakkönig ist in Ohnmacht gefallen.

Die Schwägerin   Ja, beim Anblick der neuen Richter!

Wang   Er scheint sie zu kennen! Das verstehe ich nicht.

Der Erste Gott   Sind Sie der Tabakgroßhändler Shui Ta?

Shui Ta (*sehr schwach*)   Ja.

Der Erste Gott   Gegen Sie wird die Anklage erhoben, daß Sie Ihre leibliche Kusine, das Fräulein Shen Te, beiseite geschafft haben, um sich ihres Geschäfts zu bemächtigen. Bekennen Sie sich schuldig?

Shui Ta   Nein.

Der Erste Gott (*in den Akten blätternd*)   Wir hören zunächst den Polizisten des Viertels über den Ruf des Angeklagten und den Ruf seiner Kusine.

Der Polizist (*tritt vor*)   Fräulein Shen Te war ein Mädchen, das sich gern allen Leuten angenehm machte, lebte und leben ließ, wie man sagt. Herr Shui Ta hingegen ist ein Mann von Prinzipien. Die Gutherzigkeit des Fräuleins zwang ihn mitunter zu strengen Maßnahmen. Jedoch hielt er sich im Gegensatz zu dem Mädchen stets auf seiten des Gesetzes, Euer Gnaden. Er entlarvte Leute, denen seine Kusine vertrauensvoll Obdach gewährt hatte, als eine Diebesbande, und in einem andern Fall bewahrte er die Shen Te im letzten

Wang   And unimpeachably good!

The Third God, *who is last in line, hears him, turns and smiles at him.* **The Gods** *sit.* **The First God** *bangs the mallet on the table.* **The Policeman** *brings* **Shui Ta** *in, who is welcomed by catcalls and whistles but enters with an imperious air.*

The Policeman   Prepare yourself for a shock. Judge Fu Yi Tscheng's out sick today. But the new bench looks even more eager to please than him.

Shui Ta *sees* **the Gods** *and faints.*

The Young Prostitute   The Tobacco King's fainted!

The Sister-in-Law   Took one gander at the substitute judiciary,* and out like a light!

Wang   He seemed to know who they really are! I don't understand.

The First God (*opening the proceedings*)   Are you Shui Ta the tobacco wholesaler?

Shui Ta (*very weak*)   Yes.

The First God   You have been charged with disappearing your cousin so that you could seize her business. Do you plead guilty?

Shui Ta   No.

The First God (*looking through the papers*)   We will first hear the local policeman testify as to the characters of the defendant and his cousin's reputation.

The Policeman (*stepping forward*)   Miss Shen Te was a girl who was available to everyone, pleasant, a laissez-faire sort of person, as they say. Mr Shui Ta, on the other hand, is a man of principle. The openheartedness of the young woman forced him once in a while to take strict measures. But let it be said, your honours, that he was always on the right side of the law, whereas the same could not be said of his cousin.

Augenblick vor einem glatten Meineid, Herr Shui Ta ist
mir bekannt als respektabler und die Gesetze
respektierender Bürger.

Der Erste Gott   Sind weitere Leute hier, die bezeugen
wollen, daß dem Angeklagten eine Untat, wie sie ihm
vorgeworfen wird, nicht zuzutrauen ist?

Vortreten **Herr Shu Fu** *und* **Die Hausbesitzerin**.

Der Polizist (*flüstert den Göttern zu*)   Herr Shu Fu, ein
sehr einflußreicher Herr!

Herr Shu Fu   Herr Shui Ta gilt in der Stadt als
angesehener Geschäftsmann. Er ist zweiter Vorsitzender
der Handelskammer und in seinem Viertel zum
Friedensrichter vorgesehen.

Wang (*ruft dazwischen*)   Von euch! Ihr macht Geschäfte
mit ihm.

Der Polizist (*flüsternd*)   Ein übles Subjekt!

Die Hausbesitzerin   Als Präsidentin des Fürsorgevereins
möchte ich dem Gerichtshof zur Kenntnis bringen, daß
Herr Shui Ta nicht nur im Begriff steht, zahlreichen
Menschen in seinen Tabakbetrieben die bestdenkbaren
Räume, hell und gesund, zu schenken, sondern auch
unserm Invalidenheim laufend Zuwendungen macht.

Der Polizist (*flüsternd*)   Frau Mi Tzü, eine nahe
Freundin des Richters Fu Yi Tscheng!

Der Erste Gott   Jaja, aber nun müssen wir auch hören,
ob jemand weniger Günstiges über den Angeklagten
auszusagen hat.

Vortreten **Wang**, **Der Schreiner**, *das alte Paar*, **Der
Arbeitslose**, **Die Schwägerin**, **Die Junge Prostituierte**.

Der Polizist   Der Abschaum des Viertels!

His gullible cousin took in homeless people; he exposed them for the band of thieves they were, and he also stopped Shen Te from out-and-out perjuring herself. Mr Shui Ta is known to me as a respectable, law-abiding citizen.

The First God   Are there others wishing to testify that the defendant is incapable of the crime of which he stands accused?

Shu Fu *and* **The Landlady** *step forward.*

The Policeman (*whispering, to* **the Gods**)   Mr Shu Fu is a very influential man!

Shu Fu   Mr Shui Ta is considered one of the city's business leaders. He was recently elected Vice-President of the Chamber of Commerce and he's been nominated for Justice of Peace in his district.

Wang (*calling out, interrupting*)   Nominated by you! You're his partner!

The Policeman (*whispering to* **the Gods**)   A low-down, skeevy troublemaker.

The Landlady   As President of the Charitable Trusts I would like to call the court's attentions, not only to Mr Shui Ta's impending plans to provide for his many, many tobacco workers the best in factory lighting, space and hygienics, but to the sizeable donations he routinely bestows upon the Veterans' Convalescent Home.

The Policeman (*whispering*)   Mrs Mi Tzu is an intimate of Judge Fu Yi Tscheng!

The First God   Fine, fine, but now we must inquire further as to whether anyone has anything less favourable to say about the defendant.

Wang, **The Former Carpenter**, *the old couple*, **The Unemployed Man**, **The Sister-in-Law** *and* **The Young Prostitute** *step forward.*

The Policeman   Shit from the neighbourhood sidewalk.

Der Erste Gott   Nun, was wißt ihr von dem allgemeinen Verhalten des Shui Ta?

Rufe (*durcheinander*)   Er hat uns ruiniert! Mich hat er erpreßt! Uns zu Schlechtem verleitet! Die Hilflosen ausgebeutet! Gelogen! Betrogen! Gemordet!

Der Erste Gott   Angeklagter, was haben Sie zu antworten?

Shui Ta   Ich habe nichts getan, als die nackte Existenz meiner Kusine gerettet, Euer Gnaden. Ich bin nur gekommen, wenn die Gefahr bestand, daß sie ihren kleinen Laden verlor. Ich mußte dreimal kommen. Ich wollte nie bleiben. Die Verhältnisse haben es mit sich gebracht, daß ich das letzte Mal geblieben bin. Die ganze Zeit habe ich nur Mühe gehabt. Meine Kusine war beliebt, und ich habe die schmutzige Arbeit verrichtet. Darum bin ich verhaßt.

Die Schwägerin   Das bist du. Nehmt unsern Jungen, Euer Gnaden! (*Zu* **Shui Ta**.) Ich will nicht von den Säcken reden.

Shui Ta   Warum nicht? Warum nicht?

Die Schwägerin (*zu den Göttern*)   Shen Te hat uns Obdach gewährt, und er hat uns verhaften lassen.

Shui Ta   Ihr habt Kuchen gestohlen!

Die Schwägerin   Jetzt tut er, als kümmerten ihn die Kuchen des Bäckers! Er wollte den Laden für sich haben!

Shui Ta   Der Laden war kein Asyl, ihr Eigensüchtigen!

Die Schwägerin   Aber wir hatten keine Bleibe!

Shui Ta   Ihr wart zu viele!

Wang   Und sie hier! (*Er deutet auf die beiden Alten.*) Waren sie auch zu eigensüchtig?

Der Alte   Wir haben unser Erspartes in Shen Tes Laden gegeben. Warum hast du uns um unsern Laden gebracht?

The First God   So, what do you know in general about the character of Shui Ta?

All (*simultaneously*)   He ruined us! – He blackmailed me! – He led us to evil! – He exploited the helpless! – He's a liar! – He's a traitor! – He's a murderer!

The First God   Defendant, how do you respond?

Shui Ta   I did nothing but make it possible for my cousin to survive, your honours. I only came when her little shop was in danger. Three times I had to come. I never wanted to remain. But circumstances this last time demanded my remaining. I've had nothing but pains for it. My cousin was loved, while I did the dirty work. And because I did it, I'm hated.

The Sister-in-Law   Hated! Yes! Look at my family, your honours! (*To* **Shui Ta**.) And we won't even mention our three tobacco bundles!

Shui Ta   Mention them! Why not!

The Sister-in-Law   Shen Te sheltered us; he had us arrested.

Shui Ta   You stole pastries from the baker!

The Sister-in-Law   He was never worried about the baker! He just wanted the shop for himself!

Shui Ta   It's a shop, not a hospital, you selfish parasites!

The Sister-in-Law   But we had no place to stay!

Shui Ta   But there were too many of you!

Wang   And these two? (*He points to the old couple.*) Were they selfish too?

The Old Man   We put all our savings in Shen Te's shop. And then our own shop was lost. Why did you let this happen?

Shui Ta   Weil meine Kusine einem Flieger zum Fliegen verhelfen wollte. Ich sollte das Geld schaffen!

Wang   Das wollte vielleicht sie, aber du wolltest die einträgliche Stelle in Peking. Der Laden war dir nicht gut genug.

Shui Ta   Die Ladenmiete war zu hoch!

Die Shin   Das kann ich bestätigen.

Shui Ta   Und meine Kusine verstand nichts vom Geschäft.

Die Shin   Auch das! Außerdem war sie verliebt in den Flieger.

Shui Ta   Sollte sie nicht lieben dürfen?

Wang   Sicher! Warum hast du sie dann zwingen wollen, einen ungeliebten Mann zu heiraten, den Barbier hier?

Shui Ta   Der Mann, den sie liebte, war ein Lump.

Wang   Der dort? (*Er zeigt auf* **Sun**.)

Sun (*springt auf*)   Und weil er ein Lump war, hast du ihn in dein Kontor genommen!

Shui Ta   Um dich zu bessern! Um dich zu bessern!

Die Schwägerin   Um ihn zum Antreiber zu machen!

Wang   Und als er so gebessert war, hast du ihn da nicht verkauft an diese da? (*Er zeigt auf* **Die Hausbesitzerin**.) Sie hat es überall herumposaunt!

Shui Ta   Weil sie mir die Lokalitäten nur geben wollte, wenn er ihr die Knie tätschelte!

Die Hausbesitzerin   Lüge! Reden Sie nicht mehr von meinen Lokalitäten! Ich habe mit Ihnen nichts zu schaffen, Sie Mörder! (*Sie rauscht beleidigt ab.*)

Sun (*bestimmt*)   Euer Gnaden, ich muß ein Wort für ihn einlegen!

Shui Ta Because my cousin wanted to help a pilot to fly again. I had to find the money somewhere!

Wang She may have wanted to help, you only wanted in on a big Peking salary. The shop wasn't good enough.

Shui Ta The rent was too high!

Mrs Shin I'll vouch for that.

Shui Ta My cousin didn't understand business.

Mrs Shin I'll vouch for that too! Besides she really loved this pilot.

Shui Ta Should she not be permitted to love?

Wang She should love! Then why force on her a man she didn't love, the barber Shu Fu!

Shui Ta Because the man she loved was a lumpen, a louse!

Wang That man there? (*He points to* **Sun**.)

Sun (*jumping up*) Such a lumpen you made him your field representative!

Shui Ta To make you improve! To make you improve!

The Sister-in-Law You made him into a slavedriver instead!

Wang And after he'd improved, didn't you sell him to that fine lady there? (*He points to* **The Landlady**.) She's been trumpeting about it all over town.

Shui Ta Because she wouldn't rent me the warehouse unless he tickled her knees.

The Landlady Liar! Forget the warehouses! I don't associate with murderers! You murderer! (*She storms out, insulted.*)

Sun (*determinedly*) Your honours, I must say a word in his defence.

Die Schwägerin   Selbstverständlich mußt du. Du bist sein Angestellter.

Der Arbeitslose   Er ist der schlimmste Antreiber, den es je gegeben hat. Er ist ganz verkommen.

Sun   Euer Gnaden, der Angeklagte mag mich zu was immer gemacht haben, aber er ist kein Mörder. Wenige Minuten vor seiner Verhaftung habe ich Shen Tes Stimme aus dem Gelaß hinter dem Laden gehört!

Der Erste Gott (*gierig*)   So lebte sie also? Berichte uns genau, was du gehört hast!

Sun (*triumphierend*)   Ein Schluchzen, Euer Gnaden, ein Schluchzen!

Der Dritte Gott   Und das erkanntest du wieder?

Sun   Unbedingt. Sollte ich nicht ihre Stimme kennen?

Herr Shu Fu   Ja, oft genug hast du sie schluchzen gemacht!

Sun   Und doch habe ich sie glücklich gemacht. Aber dann wollte er (*auf* **Shui Ta** *deutend*) sie an dich verkaufen.

Shui Ta (*zu* **Sun**)   Weil du sie nicht liebtest!

Wang   Nein: um des Geldes willen!

Shui Ta   Aber wozu wurde das Geld benötigt, Euer Gnaden? (*Zu* **Sun**.) Du wolltest, daß sie alle ihre Freunde opferte, aber der Barbier bot seine Häuser und sein Geld an, daß den Armen geholfen würde. Auch damit sie Gutes tun konnte, mußte ich sie mit dem Barbier verloben.

Wang   Warum hast du sie da nicht das Gute tun lassen, als der große Scheck unterschrieben wurde? Warum hast du die Freunde Shen Tes in die schmutzigen Schwitzbuden geschickt, deine Tabakfabrik, Tabakkönig?

Shui Ta   Das war für das Kind!

Der Schreiner   Und meine Kinder? Was machtest du mit meinen Kindern?

The Sister-in-Law Of course you must, because your tongue must find his asshole.

The Unemployed Man He's the worst taskmaster who ever lived. He's completely corrupt.

Sun Your honours, the defendant may in fact have made me into anything they choose to call me, but he's not a murderer. A few minutes before they arrested him I heard Shen Te crying in the room behind the shop!

The First God (*grasping this*) You mean she's alive? Tell us exactly what you heard!

Sun (*triumphant*) Crying, your honours, crying!

The Third God And you recognised it as hers?

Sun Of course! I'd know her crying anywhere!

Shu Fu You should, you made her cry often enough.

Sun And I also made her happy. But then he (*pointing to* **Shui Ta**) tried to sell her to you.

Shui Ta (*to* **Sun**) Because you didn't love her!

Wang No, you wanted the money!

Shui Ta But why did I want it, your honours? (*To* **Sun**.) You wanted her to sacrifice her friends, but the barber offered her buildings and blank cheques, so that she could help the poor. If she was to keep doing good, I had to sell her to the barber.

Wang Then why didn't you let her do good once you cashed that big cheque? Why did all Shen Te's friends become slaves in your dirty sweatshops, sorting tobacco, Tobacco King?

Shui Ta I did it for the child!

The Former Carpenter And my children? What have you done to my children?

Shui Ta *schweigt.*

Wang   Jetzt schweigst du! Die Götter haben Shen Te
ihren Laden gegeben als eine kleine Quelle der Güte.
Und immer wollte sie Gutes tun, und immer kamst du
und hast es vereitelt.

Shui Ta (*außer sich*)   Weil sonst die Quelle versiegt wäre,
du Dummkopf.

Die Shin   Das ist richtig, Euer Gnaden!

Wang   Was nützt die Quelle, wenn daraus nicht
geschöpft werden kann?

Shui Ta   Gute Taten, das bedeutet Ruin!

Wang (*wild*)   Aber schlechte Taten, das bedeutet gutes
Leben, wie? Was hast du mit der guten Shen Te gemacht,
du schlechter Mensch? Wie viele gute Menschen gibt es
schon, Erleuchtete? Sie aber war gut! Als der dort meine
Hand zerbrochen hatte, wollte sie für mich zeugen. Und
jetzt zeuge ich für sie. Sie war gut, ich bezeuge es. (*Er hebt
die Hand zum Schwur.*)

Der Dritte Gott   Was hast du an der Hand,
Wasserverkäufer? Sie ist ja steif.

Wang (*zeigt auf* **Shui Ta**)   Er ist daran schuld, nur er! Sie
wollte mir das Geld für den Arzt geben, aber dann kam
er. Du warst ihr Todfeind!

Shui Ta   Ich war ihr einziger Freund!

Alle   Wo ist sie?

Shui Ta   Verreist.

Wang   Wohin?

Shui Ta   Ich sage es nicht!

Alle   Aber warum mußte sie verreisen?

Shui Ta (*schreiend*)   Weil ihr sie sonst zerrissen hättet!

Es tritt eine plötzliche Stille ein.

Shui Ta *is silent.*

Wang   Finally, you're silent! The Gods gave the shop to Shen Te to be a small spring of goodness. And every time she tried to do good, and every time you destroyed it.

Shui Ta (*beside himself*)   Because otherwise, you idiot, the spring would have dried!

Mrs Shin   That's true, your honours!

Wang   What good's a wellspring if no water can be drawn from it?

Shui Ta   Good deeds destroy the doer!

Wang (*wild*)   But bad deeds make for a good life, right? What have you done with the good Shen Te, you evil man? How many good people are there in the world, Awakened Ones? But she was good!

When that man there broke my hand, she wanted to witness for me. And now I will witness for her. She was good, I swear it. (*He raises his hand to swear.*)

The Third God   What is wrong with your hand, waterseller. It's stiff.

Wang   It was her cousin who ruined my hand, it was him! She wanted to give me money for a doctor, but then he came. You were her worst enemy!

Shui Ta   I was her only friend!

All   Where is she?

Shui Ta   Gone away.

Wang   Where?

Shui Ta   I can't say! She had to go!

All   But why?

Shui Ta (*screaming*)   Because if she'd have stayed you'd have torn her to pieces!

Sudden silence. **Shui Ta** *has sunk into his chair.*

Shui Ta (*ist auf seinen Stuhl gesunken*) Ich kann nicht mehr. Ich will alles aufklären. Wenn der Saal geräumt wird und nur die Richter zurückbleiben, will ich ein Geständnis machen.

Alle Er gesteht! Er ist überführt!

Der Erste Gott (*schlägt mit dem Hammer auf den Tisch*) Der Saal soll geräumt werden.

Der Polizist *räumt den Saal.*

Die Shin (*im Abgehen, lachend*) Man wird sich wundern!

Shui Ta Sind sie draußen? Alle? Ich kann nicht mehr schweigen. Ich habe euch erkannt, Erleuchtete!

Der Zweite Gott Was hast du mit unserm guten Menschen von Sezuan gemacht?

Shui Ta Dann laßt mich euch die furchtbare Wahrheit gestehen, ich bin euer guter Mensch! (*Er nimmt die Maske ab und reißt sich die Kleider weg,* **Shen Te** *steht da.*)

Der Zweite Gott Shen Te!

Shen Te Ja, ich bin es. Shui Ta und Shen Te, ich bin beides.
Euer einstiger Befehl
Gut zu sein und doch zu leben
Zerriß mich wie ein Blitz in zwei Hälften. Ich
Weiß nicht, wie es kam: gut sein zu andern
Und zu mir konnte ich nicht zugleich.
Andern und mir zu helfen, war mir zu schwer.
Ach, eure Welt ist schwierig! Zu viel Not, zu viel
  Verzweiflung!
Die Hand, die dem Elenden gereicht wird
Reißt er einem gleich aus! Wer den Verlorenen hilft
Ist selbst verloren! Denn wer könnte
Lang sich weigern, böse zu sein, wenn da stirbt, wer kein
  Fleisch ißt?
Aus was sollte ich nehmen, was alles gebraucht wurde?
  Nur

Shui Ta   I can't continue. I'll explain. If the room is cleared, I will confess to the judges.

All   He's going to confess! – He's guilty!

The First God (*knocking on the table with his mallet*)   Clear the court.

The Policeman *clears the room.*

Mrs Shin (*laughing as she exits*)   Are they ever in for a surprise!

Shui Ta   Are they gone? All of them? I can't be silent anymore. I recognise you, Awakened Ones!

The Second God   What have you done with our good person of Szechwan?

Shui Ta   Then let me reveal to you the horrible truth: I am your good person!

He takes off the mask and clothes. **Shen Te** *stands there.*

The Third God   Shen Te!

Shen Te   Yes, it's I. Shui Ta and Shen Te, I'm both.

Your first decree
To be good and to live
Split me, like lightning, in two.
Don't know how it happened: to be good to others
And to myself wasn't possible for me,
To help others, and myself, was too hard.
Ah, your world is hard. Too much need, too much
    despair!
The hand you extend to the poor
Is torn from your arm! Help the lost,
And you're lost yourself. Who
Can long avoid evil, when people need to eat, and there's
    never any food?
From what source could I provide everything needed?
    Only

Aus mir! Aber dann kam ich um! Die Last der guten
   Vorsätze
Drückte mich in die Erde. Doch wenn ich Unrecht tat
Ging ich mächtig herum und aß vom guten Fleisch!
Etwas muß falsch sein an eurer Welt. Warum
Ist auf die Bosheit ein Preis gesetzt* und warum erwarten
   den Guten
So harte Strafen? Ach, in mir war
Solch eine Gier, mich zu verwöhnen! Und da war auch
In mir ein heimliches Wissen, denn meine Ziehmutter
Wusch mich mit Gossenwasser! Davon kriegte ich
Ein scharfes Aug. Jedoch Mitleid
Schmerzte mich so, daß ich gleich in wölfischen Zorn
   verfiel
Angesichts des Elends. Dann
Fühlte ich, wie ich mich verwandelte und
Mir die Lippe zur Lefze wurd. Wie Asch im Mund
Schmeckte das gütige Wort. Und doch
Wollte ich gern ein Engel sein den Vorstädten. Zu
   schenken
War mir eine Wollust. Ein glückliches Gesicht
Und ich ging wie auf Wolken.
Verdammt mich: alles, was ich verbrach
Tat ich, meinen Nachbarn zu helfen
Meinen Geliebten zu lieben und
Meinen kleinen Sohn vor dem Mangel zu retten.
Für eure großen Pläne, ihr Götter
War ich armer Mensch zu klein.

Der Erste Gott (*mit allen Zeichen des Entsetzens*)   Sprich
nicht weiter, Unglückliche! Was sollen wir denken, die so
froh sind, dich wiedergefunden zu haben!

Shen Te   Aber ich muß euch doch sagen, daß ich der
böse Mensch bin, von dem alle hier diese Untaten
berichtet haben.

Der Erste Gott   Der gute Mensch, von dem alle nur
Gutes berichtet haben!

Shen Te   Nein, auch der böse!

From out of myself! But in doing good, I died!
The burden was too much, it buried me alive.
So I did evil, and was respected, feared, I
Ate very well. Something's wrong with your world.
Oh, in me there's a great yearning to be rich and spoiled.
But there's a secret knowledge, too. My foster mother
Washed me with sewer water, and
From that I got my sharp eye. Pity used to hurt me so
    terribly,
I'd fall into ravening anger, the minute I see suffering.
Then I felt myself change, felt my lips curl back,
My teeth sharpen into fangs. The good word tasted
Like ash in my mouth. The angel of the outskirts,
I'd like to have been her, very much. I lusted to give.
A pleasant face and I walked on air.
Condemn me: to help my neighbours
To love my lover and
To save my child from want
I've committed crimes.
For your great plans, oh Gods,
This person was too poor and too small.

The First God (*with every sign of dismay*) Say nothing
more, unhappy one! What should we think, we who were
overjoyed to find you again?

Shen Te The evil person whose crimes everyone's
recounted.

The First God The good person of whom only good has
been recounted.

Shen Te No, but the bad one too!

Der Erste Gott   Ein Mißverständnis! Einige unglückliche Vorkommnisse. Ein paar Nachbarn ohne Herz! Etwas Übereifer!

Der Zweite Gott   Aber wie soll sie weiterleben?

Der Erste Gott   Sie kann es! Sie ist eine kräftige Person und wohlgestaltet und kann viel aushalten.

Der Zweite Gott   Aber hast du nicht gehört, was sie sagt?

Der Erste Gott (*heftig*)   Verwirrtes, sehr Verwirrtes! Unglaubliches, sehr Unglaubliches! Sollen wir eingestehen, daß unsere Gebote tödlich sind? Sollen wir verzichten auf unsere Gebote? (*Verbissen.*) Niemals! Soll die Welt geändert werden? Wie? Von wem? Nein, es ist alles in Ordnung. (*Er schlägt schnell mit dem Hammer auf den Tisch.*)

Und nun

Auf ein Zeichen von ihm ertönt Musik. Eine rosige Helle entsteht.

Laßt uns zurückkehren. Diese kleine Welt
Hat uns sehr gefesselt. Ihr Freud und Leid
Hat uns erquickt und uns geschmerzt. Jedoch
Gedenken wir dort über den Gestirnen
Deiner, Shen Te, des guten Menschen, gern
Die du von unserm Geist hier unten zeugst
In kalter Finsternis die kleine Lampe trägst.
Leb wohl, mach's gut!

Auf ein Zeichen von ihm öffnet sich die Decke. Eine rosa Wolke läßt sich hernieder. Auf ihr fahren die Götter sehr langsam nach oben.

Shen Te   Oh, nicht doch, Erleuchtete! Fahrt nicht weg! Verlaßt mich nicht! Wie soll ich den beiden guten Alten in die Augen schauen, die ihren Laden verloren haben, und dem Wasserverkäufer mit der steifen Hand? Und wie soll ich mich des Barbiers erwehren, den ich nicht liebe, und wie Suns, den ich liebe? Und mein Leib ist gesegnet, bald ist mein kleiner Sohn da und will essen? Ich kann nicht hier bleiben!

The First God   Misunderstandings! A few regrettable incidents! A few heartless neighbours! A little overzealousness!

The Second God   But how's she to go on living?

The First God   She can! She's strong and sturdy and she's a survivor! What endurance!

The Second God   Didn't you hear what she's told us?

The First God   Confusing, confused, improbable, unbelievable! Are you actually seriously proposing that our commandments are fatal? That we ought to renounce our precepts, denounce our eternal verities? (*Resolute.*) Never! You'd have to change the world! And how do you propose accomplishing that? Who could possibly hope to do that? No, The Laws above all, Obedience above all, everything according to Order, and all's well! (*He bangs the mallet on the table, quickly.*) And now:

At a sign from **The First God** *a rosy light appears, and music.*

The First God
Let us go home. What a remarkable place,
This little world. Its joys and sorrows
Have freshened and pained us. Yet
We shall gladly remember, from up above the stars,
Shen Te, the good person,
Bearing our spirit
On the earth below,
Carrying her little lamp in the cold and dark.
Live well, do good!

The roof opens. A pink cloud lets itself down. **The Gods** *slowly ascend on it.*

Shen Te   Oh not yet, Awakened Ones! Don't leave! Don't leave me! How am I going to look the two old people in the eyes again, they lost their shop, or the waterseller with his ruined hand? How can I fend off the barber, who I don't love, or Sun, who I do love? And look, I'm great with child now, soon, soon my son will be here, and he'll want to eat? I can't stay here!

Sie blickt gehetzt nach der Tür, durch die ihre Peiniger eintreten werden.

Der Erste Gott   Du kannst es. Sei nur gut und alles wird gut werden!

Herein die Zeugen. Sie sehen mit Verwunderung die Richter auf ihrer rosa Wolke schweben.

Wang   Bezeugt euren Respekt! Die Götter sind unter uns erschienen! Drei der höchsten Götter sind nach Sezuan gekommen, einen guten Menschen zu suchen. Sie hatten ihn schon gefunden, aber ...

Der Erste Gott   Kein Aber! Hier ist er!

Alle   Shen Te!

Der Erste Gott   Sie ist nicht umgekommen, sie war nur verborgen. Sie wird unter euch bleiben, ein guter Mensch!

Shen Te   Aber ich brauche den Vetter!

Der Erste Gott   Nicht zu oft!

Shen Te   Jede Woche zumindest!

Der Erste Gott   Jeden Monat, das genügt!

Shen Te   Oh, entfernt euch nicht, Erleuchtete! Ich habe noch nicht alles gesagt! Ich brauche euch dringend!

Die Götter singen das Terzett der Entschwindenden Götter auf der Wolke.

Leider können wir nicht bleiben
Mehr als eine flüchtige Stund:
Lang besehn, ihn zu beschreiben
Schwände hin der schöne Fund.
Eure Körper werfen Schatten
In der Flut des goldnen Lichts
Drum müßt ihr uns schon gestatten
Heimzugehn in unser Nichts.

Shen Te   Hilfe!

She looks towards the door, through which her tormentors will enter.

The First God   You can! Only be good and all will be good.

The witnesses enter. They look with astonishment at the judges swaying on their pink cloud.

Wang   Show your respect. The Gods have appeared among us! Three of the highest Gods have come to Szechwan to find a good person. And they found one, but —

The First God   No buts! Here she is!

All   Shen Te!

The First God   She hadn't perished! She was here among you! Hidden! And she will stay among you, a good person!

Shen Te   But I need my cousin!

The First God   Not too often!

Shen Te   Once a week at least!

The First God   Once a month!

Shen Te   Oh don't go, Awakened Ones! I haven't told you everything! I need you desperately!

The Gods *sing* The trio of the Disappearing Gods on their Cloud.

The Gods (*sing*)
  Flaring forth his fiery tresses,
  Our old sun sinks through the skies:
  We are going: with successes,
  Best not over-scrutinise!
  At your feet a shadow stretches
  In the sunset's auburn glow:
  Nothingness the night-time fetches:
  To the void, our home, we go.

Shen Te   Help!

Die Götter
   Und lasset, da die Suche nun vorbei
   Uns fahren schnell hinan!
   Gepriesen sei, gepriesen sei
   Der gute Mensch von Sezuan!

Während **Shen Te** *verzweifelt die Arme nach ihnen ausbreitet, verschwinden sie oben, lächelnd und winkend.*

The Gods
> Our search has led us back to you,
> Now say farewell, for we are gone!
> Praises be, all praises to
> The good Shen Te of Szechwan!

As **Shen Te** *holds her arms out to them in despair, they disappear above, smiling and waving.*

Epilog

Vor den Vorhang tritt ein Spieler und wendet sich entschuldigend
an das Publikum mit einem Epilog.

Der Spieler
> Verehrtes Publikum, jetzt kein Verdruß:
> Wir wissen wohl, das ist kein rechter Schluß.
> Vorschwebte uns: die goldene Legende.
> Unter der Hand nahm sie ein bitteres Ende.
> Wir stehen selbst enttäuscht und sehn betroffen
> Den Vorhang zu und alle Fragen offen.
> Dabei sind wir doch auf Sie angewiesen
> Daß Sie bei uns zu Haus sind und genießen.
> Wir können es uns leider nicht verhehlen:
> Wir sind bankrott, wenn Sie uns nicht empfehlen!
> Vielleicht fiel uns aus lauter Furcht nichts ein.
> Das kam schon vor. Was könnt die Lösung sein?
> Wir konnten keine finden, nicht einmal für Geld.
> Soll es ein andrer Mensch sein? Oder eine andre Welt?
> Vielleicht nur andere Götter? Oder keine?
> Wir sind zerschmettert und nicht nur zum Scheine!
> Der einzige Ausweg wär aus diesem Ungemach:
> Sie selber dächten auf der Stelle nach
> Auf welche Weis dem guten Menschen man
> Zu einem guten Ende helfen kann.
> Verehrtes Publikum, los, such dir selbst den Schluß!
> Es muß ein guter da sein, muß, muß, muß!

Epilogue

A player steps before the curtain and turns apologetically to the audience with an epilogue.

Honourable audience, don't feel cheated
If as we end you feel defeated.
We had a golden tale to tell,
But there's no way to end it well.
We've failed, we know, to be conclusive:
Definite answers proved elusive.
But since our jobs depend on you,
(Not to mention a corporate grant or two),*
We fear what your dissatisfaction portends:
You'll close down our show if you don't send your friends.
But our story, dear patrons, how would you resolve it?
The world's a conundrum! Don't ask us to solve it!
Are you disgruntled? Do you disapprove?
Should people be better? Should the world improve?
Should we have better Gods, or perhaps, none at all?
Well, we've had our say. Now, our backs to the wall,
We're turning to you to redeem this defeat.
Should you, as you sit in your theatre seat,
Choose to take on yourselves the need to defend
The good of the world, we might make a good end.
Honoured audience, do it, be brave and be just,
We've got to do better: we must, must must!

Notes

rice!', to which The Wife responds, horrified: 'Is the rice yours, too?' This inner conflict is still most evident in Shen Te's words that follow: 'They are awful'.

33 *Worked for us*: Kushner adds this implication that The Husband has already made use of the 'tight relative' ruse.

37 *The courts won't help him get his money back*: Kushner adds this stark condemnation of the justice system.

53 *Mr Shambolical*: Kushner adds this mocking title, where in the original The Nephew's joke rests in his knowledge that the cousin ('Mr Cousin') does not exist.

55 *Such ungenerous thoughts would perish on our Shen Te's lips*: The Husband's tone here perfectly reflects the overplayed politenesses and genteel language that define Brecht's play.

65 *I see that. People have told you bad things about my cousin*: At this point in the original, Shui Ta's expression is far more expansive and exaggerated – 'Her poverty was notorious, her reputation amongst the very worst, she was miserable!'

71 *First: because nobody could sell love*: Kushner increases the comedy of The Policeman's speech by having him list his reasons as follows: 'First, … Two, … And C and lastly, …'. His dumb attempt to seem capable of logical argumentation is thereby further undermined and the potential for comedy increased.

83 *Any other talents? Besides lying?*: Sun's words to Shen Te here are more cutting than in the original – 'You're not really much fun right now'.

91 *Free rice is – well it's not exactly a wonder, but it's a beginning*: Kushner has enriched the language of the original here ('I won't say a word. I'm not dissatisfied with the beginning') by playing on the word 'wonder', which is used colloquially but takes on an additional relevance in the context of the Gods.

119 *Which I think is entirely to her credit*: By using an idiom from the financial world, Kushner makes more patent the inseparability of Sun's attraction to Shen Te from his need for cash.

127 *poor mutt!*: This is the first of several times when Brecht has Sun refer to Shen Te as 'poor animal'. His two-faced dealings with her are evident in his use of this phrase in different contexts – derisory, when behind her back; loving, when to her face. This subtlety is lost in the translation, as Kushner translates it differently each time. See p. 141.

129 *I. Squeeze. Her. Tits.*: In the original, Sun says at this point: 'Because I've got my hand on her breasts? Put that in your pipe and smoke it!' This idiom is an English saying that Brecht has Germanised, and can consequently easily be rendered in English. Instead, Kushner's pointed repetition, 'I. Squeeze. Her. Tits.' effectively reflects his vile opportunism and complete lack of concern for Shen Te's feelings, as well as being a moment of pure comedy.

131 *He caresses your neck then he strangles you*: In the original, this passage forms the end of Shui Ta's speech on p. 129. This restructuring allows for the phrase 'A woman's meeting with her lover' to be followed directly by Shu Fu's entrance.

133 *that's become moot*: Kushner takes the opportunity to use legal vocabulary here (to translate 'that's no longer necessary'), bringing the dry, legal implications of Shen Te's love transactions – despite her escape from straightforward prostitution – into the language itself.

135 *hoosegow*: One of many points at which Kushner replaces the local Chinese flavour of Brecht's play with a (southern) American atmosphere, through the use of dialect terms such as this – a term for jailhouse often used in Westerns.

137 *The only intercourse will be intellectual*: Kushner allows himself a sexual pun, here, more prominent than in the original: 'There will only be an exchange of ideas'.

141 *Poor chicken*: A second translation of 'poor animal' (see p. 127).

147 *she's a fat-head*: As with Sun's phrase 'poor animal', he twice refers to Shen Te as 'fat-headed' in the German. Here, in conversation with his mother, it is spiteful and shows his true colours. On p. 152, he calls her 'fat head' to her face, which might appear somewhat tender to Shen Te, but which the audience recognises as further evidence of his spite. The echo is lost in the translation, as Kushner uses 'ox' on p. 153.

153 *Drink, ox!*: Literally, in the original, 'Drink, fat head!' *I paid you to marry them so you stay till they're wed!*: This and the following sentence are added by Kushner, emphasising Mrs Shin's money-driven character.

155 *And how do you imagine you'll manage without him?*: Sun's outburst here is extended by Kushner, making his concern at the disappearance of Shui Ta more marked.

157 *You can say that again*: Mrs Shin's allusive interjection is invented by Kushner, increasing the dramatic irony.

159 *We'll wait*: From this point until the bottom of the page, Kushner has restructured the dialogue, allowing certain passages to sing out more – such as Sun's exclamation, 'Look at me, two tickets in my pocket, and look at you, a moron who can't add and subtract'.

160 *Unerhört, diese Bedienung heutzutage!*: Mrs Yang's furious cry ('Outrageous, the service nowadays! What do you say to that, Sun?') is cut in the English version.

163 *she's my true helpmeet, waiting alongside me [...] over your unfurnished house*: Kushner heightens the terribly irony of the relationship between Sun and his mother, by adding this acknowledgement of her absolute support for him, followed by this allusion to the fact that he has sold her furniture from underneath her. This betrayal is not revealed until later in the original play, but Kushner takes full advantage of its comic potential by bringing it in here.

165 *And China trades places with Sweden*: It is rare in this version for Kushner to change Brecht's wording completely. Here, perhaps partly dictated by the metre and rhyme, he renders the original 'And pebbles roll up the river' with this more geopolitical example of a reverse of the norm.

169 *We're all banking on her*: A further example of Kushner's use of financial vocabulary when discussing Shen Te's predicament, emphasising the extent to which it is impossible to keep economic issues away from the question of goodness.

173 *Easy Street*: This addition by Kushner further locates the action in an American context.

182 *Es hat Hunger. Es fischt im Kehrichteimer*: Kushner cuts Shen Te's statement ('It is hungry. It is fishing around in the dustbin'), which is Brechtian in its simple description of the on-stage action.

205 *I've got education, not a lot but a degree. Of education, I have a degree of education, I don't have a degree*: Kushner draws on the double meaning of 'degree' to insert a joke, here, at Sun's expense.

221 *A new Yang enters the stage!*: In the original, the image is of a new Yang appearing on the 'screen'. Kushner keeps it in the theatrical sphere and so renders this moment more self-reflexive.

224 *Sie ist schwanger und braucht einen Menschen um sich*: Kushner cuts Sun's assertion that 'She is pregnant and needs somebody around'.

241 *Took one gander at the substitute judiciary*: A pun on the goose
     that has already been discussed.

254 *Warum / Ist auf die Bosheit ein Preis gesetzt*: This sentence is cut
     in the English: 'Why is evil valued and why do the good
     expect such harsh punishment?'

263 *a corporate grant*: Kushner has added this jokey aside, which
     brings the Epilogue's discussion of the requirements of the
     theatre up to date.